Somebody Gave Me Fire

By James M. Thayer

Dedicated to the One who gave me gold when I was poor, clothes when I was naked, and who bestowed *fire* upon me when I was luke-warm.

Seek First Productions, LLC - established 2012

Edited by Dona J. Dyer

ISBN: 9798987786765

Library of Congress Control Number: 2025903137

Contents

INTRODUCTION.. 1

Chapter 1 Drawn to Him... 5

Chapter 2 Hearing for Myself 14

Chapter 3 Pruning... 21

Chapter 4 In the Land of the Dying 33

Chapter 5 In the Land of the Living 52

Chapter 6 One Authentic Encounter 63

Chapter 7 Revival.. 73

Chapter 8 Glory 88

Chapter 9 Curiosities of the Spirit 121

Chapter 10 Dreams... 132

Chapter 11 Intercessory Prayer and the Kingdom 149

Chapter 12 Called into Ministry 168

Chapter 13 Witches 182

Chapter 14 Asheville.. 231

Chapter 15 Somebody Gave Me Fire 261

Chapter 16 Believer's Oppression............................ 286

Chapter 17 Drive Them Out 301

Chapter 18 Inner Healing 341

Chapter 19 Prophecy 364

Chapter 20 Tomorrow's Church 406

Appendix Healing Miracle Stories 419

INTRODUCTION

In the summer of 2023, my wife Aly and I invited a guest minister to lead one of our Freedom Nights where we focused on praying for the sick and oppressed. During this meeting, I first met a man named Jaqualin Pennyman. As I reached out to shake his hand, I suddenly felt queasy. Anxiety surged through my body, and the most peculiar sensation overtook my face. It was as if another face on top of my own was trying to peel off—as if I had been wearing a mask and something was pulling it away.

That was not the first time I had felt that way.

The year before, my wife and I were invited to our pastors' home for dinner. Joel and Savannah Ramsey were relatively new to Nashville, having recently led a ministry in South Africa. I was eager to hear about their experiences there. Their stories were captivating, unlike anything I had ever encountered in the United States. Characters new to me dotted the landscape. There were naked witch doctors, demonized people crawling on all fours, and EMTs who could distinguish between a medical crisis and a spiritual affliction in a person.

Savannah found it amusing when I used the term "exorcism" in reference to the demonized being set free. Most Christians prefer to describe the expulsion of demons as "deliverance," a term I have since adopted. This phenomenon deeply intrigued me, and their stories only fueled my curiosity. However, at some point during our conversation, I had to stand up and get a glass of water. I became nervous, and my temperature elevated. I felt somewhat out of my own body. I believed, even then, that something might be inside me that didn't belong.

The unsettling sensations eventually subsided as I struggled to suppress them, but the experience lingered in my mind, challenging my theology. I wrestled with the question: How could I, a Bible-believing, Holy-Spirit-filled Christian, be harboring a demon? I chose to stifle the hideous thought and continued on my journey with the Holy Spirit into what you may have read about in my last autobiographical book, *Stepping Out of the Boat (a year of miracles)*.

But then it happened again one day when Savannah visited my wife and me. It was a deeply shameful experience—I had to excuse myself from the conversation to drink water and suppress whatever was trying to rise up within. I wondered if others could sense it, and if so, why did no one intervene? This experience repeated several times until April 15, 2023, when I shook hands with Jaqualin for the first time.

"Brother, I really appreciate you coming to our Freedom Night and stepping in to pray for others," I said. "But I need to tell you something—I think I need deliverance. Would you pray for me?"

Later that night, Jaqualin prophesied over my life, and Jesus delivered me from that evil spirit. Thus began the most glorious year of my journey to date. I thought I'd already witnessed the majesty of God and the kindness of Jesus, but what I experienced after my deliverance far surpassed anything I'd known before. That night, Jaqualin saw a vision of me standing at the edge of a pond of anointing oil. My right toes were in the oil, but I could not go further; I've since taken the plunge. This book is about delving deeper into the things of God. It's about the transformative power of

the Holy Spirit. There are miracles beyond our com-
prehension stored in heaven, waiting for someone
with a little faith to call them down. There is a rush of
intimacy prepared for every believer who understands
the secret of the secret place. The moment we believe
our eyes have opened to the things of the Spirit, we
find more awaits to be uncovered.

*Scan the QR code to see the second half of my deliver-
ance as recorded by my wife. Notice how aggressively my
arms are shaking, and muscles contracting, towards the
end of the clip.*

Chapter 1
Drawn to Him

"You're doing such a new thing, and I thought you *already* did a new thing!" I told the Lord while pacing my living room. Ever since Jaqualin had prayed for me I was hearing clearly from God. Before that, I would have felt blessed if I heard from the Lord even once a year. Now, I was hearing Him every single day.

For the first time in my life, the Holy Spirit was drawing me into the "secret place" to simply sit in His presence. Previously, I had tried to sit with the Lord and pray, but nothing ever seemed to come of it. I wouldn't hear anything back as I prayed, and I wouldn't feel His presence. After a few minutes, I'd get bored and move on with my day. My experience was quite different now.

I'd be sitting at my computer editing a video for a client, and hear a voice in my head. It was a tempting voice saying, "Why don't you come in here, into your closet? Come speak with me." Prior, I had only felt drawn like that to sin, but this time, I was being wooed into a deeper relationship with God. I would stop what I was doing, a big smile would come across my face, and I'd sit on the floor of my closet with the door closed.

I've often wondered why ministers don't specify what they do in the secret place. Perhaps they fear the "reward" Jesus mentioned in Matthew 6 will be taken from them. I want you to know exactly what I experience because God has the same thing in store for you. Jesus told us to pray in secret—away from other people—in a private place. He said that the Father will be "in secret." The most significant "secret" of the secret place is that it is where the Father has *positioned* Himself for deep intimacy. When I go into a room to pray to God, the first thing I do is *expect* Him to be there.

Often, I will feel the presence of the Holy Spirit immediately when I cross the threshold where I'm praying. He alights on my hands—resulting in a tingly sensation. Sometimes, the weight of the Holy Spirit will come upon me. The secret place is where God's glory washes over us. It is the place from which our ministry flows. I've had people prophecy over me, saying,

"What you do in your secret place directly impacts what you are doing outside of it." I believe it, too! After God started to draw me into this intimacy, I began to see more extraordinary manifestations of the Spirit in my life.

Upon entering my prayer place, I'll often kneel or stand and then play worship music on my phone as I praise God. This will usually transition into praying in English, which tends to give way to praying in tongues after several minutes. I will intercede during my prayer time. I'll touch on intercession more later in this book, but for now, know when you're praying for other people or seeking breakthrough, you are often engaging in intercessory prayer.

Frequently, the Holy Spirit directs my worship and my prayers. He will tell me what I need to be praying for, and He will tell me when I need to stop praying altogether. My secret place time usually ends in the same way—I sit like Mary at the feet of Jesus and wait to see if He has anything to tell me. Sometimes I'll fall asleep on the floor, in His glory.

Before delivering a sermon or ministering to sick people, I almost always go to the secret place to receive wisdom and revelation.

"What should I preach? What insight do you have for this sick person?"

I will ask these types of questions and then wait to receive a word or vision from the Lord. I do not always receive an answer, but more often than not, I do! I have found God is always speaking; the question is whether we are in a position to hear Him or not. Jesus said some don't have ears to hear, and before my deliverance I think I was one of them to a degree.

You might be wondering why I needed deliverance, to begin with. I will dedicate an entire chapter to answering the question, "Can Christians have demons?" later on, but for now, I'll give you my story.

As Jaqualin prophesied over me that night and saw me unable to move forward into the pond of oil, God explained some things to me. First, the demon would manifest around certain people and not others because those people had a substantial prophetic gift upon their lives. As I heard this word, I remembered all the times I had manifested—around Savannah Ramsey, Kristina Hurley, and Jaqualin Pennyman. All of these people move in the prophetic. Second, as I prayed on it later, God convicted me of sin. He told me I had been verbally cursing myself for a very long time.

I had agreed with my enemy, saying, "Prophecy is not for me." I would declare this openly to people I was ministering to, "I operate in healing, but if you need prophecy, you can talk to my wife." Wiser believers, like my good friend Joel Cosand, would tell me not to say such things, but no one warned me that if I agreed with the enemy's voice over God's word long enough, a demon would take residence. I've since determined this was a religious spirit born out of a false doctrine I once believed about the gifts of the Spirit. As I mentioned in my last book, I used to assert that people were assigned spiritual gifts at birth. Since I never saw me prophesy, I figured it just wasn't for me.

But God's word tells us something different. Paul wrote to the church at Corinth that they should "eagerly desire the gifts of the Spirit, especially prophecy

(1 Corinthians 14:1)." By encouraging people to desire something eagerly, he likewise indicates that some people *lack* something. Simply because a person has never prophesied before does not mean God doesn't wish that for their life. Instead, we should carefully follow scripture—desire it and receive it with open hands. We should never close ourselves to what the Spirit might be trying to do in our lives.

One thing Jaqualin saw was a colon, the ":" symbol. On one side were things I was unlearning, and on the other were things I was busy trying to learn. I immediately told him what he saw: "It's false doctrine."

Many of you reading this book have grown up similarly to myself. You've loved Jesus since the moment you met Him, and yet you don't feel like you're living the "abundant life" He promised (John 10:10). You read the gospels and Acts, and you look at your church and wonder, "Where are all the miracles?"

Understand this—there are many revelations our ancestors failed to pass down to us, and there are many false doctrines they *did* pass down to us. The Spirit of God will discern and divide these things if you allow

Him. If you shut Him up, you have no hope. He is the one who inspired scripture, and so only He can make it mean more than ink on a page. We can read a passage of scripture a hundred times and fail to grasp its true meaning if we aren't partnered with the Spirit. Meanwhile, if we are partnered with *unclean spirits*— knowingly or unknowingly—they will place a filter on what we hear. In my case, one was filtering out the rhema (spoken) word of God. It is why I could never get into the secret place—why that time was unbearably dry.

God called Moses into a secret place, to a burning bush (Exodus 3). As he entered, he was told to take his shoes off because he was on holy ground. Because of Christ, you can have even greater intimacy with the Lord than Moses. Moses' sins were not atoned for; ours are. The Bible says we can boldly approach the throne room of grace (Hebrews 4:16). Have you seen the throne room of heaven? I have, once, and I'll talk about that experience later on. But I was able to have that experience because Christ made a way by the tearing of His flesh—like the veil torn in the temple (Hebrews 10:20). Every time you go into the secret place, you must imagine you are right there at the foot of the throne. It is your birthright as a believer. In that place you'll find protection, nourishment, and spiritual growth.

Moses also met with the Lord on the mountaintop, and when he came down, his face shined with the glory of God (Exodus 34:29-35). It was so bright and convicting that no one could bear to look at him, so he had to wear a veil. God was so terrifying to the Israelites that even though they were invited to the mountain themselves to meet Him, they refused the invitation and begged for a mediator—Moses (Exodus 20:18-21). We have a superior mediator in Jesus (1 Timothy 2:5-6). He has made us all spotless before God. We no longer fear His wrath, and that is why we approach His throne to receive grace.

Don't refuse the invitation. God is waiting in the secret place, longing to meet with you. He has many things to tell you, and just as Moses came away with the glory on his face, you will go away with the glory in your spirit. You will carry that glory with you, resulting in the miraculous happening everywhere you go. I have a theory that as we breathe in the secret place, we are filled with the glory of God. This is the last thing Jaqualin revealed to me that evening. He said God would give me His glory—that I would one day walk into places and people would be healed and delivered simply because the Spirit would be there. He said I had desired this glory like Peter—whose shadow healed and whose words welcomed the Spirit to fall upon those who heard him preach. This is what I desire in the same way I desire prophecy. I want every good gift the Lord has for me. I'm done counting myself out, and I encourage *you* to be done counting *yourself* out. God is not a respecter of persons (Romans 2:11). He's just looking for someone, anyone, who will say, "Yes, Lord."

Chapter 2
Hearing for Myself

One night prior to my deliverance, I woke up from a nightmare. Or was it a prophetic dream? At the time, I could not tell because it sounded like the voice of the Lord, and yet something seemed off. In the dream, I was suddenly pulled out of my body, and I could see my wife and I sleeping in bed. A commanding voice spoke, "You shame me when you devour me. I will speak to you through her." The voice was talking about my wife, the only one of us operating in prophecy at the time.

I shared the dream with Aly, and I pondered the rebuke. What did it mean? Was this Jesus talking about taking communion (devouring) improperly? Was this God telling me my ministry would be bifurcated —that Aly was the only prophetic one, confirming my suspicions? It wasn't until after I was delivered that I came to believe this was a demonic dream—for God was now speaking to me daily.

Those first two weeks after Jaqaulin prayed were absolutely bonkers. Not only was I being drawn into the secret place, but my hands were electrified almost 24/7. I
could hardly leave my house in the morning without
receiving direction from the Lord. For example, one
day I had a reality series pilot shoot scheduled for that
afternoon. As I reached for a shirt to get dressed, the
Spirit told me, "Not that one." So I put the shirt down
and heard something like, "The fish shirt." I knew this
was my Chosen (TV series) shirt, so I put it on and
went to the film shoot.

About two-thirds of the way through, one of the ac-
tresses noticed my shirt and commented on how she
loved "that show." She was one of about six women
there staring at my shirt, but she was also the only one
who commented on it. I knew the Lord had something for this lady, so I caught up with her on the sidewalk as she walked off set. I told her that the Holy
Spirit directed me to wear my shirt that day because
God had something for her. The Holy Spirit immediately came, and she began to cry. As the conversation
unfolded, she revealed she had just gone through a
messy divorce where her husband was unfaithful. She
was trying to pick up all the pieces for her children

and seeking happiness in the world. She was a believer, but she was broken and lost. She began to shake uncontrollably, which can be a sign of the Holy Spirit and also of a spirit of fear—I discerned this was the latter. So I asked if I could pray for her, and she got free from that fear, along with depression. She instantly felt lighter, and a laugh came to her. I asked the Lord to fill her with peace and joy.

Another time, I woke up, and the Lord showed me a shirt pattern with specific colors. Later that day, I'd meet a woman at my kid's soccer game wearing that same shirt and be able to pray for her family. This was about the time in my life that God began to tell me where to eat, even if it was incredibly inconvenient.

One time, I woke up in Asheville, NC, excited for a fantastic breakfast as the food in that city is excellent. Then I heard the Lord say, "Eat at Burger King." Friend, I did not want to eat at Burger King.

Sometimes, when you're wondering if you're hearing the Lord or making stuff up, ask yourself if your flesh would choose to do what you're hearing, and often you'll say, "No," which helps clue you into the fact the voice is probably external.

I tarried and took a shower. The Lord spoke again to me, "Hurry up, you need to leave," so I cut my shower short, dressed quickly, and hopped on the elevator. As I entered, a man who worked for the hotel joined, and I began to witness to him. At the next floor, a woman jumped on the elevator and she heard me witnessing to the worker. She chimed in and said that Jesus had changed *her* life, also. I followed this woman out and met her as she sat at a table. "Thank you for witnessing to that man with me," I said. I told her a bit about how the Lord uses me to pray for sick people and then offered to pray for her.

She had a broken shoulder, which caused her pain, so I laid my hand on it, prayed, and Jesus healed her! She was very excited, and I spoke to her a little longer, but I needed to get to Burger King. Looking back, I believe the Lord told me to hurry up and leave because I needed to meet those two people in the elevator. Since I chose to listen to the voice of the Spirit over my desire for a long shower, two people were touched by the Kingdom of God.

I jumped in my car and asked my phone to show nearby Burger Kings. As I was about to hit the closest option on the map, I heard the Lord say, "The second one." So even though the restaurant was farther away, I obeyed and clicked the second option on the screen, and off I went to my stomach's chagrin. When I arrived, I tried to discern why I was there. I spoke to the employees but couldn't get anywhere with them. So I took my lowly breakfast to a table and noticed I was the only customer in the store. "God, what am I doing here?" I asked. Maybe I heard wrong—which does happen. I was hungry, so I shoveled food in and sat by myself.

Suddenly, a woman emerged from the bathroom. I watched as she limped over to the kitchen door, wearing a work uniform. I knew she was why God sent me, so I approached her and asked how her day was going. She was having a very rough time—there were family issues and money issues. She was also suffering from some pain in her joints. I asked if I could pray for her, and I did. Then (and this is key), I gave her the amount of money the Holy Spirit told me to give. She began to weep. Not only was her body feeling better, but it was like an enormous burden had lifted off her soul. I returned to my seat, finished eating, and headed for the door. On my way out, though, I was spotted. The woman I had prayed for was pointing at me. She was telling her co-workers about what had happened, which allowed me to pray for the person I couldn't get anywhere with upon first arriving.

You might think that's the end of the story, but the chain goes on because the Lord plays 4D chess. The woman I prayed for found me on social media. She then messaged and asked if I would pray for members of her extended family. I believe I prayed and prophesied over three different members—and the miracles were outrageous. One man had a severe impediment to walking, and as I commanded his healing over the phone, he began to freak out in amazement. He told me he was now walking and didn't have to use his cane. It was a radical healing. Another man I prayed for had an issue with his eye that was going to require surgery. I prayed for him over the phone and the issue left! At the same time, I was able to pray for his wife, who got delivered from anxiety/depression issues.

All of those people were touched because I woke up one morning and chose to listen to the Holy Spirit over my flesh. Did I have terrible indigestion after eating Burger King for breakfast? You bet. Would I trade the advancement of the Kingdom for a good meal? No way. We must learn from Esau, who traded his birthright to Jacob for a single meal. In essence, he traded something of immense value for temporary satisfaction. When God is calling you deeper, it will cost you something.

Chapter 3
Pruning

Jesus can't use you if you're the owner of your life. He was very explicit when He said, "Whoever wants to save their life will lose it, but whoever loses their life for me will find it (Matthew 16:25)." It doesn't *only* matter if you can hear from the Lord. What matters is if you *obey* the Lord (James 1:22). Very anointed people have walked this Earth squandering their gifts like the man in the Parable of the Talents (Matthew 25). Hearing from God is a gift. Don't take it lightly, and cultivate the fear of the Lord concerning it.

I've walked through several seasons of pruning. The Lord wants holy vessels committed to Him, and I have not always been that (nor do I feel I've obtained it yet, either). There were times I was so caught in the sin of lust I had resigned myself to believing I might never be free. Yet God was faithful to free me one night when I resisted to the point of sickness (Hebrews 12:4). On the other hand, there came a point in our lives where my wife and I asked each other, "Do you sin

anymore? I don't feel like I sin anymore." We were na-
ive and only felt that way because the Spirit hadn't yet
ramped up the conviction. At this time, I was struggling with something I heard from the Lord. He
wanted me to get rid of my Magic the Gathering collection.

Magic is a card game. It is one of the most complicated games ever created, as it is decades old, and the
creators are constantly adding new mechanics. It was
my favorite game in the world, something I had played
since elementary school. I'm good at it too—having
won three local tournaments just a year prior to me
hearing from the Lord, "I want you to get rid of all of
it." This command made no sense to me. I had read
the Bible; I didn't believe the cards were actually sorcery—it was just fun artwork and a competitive game
like chess. I knew Romans 14 concerning conditional
sin and had never felt any conviction over playing the
game.

It wasn't only my favorite game to play, but I had a
couple thousand dollars invested in it and hundreds of
hours building decks. At the same time, my wife was
hearing from the Lord that she needed to get rid of all

her Harry Potter stuff. You name it, and my wife had a Harry Potter version of it—sugar cauldron, wand makeup brushes, hardback books, softback books, all of the movies, etc. She also didn't understand why God would call her to eliminate all those things. It was just fantasy and not *real* magic.

So, for two weeks, I kept hearing the same command, "Get rid of the cards," and I kept rationalizing it away. Then, one day, I was cleaning out my garage, and I heard plain as day, "If you are going to be lukewarm, I will spit you out of My mouth (Revelation 3:16)." That put the fear of God in me. I quickly ran inside and got rid of my entire collection. Around this time, my wife also got rid of *her* geeky collection in obedience to God. We didn't understand why, but we didn't need to.

About a year later, we found out that God was sending us to minister to ex-witches. Although the stuff wasn't real to us, to a New Ager (a person who incorporates eastern religion and witchcraft into their life), they were stumbling blocks. God was calling us to be above reproach (1 Timothy 3:2), so when these people came to our home for ministry, they couldn't look at the cauldron on our counter and say, "If Aly and James do this stuff, it must be fine."

Similarly, something gradually began to change with my drinking habits. Ever since college, I had been a connoisseur of cocktails, offering them to guests whenever they visited and enjoying them myself about twice a week. Never in my life have I been drunk, but I used to drink frequently and socially. Again, when it came to this topic, I referenced Romans 14 as well as many other passages of scripture that not only allow the consumption of alcohol but recommend it, such as in Proverbs 31 or when Paul told Timothy to drink wine for his upset stomach (1 Timothy 5:23).

Over time, I began to drink less and less. I thought about it less and, frankly, just cared about it less. I didn't consciously decide to change that in my life; I simply fell into it. It was almost as if the Spirit was doing something in me that alcohol maybe used to do. The Bible tells us not to be drunk on wine but to be filled with the Holy Spirit (Ephesians 5:18). I find it interesting that at Pentecost in Acts chapter 2, the apostles, now clothed by the Holy Spirit in power, are accused of being drunk. The Spirit of God is a far better high than anything you'll find on Earth. In Him is an inescapable joy I have seen poured out in rooms like an intoxication—people laughing for seemingly no reason other than the fact the Spirit is upon them.

One day, I was vacationing with my extended family when my father and brother offered me a new liquor they had just purchased. Usually, I would jump at the chance, but I consulted the Holy Spirit on the decision, and He told me, "No." I politely declined and sat down on the couch to socialize with everyone. After a while, my cousin's young teenage daughter walked into the room and sat across from me. The Lord began to speak about her. I told her, "I see you journaling, and studying the Bible. You're using multiple colored gel pens." She confirmed that was something she often did. I then told her I felt like she would write fiction novels one day.

The Spirit took a turn, and I said, "I see you specifically drawn to loners—people isolated in social situations without many friends, and I believe you'll have a ministry with these types of people—that God will begin to supernaturally give you words of encouragement for them." She confirmed that she, indeed, often felt drawn to such people. I then got the impression that one day, the Lord would begin to speak to her in dreams, and I felt like this would start in her 20s. Finally, God showed me her in the secret place and told me her relationship with Him was very sweet.

This girl embodies the qualities I hope to instill in my children. So when the Lord showed me all of that, He was prophesying to her, but He was also telling me how I need to encourage my kids to have their own intimate relationship with Him; that her model behavior stemmed from it, specifically. The prophetic ceased, I stopped talking, and I quickly remembered this young girl belonged to a denomination that most likely thought the gifts of the Spirit had ceased. She was deeply encouraged, and perhaps it was the first time she had witnessed a demonstration of the prophetic. I truly believe that if I had been drinking before she arrived, I likely wouldn't have been used in the same way at that moment. The Spirit moves with purpose, even when we don't fully understand His reasons.

Jesus was clear about the pruning process when He said, "I am the true vine, and my Father is the vine-dresser. Every branch in me that does not bear fruit

He takes away, and every branch that does bear fruit He prunes that it may bear more fruit (John 15:1)." Pruning is a difficult process, and it often hurts. God might prune something as simple as watching a certain show, or He might tell you to stop hanging out with your best friend. No matter what the Lord calls you to do, your job is to be obedient. He is doing it for your benefit because He promises that on the other side there will be more fruit in your life. That fruit is to the glory of Jesus.

One of the things that had me bound the most throughout my post-college life was politics. I was an avid debater, and politics offered an outlet for that addiction. My membership to various online forums was dominated by political thought shooting from my fingertips into the keyboard. Looking back, this was a great hindrance to me being used by God to advance His kingdom in any way of eternal significance. Without realizing it, I had put my faith in the government (even the absence of it) to save my nation. The devil doesn't quite care in which direction he makes political fanatics. He wins when we take our eyes off the unseen spiritual war and focus on anything else.

According to his military doctrine, a distracted Christian is just as inept as one bound in sin.

So the Lord came to me one day and told me to stop frequenting many online forums and social media websites—including the ones I felt were intellectual and "high-brow." I obeyed, and like the liquor, my taste for politics slowly drained from me. My online writings turned from politics to focusing on the Kingdom of God.

Previously, I mentioned a time in my life when I felt like I no longer sinned. Let me regale you with a cautionary tale. I had a friend, we'll call Brian, who was diagnosed with "end-stage cancer." Many faith healers, including myself, had prayed for this man without any signs of physical healing. I first met him on social media when I saw he commented something quite bitter concerning healing. I reached out to him to pray. He was delivered of a heaviness of spirit over the phone, but that was it.

Around this time, the Lord began to impress upon me the need to water baptize people. I made plans to fix the dead hot tub my wife and I had been gifted, and to use it as a baptismal. Then, one day, I heard a sermon where a minister talked about the North Georgia Revival and their experience immersing people in water. Sick people would go into the water, be immersed, and come up healed. These healings were well documented, and something in me said I needed to get Brian to this revival meeting.

Interestingly enough, Brian kept hearing words from people that indicated a washing or healing through water, so he was on board. He flew down to Nashville, and we drove to the revival, which was held in a large warehouse-type structure. Hundreds of people were lined up outside the doors, and as soon as we entered, I noticed a throng of people circling the auditorium in prayer. The presence of the Spirit became tangible as a couple thousand of us began to worship God together. In front of the stage to the left was a swimming pool, and on the other side was a traditional baptistry built into the wall. Later, I'd discover an entire wing existed backstage of multiple small swimming pools, bathrooms, and lockers. Dozens of workers would direct hundreds of people through what seemed to be baptism on an industrial scale.

At the time of worship, though, I didn't know anything about the place—I just knew my friend had cancer, and we both felt led to see him dunked and come
up healed. A preacher came on stage to deliver a message, followed by another who was prophetic, and
sometime during this man's sermon, the Holy Spirit
fell on me. I began to shake and weep. My arms became electrified as I sauntered to the altar and knelt
before God. The Holy Spirit began to reveal my sin. I
was prideful and arrogant, and even though I did not
believe it in my mind, my heart thought I was the one
performing miracles and seeing the sick healed. The
Holy Spirit gently told me I would be useless to Him if
I maintained this pride. I thought I no longer had sin
in my life, but the Lord showed me deeper pruning
was required in my heart. Still, to this day, I practically
beg the Lord to remove pride from it.

As I approached the waters, still weeping horribly and
my arms shaking, people tried to console me. They
thought I was maybe sick or scared, but instead, I was
cut to the heart by the word of the Lord. He was tilling
up rocky dirt so new seeds could be sown. The power
of God became almost unbearable when I stepped into
the water. There, in front of a massive crowd, I

confessed my arrogance and was prayed over by the pastor. He prophetically saw me traveling the world preaching the gospel, and he prayed something radical—that when I left those nations, the people would forget what my face looked like. He then dunked me, and I went to the changing room.

Eventually, it was Brian's turn. He told the pastor about his cancer, was prayed for, and immersed. When he came back up, he could immediately move his body in ways he was incapable of doing just moments before. All of Brian's symptoms left over the next couple of days. He was doing squats and going on long walks while taking videos of these improvements and sending them to his wife back home. Even though Brian was free for a time, eventually, all his symptoms returned, and he has not been free since. I'll be going into detail about complicated deliverances and healings later in this book, as well as a reference to maintain one's freedom in Christ.

But I had learned a valuable lesson—to take Jesus at His word. When He said the Father would prune us if we're bearing fruit, He wasn't kidding. The Spirit has continued to remove addictions and distractions from my life, ranging from mindlessly scrolling on social media to gluttonously snacking for comfort. I have come to covet His conviction. As believers, let's be brave and pray as David did:

"Search me, God, and know my heart;
test me and know my anxious thoughts.
See if there is any offensive way in me,
and lead me in the way everlasting."
-    **Psalm 139:23-24**

Before Brian flew home from the North Georgia Revival, I took him with me to hospitals to pray for the sick. At that time, I was in hospitals every week— sometimes multiple times a week and even visiting several hospitals in a single day—praying for the sick and dying.

Chapter 4
In the Land of the Dying

Hospitals are dark. I'm not talking about physical illumination but rather their spiritual atmosphere. One of the first people I was called to pray for in a hospital was a 9-year-old girl I will call Anne—and her story highlights the best and worst aspects of hospital ministry.

Anne's case was in the local news: she had been diagnosed with T-cell lymphoma many months prior and was dying. I heard about her through my mother-in-law, who knew Anne's mom. She asked if I would pray for the girl, so I contacted the mother and went as soon as possible. As I entered the hospital, fear gripped me. It was a tangible anxiety that lingered in the hallways and elevators. Despair hung so thick in the atmosphere you had to wade through it. Never in my life had I experienced such a thing in a hospital— even when my mother was dying of cancer. But this time, I had become far more sensitive to the Holy Spirit and more discerning of the spiritual climate of territories. I began to rebuke these attacks as I made my way to Anne's room, but they seemed to cling to me to some degree.

When I got there, I learned the day prior Anne had been given 48 hours to live. The doctors told Anne's mom to call in the rest of the family to say their good-byes. At this point, it wasn't the cancer that was snuffing out the girl's life—it was an undiagnosable lung condition. Doctors thought it might have been a fungus, but even antifungal medication wasn't helping. Nothing they threw at it put a dent in it, so Anne would asphyxiate within the next day, they suspected.

The girl was bald from chemo, passed out, with labored breathing. Worship music was playing on a cell phone. I introduced myself to the mother and grandmother and offered to pray for them first, which they accepted. This has become routine for me when it comes to hospital ministry. The family of the sick person is almost always under some demonic attack—usually not sleeping well, riddled with anxiety, and sometimes under the yoke of depression. In one case, the family was even afflicted by witchcraft.

After praying for the mother and grandmother to be free from anxiety, I turned to Anne, laid hands on her, and told her to be healed. The next day, Anne's mom texted me that the fluid in the girl's lungs had disappeared but that she was now being put on a ventilator to give her lungs rest.

Praying by myself that morning, I got a vision of a little girl who looked like Anne, but she had long, curly dark hair, and she was getting transferred from a hospital bed to a wheelchair because she was being discharged. Later that day, I hopped in the car and went to pray a second time. This time, I asked the Freedom Night team (fellow ministers) to pray for me, and as I drove, I asked the Spirit to baptize me again in fire. The presence of God filled my car, and my arms began to feel like lightning was shooting down them the nearer I got to the hospital.

I remembered my last visit—all of the darkness I encountered the moment I entered—and chose to pray against those attacks preemptively. I prayed in the Spirit the entire way to the waiting room. While pacing, my arms on fire to the point of pain, I asked God, "What should I say to her?" The response was simple,

"Tell her to live." The nurses' station buzzed me in, and I proceeded to Anne's room. She was on a ventilator, unconscious, and under a doctor-given paralytic. I so wanted to talk to her, but as is the case with many hospital visitations, I couldn't. I laid my hands on Anne in the presence of her mother, and I called out to her, "Anne, in the name of Jesus, live!" After praying, I felt quite confident, and with a big smile on my face, I went home.

A couple of hours later, Anne woke up kicking and screaming, trying to rip the ventilator tube out to leave the hospital. This is what her mother texted me, "The doctor is so confused because he said with how she was, she should be needing way more support, and there's no way she should be sitting up. He said, 'I'm scratching my bald head.' He's an older Polish man."

Then, early the following day, I received another text, "[Anne's] white count jumped from 1.1 to 8 today. She's not been at 8 since before she was diagnosed."

A couple of hours later, she texted, "2 doctors just said, 'We've never seen anything like this before.'"

Anne, indeed, was wheeled out of that hospital a couple of weeks later, just as I saw in my vision. Her mom posted to her followers, "We saw [Anne's] pulmonologist who did some breathing tests and an x-ray of her chest. She was hesitant to reduce steroids because this type of lung disease takes months to a year to get better. This morning, she called to tell me that [Anne's] x-ray showed NORMAL. THEN—her oncologist called to let me know that the mass in her chest is COMPLETELY GONE. As of right now, there is no evidence of disease in her body."

Before her discharge, I met an awake Anne on a third visit to the hospital. She didn't know me, of course, but I had grown to love her with the love of her heavenly Father, and I shared with her about Jesus as best as possible. On this visit, I asked Anne's mother, "Is there anyone else on this floor you know of who I might be able to pray for?" She told me the floor was pretty empty after the weekend and that there was only one guy on the floor they had brought in the night before.

This man was intoxicated and belligerent—screaming and cursing. Anne's mom exclaimed she could not

believe they would bring such a man onto the same
floor as her daughter. I asked her, "Where is this man?
I must pray for him." She pointed to a door across the
way, and I went.

When I arrived at the door, I peeked through the little
window and smiled at a woman who spotted me. She
smiled back, and I gestured for her to open the door,
which she did. I popped my head in and saw a grown
man sitting beside the woman, as well as a young man
(probably 17 years old) sitting on the patient table,
wearing nothing but a hospital gown, looking as de-
jected as a person possibly could.

"I was here today praying for a girl across the way and
thought I'd poke my head in and ask if anyone needed
prayer?" I announced.

The older woman and man, obviously the teen's parents, smiled and shook their heads, "No." A pause settled in the room. "I do," the teen started, "I experienced a miracle last night." I took this as my invitation
to proceed, walked to him (we'll call him Justin), and
shut the door behind me. "Oh yeah? Tell me about
this miracle," I responded. Justin then told me about

the night before—how he got in an argument with his parents, drank a bottle of liquor, hopped in a car, and drove as fast as he could down i65. He said the "miracle" was the fact he got pulled over safely, and no one got hurt. I told him, "People abuse alcohol and drugs because they are coping with something; what are you coping with?" He replied to me, "I'm depressed, anxious, and suffering from OCD as well as bipolar disorder."

I told Justin that was a lot of stuff to be struggling with and that my God could take it away from him in an instant. I shared my testimony with him about being freed from depression, and then I shared the gospel message of salvation. As I was about to move on to praying for his deliverance, I believe the Lord stopped me and planted a thought in my mind.

"Before I pray for you, do you want to make Jesus your Lord?" I asked. My words lingered in the air as the young man thought deeply. Justin then began to cry and, through tears, stated plainly that he wanted to give his life to Christ. I led him through a prayer of repentance, and then I took his hand and rebuked the horde of demons plaguing his mind. As I did, I saw the spirits coming off his face one at a time; it was incredible! After his deliverance, I asked him how he felt, and he said, "Amazing!" He and his parents all three wept and rejoiced together! I then told Justin about the Holy Spirit, and he enthusiastically received Him.

Justin later told me that he knew I was sent to him by God. He recalled a buddy's story, "My friend was in a mental health facility when a man came, prayed for him, and he encountered God. You were that man for me today."

In America, we have a saying that the Church is a hospital filled with broken people. In my experience, though, the vast majority of broken people will never step foot in a church. Justin was headed to a mental health facility for a week after our encounter—a place *filled* with broken people. I told him he had an excellent opportunity to evangelize there—that the same power in me was now in him. As the Church, we need to find inroads into the lives of the lost. We will make more significant headway reaching them if we walk into the mental health facility than we will by walking into church. I know that sounds obvious, but despite this, I believe such a strategy is overlooked by the modern Church.

You do not have to go far out of your way to seek the lost. Notice I was already at the hospital, and Justin just happened to be on my way out the door. I'll delve deeper into this topic in a later book on evangelism.

After leaving the hospital, I texted Anne's mother about what had happened and asked her if she had a Bible she could give to the young man. It turned out her husband's Bible was at the hospital, so she gifted it to Justin and wrote back to me about how the entire atmosphere in his room had changed from the prior night—there was peace.

Many days later, Anne's mother reached out to me asking if I would come and pray for a 19-year-old woman dying of cancer whom Anne had become fast friends with. I took this to the secret place before the Lord, saying to Him, "You've anointed me to heal the sick; this woman is sick, so I will go pray for her to be healed."

I heard clearly, "I have anointed you to heal the sick, but not her." I stopped praying and began to rebuke Satan for saying such a thing to make me doubt. I picked up my things and hurried to the hospital. I felt the same lightning surge through my arms as I approached the hospital. Praying in tongues as I walked to the dying woman's room, I was met by three generations of her family. There was the sick girl, whom I'll call Chelsea, her grandmother, who went by "Gram," and the great-grandmother, "GG." GG was a practicing Catholic, Gram wanted nothing to do with Jesus, and Chelsea was on a ventilator with sores all over her unconscious body.

As I spoke to Gram and GG, the Lord began to drop words of knowledge concerning Chelsea's life into me. I asked them if she ever dealt with depression or suicide, and she had. Her home life growing up was traumatic, which is why Gram had been raising her. And even while in college, she had constant thoughts of killing herself. Gram told me that one time, Chelsea, in rage and depression, said to her, "I'll just get cancer and die!" Sure enough, she was now dying of cancer.

We mustn't curse ourselves. Satan wants nothing more than for our thoughts to align with his thoughts. Too many people flippantly say things like, "I'll never do X" or "I'm not worthy of Y." These are demonic thoughts that get pushed into our minds based on circumstances we go through. Once verbalized, they become curses. Should we curse ourselves long enough, it invites the demonic to take residence and enforce the curse. I find many people who have dealt with auto-immune disorders have likewise gone through periods of self-hatred or an inability to forgive themselves for things they've done or failed to do. The antidote for all of this is to give up Satan's thoughts, as well as our own thoughts, and to receive God's thoughts toward us. We don't need personal prophecy or inspiration to know what His thoughts are—we needn't look further than what is written in scripture.

I started with GG and asked if she needed prayer for anything. She was demure, so I asked her if she had any pain in her body. She had an arm she could not lift above her chest, so I prayed for it to be healed. Her eyes grew wide as she raised her arm slowly, and without pain, she fully elevated it. This was wholly outside the framework of what she knew about how God healed people, and she began to testify to Gram about what was happening. This opened Gram up to let me pray for her.

Gram said she dealt with bipolar disorder and a whole host of other mental issues. I took her hands, and something extraordinary happened. The power of God struck Gram through her soul, and Jesus sovereignly began to free her from all demonic oppression without any manifestations. After, I asked how she felt, and she said, "When you took my hand, it felt like I was floating!" Gram became a believer after that encounter with God.

I then turned to Chelsea and laid hands on her, commanding her healing. The next day, her lungs had drastically improved, but weeks later, the cancer took her life. As soon as I heard the news, I was instantly reminded of the voice I heard in the closet, "I have anointed you to heal the sick, but not her." I now knew I had heard from the Lord and repented for confusing His voice with the voice of Satan. He had spoken something I didn't like, and instead of falling in line with His word, I persuaded myself against it.

One of the reasons I like being able to talk to the people I'm ministering to is it gives me a chance to lead them to Christ or, if they are already a Christian—repentance. Repentance means "Changing your mind." If Chelsea had been awake, I maybe could have told her that her life was worth living—that God had loved her deeply and pursued her since before she was born. Perhaps she would have broken the agreement with the spirit of death that was killing her, and maybe that thing would have left her when I prayed. On the flip side, I believe if I had perfect faith, the thing would have left her even if she *had* made an agreement with it. I believe in her situation, my faith was too weak, and her agreement with death was too strong—but only God knows the truth.

I once prayed for an all but brain-dead boy in the hospital who was not healed. This boy's case was high profile—making national news. I was invited to pray for his healing through a chain of people, and I firmly believed the Lord wanted me to go. My disciple and co-worker in the gospel, Ethan Sherrer, and I went, and pretty immediately upon entering the hospital, Ethan got attacked. He was overcome with fear. I prayed for him, but it didn't abate much. When we got to the hospital room, I heard the word "witchcraft."

To this day, I'm not sure why witchcraft would be involved with this boy, but it could have been a family member practiced it (even if they were ignorant of what they were doing), or due to the publicity, there could have been a coven cursing the child and his family, or most controversial of all—people who worked at the hospital may have been cursing him. At roughly 2:00 AM each night, the child was getting attacked. Things would be steady, and then they'd go haywire. This is a sure sign of witches cursing someone. I'll dedicate an entire chapter to discussing witchcraft later in this book.

Ethan and I laid hands on the child, prayed for him and the rest of the family (the father experienced miraculous healing), and then left to sit in the lobby. There, we prayed to break all witchcraft that had come against the child. We did not do this in front of the family as they were not really believers, and it would have been too far outside their realm of understanding.

From that night onward, the attacks ceased, and the child's father recognized this difference. The family's sleep improved, and the mom's countenance changed dramatically. The child's brain started to regulate his body temperature again. Yet, about a week later, the boy wasn't improving, so the family took him off life support, and he died. I sucked up my pride and texted the father my condolences and told him something similar to what I usually tell people in that situation: that if Jesus in the flesh had prayed for his son, he would have lived, but that I did not have enough faith to see his son recover.

Since the case was so high profile, with thousands of Christians praying for the child's recovery, and since my social media followers figured out I was praying for the boy (despite me never mentioning his name), I felt I needed to own up to the failure and posted a simple message about how my faith wasn't enough; how I needed to get into the secret place and ask the Lord to increase it; and how we shouldn't be despondent about this—but rather keep praying for sick people. Unfortunately, not everyone took my post well, and I received much pushback and outright disdain for my theology.

Most of the Christians who took umbrage said the real reason the boy died was "because it was God's will." My brother called me and said he prayed about what I had written and knew that my faith was, indeed, great enough to see the boy healed. Many people checked in on me to see if I was depressed, although I was far from it. To those who wanted to argue with me, I turned their eyes to Matthew 17 and the story of the demonized little boy whom the disciples could not heal. When the disciples asked why they couldn't heal the boy, Jesus responded it was because of their *unbelief*. He recommended prayer and fasting.

This passage seemed so straightforward that I hardly understood where those Christians were coming from. The secondary implication of saying "it was simply God's will for the child to die" is the fact I honestly doubt the child knew Jesus when he died based on my interaction with his family (although I hope he did). Just like the case of Chelsea dying, I don't believe she had given her life to the Lord. If it was God's will for unsaved individuals to die, then you must also say it was His will to send them to hell, and yet scripture tells us that God doesn't desire a single soul to perish (2 Peter 3:9). Ultimately, people get sick and die in hospitals because of Satan. He is the one to blame, not Jesus. But when a person isn't healed whom we pray for, the most humble thing we can say is, "I have unbelief I need to get with Jesus to deal with."

The wife of a pastor I know died from cancer. The pastor, himself, is an anointed man who has prayed for a multitude of people dying from cancer and seen them healed. When a friend of his asked, "How do you deal with the fact your wife died from a disease you've seen healed in so many people?" he responded, "I pray for the next one."

There is no point in entertaining condemnation or shame over healing failures. The best thing you can do is pick up your cross a little higher, climb Golgotha, and ask Jesus to crucify your unbelief even more. I believe in *perfect faith*. I believe Jesus had perfect faith, and I can have it, too. I doubted for a while, but I have met two people who had faultless streaks of healing for extended periods. When he was first baptized in the Spirit, one of these men didn't have a single healing failure for years. Every single person he prayed for, Jesus healed. The same was true for the other man for at least one year; even those in comas would pop right out of bed after he laid hands on them.

Both men endured moral failings or Job-like seasons, doubt crept in, and neither has seen such unrestrained power in healing ever since (even though they both still pray for the sick years later).

Jesus said we'd do the same works He did, and even greater ones (John 14:12). It was Jesus who said with a little faith, "Nothing would be impossible" (Matthew 17:20); He doesn't put any restrictions on what we can do (John 15:7). If we lack perfect faith it is because we have not asked for it (James 4:2), as faith is a gift (1 Cor 12:9), nor have we believed we would receive it (Mark 11:24). I must confess I know these truths. Yet, they have not sunk into my heart as they should.

Jesus gave His disciples a to-do list before He sent them out in pairs. He told them to preach the Kingdom of God was at hand, to heal the sick, cleanse the leper, drive out demons, and *raise the dead* (Matthew 10:8). So when a widow called me one day as I was headed out of town with my wife, asking me to pray for her husband to come back to life, that's precisely what I did.

Chapter 5
In the Land of the Living

One day, my wife messaged me with a screenshot of a social media post. In the post, a woman named Rachel (for the purposes of this book) was pleading with the general public, "If anyone believes in the laying on of hands for healing, please come and pray for my husband Tim in the hospital." I had been in and out of hospitals for months, watching some people get radically healed by Jesus and others die. It had become routine, so I asked Rachel when the best time I could come was.

Around that time, the intercessors for my ministry were independently telling me I was not allowed to minister by myself, but I always needed a second person with me. This was for both physical safety and purity in the ministry. Incidentally, Ethan Sherrer, whom I mentioned previously, had been told by God months prior to follow me. I'd been bringing him along for hospital excursions, and we had been evangelizing together in local parks. Neither of us knew what a crazy ride we were in for when we crossed the threshold into Tim's hospital room. He was emaciated, pale, and languished. His oncologist had given up on him, and he was supposed to die soon.

I'd later come to find out the reason Rachel created that social media post was because, days prior, she was surrounded by a team of hospital staff that was urging her to let Tim die. It was a big decision to make, and although she was estranged from God, she asked for a moment to pray about it. Sitting in her car outside the hospital, she prayed for wisdom, and maybe for the first time in her life, she felt the power and presence of the Holy Spirit. It overwhelmed her in the vehicle, and she began to hear from the Lord. He told her many things, and one of them was that there would be people coming to the hospital who would lay hands on Tim and pray for his healing. She would know they were from Him because they would come in pairs.

Thus, when I told Rachel that I was bringing my friend Ethan with me, it confirmed that God had sent us. So we laid our hands on Tim and rebuked the cancer. About an hour later, Tim said he felt the cancer leave him. Whereas his liver was in complete failure, it was healed overnight to the shock and embarrassment of the staff. Tim went from hospice to home within a week. Ethan and I moved on with our lives, praying for other people, and we thought that would be that.

It wasn't. Roughly a week after Tim went home, he had to be rushed to the hospital. All of his symptoms returned with a vengeance. Over the next nine months, we would see God do one miracle after another in his body. When his lungs would be going out, God would heal them. When he started peeing blood, he'd be prayed for, and the next day he'd be healed.

One day, I went in to pray for him and asked Rachel if she wanted to make Jesus her Lord. She did and was baptized in the Holy Spirit. For the rest of the day, she walked with the heavy weight of God's glory on her body—feeling drunk in the Spirit. This event marked a massive reversal in her life concerning how she pursued Tim's healing.

I did not know it when Ethan and I initially went to pray, but Rachel and Tim had been pursuing healing everywhere they could—from hypnotherapists to New Age shamans to healing rocks. For example, even after

Tim was first healed, he listened to hypnotic audio recordings while he slept at night. The family didn't know this was all demonic, but now Rachel's eyes were opened, and she determined to throw everything away and put her complete trust in Jesus.

There was another difficulty. From a childhood of severe trauma and an adult life filled with sinful choices, Tim had developed the mindset that he deserved to be punished. He had an arduous time forgiving himself and those who had abused him. These mindsets were the gateway to demonic oppression in his life. So even when miracles happened, he would fall back into self-hatred and bitterness, giving into his soul's deep wounds, and the sickness would return or evolve.

Tim needed a new identity in Christ, and although he professed Jesus with his lips, it was hard to determine if he knew Jesus in his heart. It was harder still for him to allow Jesus to change his heart because he didn't feel worthy of love. The nine months we ministered to Tim were filled with too much detail for this book, but I want to tell you what began to happen at the end of his life.

There was a moment when Tim was healthy enough to leave the hospital that Rachel was able to bring him on a bed to our church. She laid him down near the altar. Prior, I had told Rachel, "What bothers me is these demons never manifest. Usually, for someone as demonized as Tim, there will be manifestations under the glory of God, but we never see them." That day, we prayed for Tim, and for the first time, after rebuking a demon in him, he jumped and said, "It felt like I was jumping out of my skin!" This was an evil spirit that had come in through bitterness towards his adoptive mother—a woman he was able to forgive that day.

From there, the manifestations became greater. Demons began to talk out of Tim when Rachel would pray over him. He would growl. On one occasion, Rachel let her pity for Tim get the best of her, and she told a manifesting spirit it could enter her if it would leave him. Immediately, she began to throw up violently; she said she was sicker than she had ever been before. From that day on, her vocal cords were damaged.

Demons will try anything to get you to stop a deliverance session. They are desperate to complete their assignment from Satan and to maintain their "home" inside a person. They have tried to intimidate me, "You have no power here! I hate you! You don't have enough authority!" I have had them try to make me pity them, "If I leave, I'll be destroyed!" They will sometimes feign leaving a person. They have a hundred different tactics, and you and I need to rely on the Holy Spirit to discern what to do in each situation.

One fateful day, while Tim was back in the hospital, I had additional ministry friends in town staying with me. Four of us decided to pray for Tim and hold a deliverance session with him to finally end things. The reason the demons were now being vocal was because they knew their time was up, and this was precipitated by the fact Tim was finally accepting Jesus' forgiveness and throwing his heart and mind behind God's word over his life. Their right to him had ended, and our job was to evict them.

Long deliverances can get tiring. The longest one I have done consecutively was 6 hours—a story I'll share later when I write about the topic of New Age. When you're in a spiritual battle, it pulls on your soul, which draws on your body. That's why having multiple ministers dealing with heavily oppressed people is wise.

The four of us visited Tim at the hospital, and we waited on the Holy Spirit. God told Ethan there were spirits in Tim's mind, body, and soul—and that we should focus on the one in the mind. The Spirit showed *me* a vision of a row of candles. Some were burning, and some were not. I believed the instruction was to pray over the systems in his body that were not working (there were many), one at a time—to light the candles. We began to pray over individual organs and systems, commanding them to be healed and for spirits of sickness to vacate. When we got to Tim's stomach, where the cancer had spread the most, it began to heat up. Tim groaned in pain as his stomach caught fire. Looking back, I made a mistake here. I believed it was the Holy Spirit healing him, but it was actually the cancer spirit *responding* to the Holy Spirit. I should have pressed in for deliverance but didn't. Ethan prayed against the spirit in Tim's mind.

After we prayed for all of the systems, we regrouped. While consulting the Holy Spirit, a demon inside Tim began to speak to Rachel. It told Rachel it would leave, but only if it could enter into another man. It gave the man's full name and the town he lived in. Rachel forbade it from entering that man. She did not know who the man was, nor did Tim. Only the demon knew who it was talking about, and since we were in a well-known hospital, I figured it was a man who was probably in a room nearby.

Since the spirits were manifesting heavily now, the four of us formed a line and began to pray for deliverance—taking turns at the head of the line. Evil spirits started to come out of Tim as he coughed violently. He reported feeling them leave him.

Ominously, Tim began to stare off into space behind my shoulder. I looked back there and could see nothing. I then asked him, "Do you see something?" He responded, "I see a little girl behind you." I figured this was demonic, so I rebuked the "little girl." When my second time at the head of the line came around, I felt such optimism. Things were going great! Demons were fleeing this man, and he was improving. I then began to tackle what I figured was that cancer demon in his stomach. All of us could physically see it coming up his stomach, up his chest, and into his throat—like a physical lump. When it got to his throat, though, he began to choke. The demon cut off his airway, Tim became fearful, his oxygen levels plummeted, and suddenly he began to code. I told the demon to "bind its manifestation," and the choking stopped, but it was too late. The rapid response team of doctors and nurses burst into his room and began to treat him by turning up his oxygen levels.

As the staff treated him, Tim looked at me and said, "I don't think I can do anymore." His strength was spent after about an hour of deliverance, which came on the tail end of nine months of a liquid-only diet. Most people who go through intense deliverance need to sleep a long time afterward—it is incredibly draining for both the person being freed and the minister waging war on their behalf in partnership with the Holy Spirit. I refuse to do deliverance on people who do not want it, so since Tim was waving off continuing, I decided to head out, and we'd tackle it again another day when he had his strength back.

"Bye, Tim; I love you, man," I said as I left.

"I love you too, buddy," he replied.

Less than a week later, Tim died. Rachel called me on the phone. She arrived at Tim's room a couple of hours after he passed, put me on speakerphone, and asked me to pray for his resurrection. I prayed for Tim to come back to life for about thirty minutes. Again, at his funeral, Rachel and I prayed for Tim's resurrection secretly.

Very few people have that kind of faith. Jesus is Lord of all and holds the keys to death and life in His hand. He raised the dead in His life on Earth and told His disciples to do the same. Today, Jesus still raises the dead through ministries such as David Hogan's. There's a story in a book called *Raised from the Dead* by Reinhard Bonnke about a woman's faith to see her husband raised even after he was partially embalmed. Spoiler: Jesus raised him from the dead.

Even though Tim didn't come back to life here on Earth, this story has a happy ending. By the end of his life, Tim had finally made Jesus his Lord and was at peace with his past and himself. God miraculously extended his life by nine months to see His son set free from sin and bitterness.

Around this same time, a minister friend of mine lost his sister in an auto accident. He had the faith to see her raised from the dead and consulted his mentors to get their thoughts. Almost everyone gave him the same report, "She doesn't want to come back." Despite this, he prayed over her body for hours. She was not raised, either.

It would be difficult to see the land of the living, to see Christ in all His glory, and then want to return to our broken world.

Chapter 6
One Authentic Encounter

Jesus said He did not come into the world to condemn it but to save it. As believers, we are given the same mandate—to seek and save the lost. We don't do the saving, but we certainly preach the good news of Christ's salvation.

"How beautiful upon the mountains are the feet of him who brings good news, who publishes peace, who brings good news of happiness, who publishes salvation, who says to Zion, 'Your God reigns.'"
  -   Isaiah 52:7

The world is broken but not beyond repair. Jesus told us to pray for God's will in Heaven to be done on the Earth (Matthew 6:10). Christ was the first of this invasion, and with Him came a royal caravan of heavenly goods. If you've seen the movie Alladin, you know the scene where he is coming into Agrabah, and there is a procession of goods from his kingdom with him. There are elephants, gold, exotic items, and beautiful people. The purpose of this caravan is to show off all the good stuff found in Alladin's kingdom.

Similarly, when Jesus came into the world, He brought good things from His Kingdom, such as healing, deliverance, salvation, restoration, peace, miracles, and the Holy Spirit. He brought a remarkable reversal of darkness. John 1 tells us that "light was coming into the world" and that the light was the "life of Christ." He tells us that the world's darkness could not overcome that light. In Matthew 4, he writes that the people living in Capernaum who were dwelling in great darkness had "seen a great light," in reference to Jesus.

Jesus did not come to establish a new *religion* but a new *Kingdom*. He used imperial terms to describe His Kingdom because the Jews of His day would recognize their use by Rome. For example, Jesus came to establish His Church, and that word in Greek is "ekklesia." It referred to a general assembly for political reasons—think the Roman senate. Such assemblies implemented policy. For Rome, that would be the policy of the emperor. For the Christian Church, that is the policy of Christ, the head of the Church

(Colossians 1:18). We have been delegated responsibility by Him to see His Kingdom come.

Another word the bible uses is "apostles." These were the twelve main disciples of Jesus, and later, more were added, such as the apostle Paul. Their job was to establish the Kingdom in new territories. Rome likewise had apostles—and no doubt Jesus' followers understood what He wanted by how the Romans used apostles. The emperor would send out an armada of ships to new territories, and the center ship would be called the "Apostolos," the apostle ship, or the admiral ship. In this fleet would be all the manpower and resources necessary to colonize a new territory reflecting the Roman way of life.

These apostles (literally meaning "sent ones") would take with them the "gospel of Rome," which would be the "good news of Rome." This gospel would be presented to people groups; the apostle may have conveyed how Rome would provide the greatest army in the world for their protection, aqueducts for sanitation, and he may show off various unique and sought-after objects found in the Roman Empire. The goal would be to have the local people become part of Rome. If they resisted, they'd be crushed.

Similarly, you and I are supposed to take the "gospel of Jesus" to the ends of the Earth—finding people not already part of the Kingdom of God and presenting the unique and sought-after objects found in our Kingdom. This is why healing is such a gift to the world: it authenticates the evangelist's message (an evangelist is someone who preaches the gospel). Each Christian can leverage the caravan of good things Jesus brought into this world to persuade others to leave a rebellious kingdom of darkness and step into the Kingdom of Light. We can heal the sick, drive out demons, raise the dead, and perform miracles for the sake of those we preach to.

"And the master said to the servant, 'Go out to the highways and hedges and compel people to come in, that my house may be filled."
- **Luke 14:23**

One significant difference between those sent by Rome and those sent by Jesus is we are able to introduce people to our King. Each person we minister (that word means "serve") to can have an authentic encounter with their Creator. It is why I am a believer today—I met Jesus. I didn't simply hear about Jesus, and I didn't just have an intellectual understanding of Jesus. No, I met Him like Paul met Him on the road to Damascus.

Paul was a Pharisee, and as such, he had the Pentateuch (the first five books of the bible) memorized. His righteous deeds and works were unmatched. Even today, you'll be hard-pressed to find a Christian with five Bible verses memorized, let alone five entire books. In Philippians 3, Paul wrote, "If anyone else thinks he has reason for confidence in the flesh, I have more: circumcised on the eighth day, of the people of Israel, of the tribe of Benjamin, a Hebrew of Hebrews; as to the law, a Pharisee; as to zeal, a persecutor of the church; as to righteousness under the law, blameless."

Paul knew more *about* God and His law than practically anyone alive today. But before he met Jesus on that road, he didn't know Him. He knew *of* Him but didn't *know* Him—and he certainly wasn't known *by* Him. That difference matters.

Many people living today know about Jesus. Most Americans grew up in church and could tell you some basic Bible knowledge, but this is akin to knowing about Michael Jordan and being able to rattle off a few of his basketball career stats. If you showed up to Michael's house spouting off all of your knowledge, he still wouldn't invite you inside. If you want to get into Michael Jordan's home as a guest, you better have an intimate relationship with him.

The same is true of Jesus. Many will come to Him at judgment and they will be turned away when He says, "I never knew you (Matthew 7:23)." We want to already know Jesus before we show up at His home. As Christians, it is our job to make that introduction to others and to give them the encounter that Paul had— which changed his entire life trajectory. When Paul met Jesus, his eyesight was taken from him. That's very poetic. You're talking about one of the worst of men who thought he was one of the best of men, encountering the actual best of Men—Jesus Christ—and understanding that he was actually nothing. He fell to the ground and gave way to the glory of Jesus. There is something so devastating about religion because it warps us into thinking we are fine when we are actually at the tip of the spear of the wrath of God.

Paul was walking on the road to Damascus, and he had eyesight; he met Jesus, and his eyesight was taken. But he finally recognized who Jesus was. He thought he could see, but he was blind; when he met Jesus, he may have been blind to the world now, but he could finally see. All of his good deeds melted into nothing. Like Isaiah, Paul finally knew they were like filthy rags (Isaiah 64:6). He went on to write in Philippians 3, "But whatever gain I had, I counted as loss for the sake of Christ. Indeed, I count everything as loss because of the surpassing worth of knowing Christ Jesus my Lord."

Did you catch it? He finally *knew* Christ, not just *about* Him. And that is the encounter all of us need with Jesus.

One time, I was doing altar ministry at my church when a woman came down. She was struggling with addiction, and somewhere during our conversation, I asked her a pointed question: "Is Jesus your Lord, or just your Savior?" I explained the difference—to make

Jesus our Lord is to have lordship to Him. It means we have laid our rights and lives down for His sake. It means He has the ultimate authority over us, and we must obey Him. Many Christians have only made Jesus their Savior—cosmic fire insurance against hell. They have not counted the cost to follow Him, and as such, their lives are never any different upon meeting Him.

Jesus didn't call us to merely believe in Him. Remember, the demons believe in God (James 2:19) but do not obey Him. Instead, Jesus called us to deny ourselves, pick up our cross, and follow [Him] (Matthew 16:24). *Denying yourself* means laying down any claim you have to your own life. To *pick up your cross* is to count your old life, before Jesus, as dead—along with all your old passions and desires. To *follow* Jesus is to obey Him and to live as He lived. The term Christian means "little Christ," yet many believers do not look anything like Jesus! They commit the Old Testament sin of "taking the Lord's name in vain (Exodus 20:7)." To take His name in vain is to count yourself as His follower (in our case, a Christian) and to fail to follow Him.

You will then be *false* like an "apple tree" bearing oranges (Luke 6:44). In the end, Jesus doesn't have time for this kind of believer. They are lukewarm like the Laodicean church in Revelation, and He will spit them out of His mouth (Revelation 3). Such believers are a hindrance to the Kingdom of God because they live as hypocrites and offer a poor witness to their friends and families. They look like the rest of the world and do not bring the light of Christ with them into the darkness.

This woman who had come down to the altar to get free from her addiction was honest with me. "I don't believe I can make Him my Lord," she said. I did not get offended but felt pity. I want to see the lost saved, and this woman was lost. So I offered to pray for her anyway, but not simply for her addiction to leave. I prayed that God would remove her heart of stone and give her a heart of flesh. As I held her hands, she grew faint; the fire of God struck her, and she fell to the ground. Her breathing became labored as heat grew in her chest, and suddenly, little specs of gold began to appear on her neck and head. Later, she told me that her head felt like it was on fire. I commanded any unclean spirit in her to leave, and after this was all over, I asked her to stand back up.

Again, I asked her the pointed question, "Do you think you can make Jesus your Lord *now*?" Through breathless shock, she said, "Yes!"

What changed between when she first came down to the altar and rejected Christ and when she accepted Him? The woman finally met Him in person. She had an authentic encounter with God, and once a person has an authentic encounter with God, they can't leave the same. Everyone is searching for a similar experience, and it is the Church's job to offer that experience. For too long, the church has just provided coffee and entertainment. If we want to see revival, if we're going to see an awakening, we will have to offer something the world doesn't possess.

Chapter 7
Revival

When my neighbors, David and Jaime, first moved into the house next to mine, I distinctly remember our first conversation. After introductions, I warned them, "We hold meetings at our house sometimes, and about 50-60 people will come, so the driveway will be full. We basically pray for sick people, and God heals them; miracles happen at each event." Several months later, an extended family member of theirs would grab a copy of my book, *Stepping Out of the Boat (a year of miracles)*, and it would change her family's life forever.

One can never be too cautious about the books they read. When I was in high school, a fellow student left a C.S. Lewis book on a desk backstage during one of our play performances. I picked it up, read it, and my life was never the same.

More recently, I ministered to a man who, out of a desire to understand his friend's beliefs, read an occult book. That single decision became a gateway for demonic influence to take hold of his mind, and it took nearly five hours of deliverance to set him free. There is undeniable power in the written word.

The woman who picked up *my* book happened to be Jaime's mother, and upon reading it, she sent me an email stating that she had never read anything like it before. Her background was cessationist (meaning her denomination of Christianity did not believe the Holy Spirit still moved in power through the Church). She loved the book so much that she gave away a dozen copies to friends and family who wanted it—yet it sat on Dave and Jaime's shelf for months and months. That is, until one day, their newborn daughter was born deaf.

Jaime's baby had failed three hearing tests back-to-back. Neither ear was functional. At the same time, one of Dave's buddies back in California had to go to the ER multiple times due to fainting spells and other complications. Our neighbors knew about the miracles we claimed, so they contacted my wife and I.

The day Dave told me about his friend, I called the man and rebuked a demon causing his sickness. Over the phone, I asked him how he felt, and he said it was a wild experience—that he felt very light. He was freed, and Jesus healed him! I would meet him in person months later to find out he was still healed and his wife had given her life to Jesus after having her own encounter with Him.

The next day, my wife went over to chat with Jaime and lay hands on her newborn. She gently commanded her ears to open and left. That following morning, the baby had another hearing appointment, and this time, she passed her hearing test in both ears—perfect hearing. Yes, Jesus still opens the ears of the deaf!

Before I tell you the full extent of what happened in this family, I want to point out something from John chapter 6. In verse 3, it says, "And a large crowd was following [Jesus], because they saw the signs that he was doing on the sick." Notice how healing *from* Jesus drew people *to* Jesus. God's kindness draws people to repentance (Romans 2:4). This is the same crowd who would sit and watch Jesus multiply the loaves and the fishes. Later in the chapter, we find Jesus and His disciples have gone across the sea and the crowd that came to hear him preach followed. But when they meet up with Jesus again, they receive a rebuke.

"'Truly, truly, I say to you, you are seeking me, not because you saw signs, but because you ate your fill of the loaves. Do not work for the food that perishes, but for the food that endures to eternal life, which the Son of Man will give to you. For on him, God the Father has set his seal.' Then they said to him, 'What must we do, to be doing the works of God?' Jesus answered them, 'This is the work of God, that you believe in him whom he has sent.'"
  - **John 6:26-29**

Suddenly, this crowd was no longer following the signs to find Jesus but was finding Jesus to get the signs. Jesus worked to correct their faulty thinking, for a sign always points to something greater than itself. If you're traveling down the highway and see a sign for an upcoming rest stop, you hopefully have the good sense to visit the rest stop and not obsess over the sign itself. Miracles point us to Jesus, and that's precisely what the miracles Dave and Jaime witnessed did.

So soon afterward, Jaime picked up her copy of my book and read it in less than a week. She had many questions, so we set up a time for her family to come over for dinner to discuss. This conversation led to both her and Dave's salvation. Both were delivered, and Dave received healing in his back. When he was nineteen years old, he drove off a cliff in his car and pulverized his lower spine. He lived with spinal pain for the next 21 years until Jesus healed him on the night of his salvation.

Immediately, this family became evangelists for the gospel. Dave, who had grown up in a secular home and had never read the Bible, began to pray for sick people in parking lots and witness to telemarketers who called him. Jaime, who spent 30 years in a cessationist Baptist culture, began to have vivid prophetic dreams and visions. Both of them, just a couple days after their salvation, had an angelic visitation at 4 a.m. in their home.

My neighbors are successful entrepreneurs. They chased and caught the American dream, but they still felt empty. Jaime had made money her god, and it wasn't satisfying her. Dave just didn't know what he didn't know, as no one had introduced him to Jesus before. These were people who had the whole world but were still poor. Yet Jesus stated in Matthew 5, "Blessed are the poor in spirit, for theirs is the Kingdom of Heaven." The Kingdom came to my neighbors one night, and they received it gladly. Their lives were forfeited to Christ, and He began to use them to reach their friends and family. From those seeds sown in their hearts came forth fruit—and pretty soon, the world around them began to catch fire for the gospel.

First, one brother was saved from suicidality and a host of evil spirits. He gave his life to Jesus on their couch, and a small team (including Jaime) and I drove those tormenting demons out of him with the Fire of God. He entered rehab—breaking a generational curse upon their family where every male (except one) had been an alcoholic.

Witnessing that experience, Jaime's father gave his life entirely to Jesus, and the Holy Spirit clothed him.

He started to pray for his children, and witness to un-believers on airplane rides and street corners. He be-came the spiritual leader of his family that his wife al-ways dreamed of. He told me, "That night my son got delivered, I felt like Thomas who put his finger in Je-sus' side. Except I put my whole hand in."

Then, another brother gave his life to Christ at the very moment he thought his life was over and done. He was delivered in my living room and, like the woman I mentioned at the altar previously, had to en-counter Jesus to go all-in. Like many others I've met, he didn't believe he was worthy of Christ or deserving of the same experiences his family members had. He was wrong.

He, too, went into rehab—voluntarily doubling his time there and eventually working there to see other men set free. I spoke to him on the phone a few months after he first entered the program, and I felt the Holy Spirit fall on me. I knew he was a changed man, and the Spirit of God had taken residence in him. He was actually calling to invite me to speak to the other people living at the recovery center!

And then Dave's parents visited my church on Salvation Sunday when I happened to be preaching. They came down to the altar, and I was blessed to lead them through a prayer of repentance to give their lives to Jesus. Another brother then had a radical encounter with Christ, and an uncle's life drastically changed as this fire-lit family got him to enter the same rehabilitation program as the other two men. Four aunts received a touch from Jesus at four different times! A revival rushed through this family as each member laid down their life on the altar of God and became a living sacrifice for Him.

Such a revival is ushered in by prayer. My wife had been interceding for our neighbors heavily. She had been dreaming prophetic dreams (I'll talk about these in a later chapter) for a year before the first domino fell. But once it fell, that revival became a question of obedience. Many people encounter Jesus, but not all choose to lay their lives down for Him. Many people are healed, but very few tell their family, friends, and strangers about the miracle God did in their life. Dave and Jaime's family kept laying it down for Christ, and He kept picking up and ordering it correctly in response to their obedience.

Tragically, less than a year after making Jesus His Lord, my friend Dave passed away. Jaime asked me to present the gospel at Dave's Celebration of Life where at least thirty of his friends and family decided to make Jesus their Lord.

Revival is an outpouring of God's Spirit. It can't be forced, but it can be courted. It starts with you and me. Are we willing to surrender our lives to the point we can see God move through us? Sometimes, we shouldn't be asking for *more of the Holy Spirit* but for the Holy Spirit to *consume more of us*. The Bible says God is a "consuming fire (Hebrews 12:29)."

Tell me, what is an altar suitable for? It is a place where things go to die. It is also a place where things get set on fire. What are the things in your life you need to lay on the altar for God to consume? What areas of your life do you need to lay on the altar for God to set ablaze? For Jaime, it was her love of money. The proof that she had put that to death came one day when she found out her roommate had drunk 24 beers, passed out in the bathtub of her home with the water running, and caused $100,000 in water damage. She later recalled that had it happened before her conversion experience, she would have flipped a lid. But now that she was in Christ—her concern was for her roommate to get help, and she recognized God's mercy in keeping him alive—for he probably should have drowned.

Without laying down our lives for Jesus, we will not see revival. A friend once asked me, "Why do you think our church hasn't seen revival yet?" I told him simply, "Because of me. I am the problem." I explained that I can't expect others to be more hungry for Jesus than I am. My life is not fully surrendered to the cause of the gospel, even if I'd like to think it is. More of my flesh still needs to be laid on the altar.

There is more of my old corpse that needs to be crucified. And in the end, more of me must be set on fire for God. You see, Somebody did give me fire—His name is Jesus. The real question is, what will I now do with it? Will I quench it? Will I trade it in for binge-watching television or scrolling on social media? Or will I run around this Earth setting everyone else on fire I can grab hold of? The day the Church chooses the latter, we'll see a revival like my neighbors saw in their family—but throughout our whole world. A billion-person harvest has been prophesied on this planet—a revival like the Church has never seen before. It won't come unless the Church finally grabs hold of God's vision for itself.

On June 30th, 2024, I ecstatically prophesied through tears during prayer at my church. I heard the Lord say to His Church, "You can't bring anything to Me I haven't first given you."

You see, the Lord clothes His Church in gold, like the temple of the Old Testament. He makes beautiful clothes and perfume for us—a fragrance for His pleasure. In Revelation 3, Jesus says to the Church, "I counsel you to buy from me gold refined by fire, so that you may be rich, and white garments so that you may clothe yourself and the shame of your nakedness may not be seen, and salve to anoint your eyes, so that you may see."

The Church must understand it is poor, naked, and blind, in our present day. Even the best of our churches lack the fear of the Lord. There are great miracles done throughout the churches of America right now, and yet believers are mistaking those miracles as a benchmark for success. Miracles aren't a benchmark; they are unmerited favor. The miracles are there so the Church will repent. Far too many Christians are living in unrepentant sin, lukewarmness, and unforgiveness. God's grace is being poured out all over the planet right now, taking the form of signs, wonders, and miracles. But again, what do signs do? They point us to something greater.

"Then [Jesus] began to denounce the cities where most of his mighty works had been done, because they did not repent. 'Woe to you, Chorazin! Woe to you, Bethsaida! For if the mighty works done in you had been done in Tyre and Sidon, they would have repented long ago in sackcloth and ashes. But I tell you, it will be more bearable on the day of judgment for Tyre and Sidon than for you. And you, Capernaum, will you be exalted to heaven? You will be brought down to Hades. For if the mighty works done in you had been done in Sodom, it would have remained until this day. But I tell you that it will be more tolerable on the day of judgment for the land of Sodom than for you.'"
  - **Matthew 11:20-24**

The Spirit is being poured out heavily in a bid to win us back to our first love—Jesus. Too many of us are holding onto our baggage. We are trying to keep the old corpse alive that Jesus came to replace. If revival came to the modern Church of America today, it wouldn't know what to do with it.

As I prophesied that day, I heard the Lord say, "Come up here with Me," and I was reminded of Ephesians 2:6, where Paul says we are "seated...with him in the heavenly places in Christ Jesus." The Church seems to think it is stuck on the Earth, and as such, it is operating like any other Earthly organization. The last several decades have seen Jesus' Church following the way of corporations and utilizing marketing gimmicks to fill pews. It has been a losing strategy.

The final words to come out of my mouth through sobs that morning were, "We are the ekklesia, the Church. We're given authority. If the Church ever caught a vision of who we are, we could have everything. There wouldn't be so many lost people if the Church just knew who it was."

We're having an identity crisis right now. On the one hand, the kingdom of darkness has advanced to unimaginable degrees within the current generation; on the other hand, the vast majority of our churches refuse to engage in spiritual warfare. We've been given authority over all powers of darkness (Luke 10:19), but we fail to wield it. A third of Jesus' miracles were casting out demons; most modern churches fail even to teach such things exist.

I hear Christians all the time say they want to go overseas to preach the gospel in third-world nations, but they won't even go across the street to preach the gospel to their neighbors. Believers hopped up on emotionalism from a conference talk a big game about how on fire they are for Jesus, but they would rather spend hours in front of the TV than thirty minutes praying to Him. Preachers will spend hundreds of hours on a seminary degree to learn about God in the way an astronomer learns about the stars—but never touches them.

In the Old Testament, seeing God's face was a death sentence. Yet, under the second covenant, we *must* see the face of God, or we will perish. In the words of

Leonard Ravenhill, "Forbid it, Almighty God! I know not what course others may take, but as for me, GIVE ME REVIVAL in my soul, in my church, and in my nation—or GIVE ME DEATH."

Chapter 8
Glory

As you read what I am about to write, expect the manifest presence of the Holy Spirit to come upon you. Do not read this chapter lightly, but pray as you go, for I'm about to write about things I've only seen pieces of. Imagine a window covered in crusted mud. The Lord has scratched a bit of the mud away here and there, and the radiance of His glory has shown through like pinpricks. I believe the day He throws open that window; I will not know what to do other than sink into the floor and submit my whole way of life to Him to a degree I did not know was possible. I long for this day.

In Isaiah chapter 6, the prophet of God has an encounter with the Lord that wouldn't be repeated to that degree until John penned the book of Revelation.

"In the year that King Uzziah died, I saw the Lord sitting upon a throne, high and lifted up; and the train of his robe filled the temple. Above him stood

the seraphim. Each had six wings: with two, he covered his face, and with two, he covered his feet, and with two, he flew. And one called to another and said:

'Holy, holy, holy is the Lord of hosts;
the whole earth is full of his glory!'"
-   Isaiah 6:1-3

Take note of the creatures Isaiah sees. He calls them seraphim, closely related to the Hebrew word "flame." These are powerful angelic beings that somehow come near to the Lord, whom the bible says "dwells in unapproachable light (1 Timothy 6:16)." Curiously, their faces and feet are covered by their wings. Why? You can take this with a grain of salt, but I speculate that they can't look upon the glory of the Lord unfiltered—and they don't dare expose their feet, which touch creation amid the holiness of God.

When Moses saw the burning bush in the desert, God called him. As he approached the bush, the Lord instructed Moses to remove his sandals "for the place on which [he was] standing [was] holy ground (Exodus 3:5)."

Again, when Peter questions Jesus about washing his feet, Jesus responds, "The one who has bathed does not need to wash, except for his feet, but is completely clean (John 13)." In both cases, the Lord deals with the part of the person that touches the world—or fallen creation. Unmistakably, there is a more profound spiritual mystery here that I do not understand. What I do understand, though, is this: the holiness of God is something creation can not bear under. Even the most angelic of beings cover their faces and feet in the presence of Almighty God.

The seraphim call out to one another that the Lord is *holy* and that His *glory* fills the Earth. One emanates from the other, and neither exists without the other. Both reference the nature of the Lord—something inescapable which all creation is judged against. Yet God's glory is not an impersonal force but the third Person of God. The Holy Spirit is alive and active, and when He enters the room, you know it. Isaiah understood this as he went on to write:

"And the foundations of the thresholds shook at the voice of him who called, and the house was filled with smoke. And I said: 'Woe is me! For I am lost;

for I am a man of unclean lips, and I dwell in the midst of a people of unclean lips; for my eyes have seen the King, the Lord of hosts!'"
   - Isaiah 6:4-5

Isaiah encountered God's holiness and glory, and the prophet's only response was to fear the Lord and renounce himself in ruin. We call this feeling *conviction*. The Lord mercifully reveals our sinfulness in the light of His holiness so we might repent. Out of God's mercy, there is provision for our sin, and in the case of Isaiah, an angel grabs a hot coal from the altar of the Lord and touches his lips with it—absolving his sin.

For the Christian believer, the atonement of Jesus made us perfect. Still, it continues to make us holy (Hebrews 10:14). Because we are justified before God (meaning, due to the blood of Christ we have never sinned according to His ledger), we have the right to enter His throne room and petition Him for grace in our time of need (Hebrews 4:16).

But the glory of the Lord is not something to be bound or studied, and it is not limited to causing conviction in His creation. The glory is, in some mysterious way, a substance or currency. It is a realm, a spiritual reality that supplants creation when the two collide. It is the atmosphere of Heaven—emanating from God Himself. It is a place inside the Lord where we dwell, but most of us are unaware of it. In the glory, miracles come easy. One doesn't have to command healing—healing simply manifests, and demons flee.

You may have read about the Asbury revival. A handful of students began to worship Jesus and just never stopped. Soon, over 100,000 people visited the school to step into the glory of that tiny chapel. Each reported the same thing: The presence of God was thick and sweet, causing conviction and peace. Many backslidden believers rededicated their lives in this atmosphere. There wasn't a great evangelist there who put on a crusade. There weren't well-trained prayer teams releasing the power of God into the masses. No, there was simply the *Presence*. For a time, Asbury became a place where the glory realm touched the Earth. Indeed the Kingdom of God invaded there in power.

In Christ, there is *authority*—it is the *right* that enforces the rules of the Kingdom, and makes demons leave when we tell them to. In Jesus is also *faith*, which the Lord told us was a substance that could move mountains (Matthew 17:20). But then there is His *glory* where there is an ease. It is truly the place of rest God promised us (Hebrews 4). Many believers want to die and go to Heaven, but Jesus instructed us to live and bring Heaven to Earth (Matthew 6:10). We can rest *here* as though we were *there* (Ephesians 2:6) if you're willing to believe it. That is why you can sit in the secret place and feel the glory of the Lord coming upon you—resulting in such incredible peace that you want to lay down. The Lord is washing you in His glory, and although you are unaware of it, He is preparing you for what's to come in your life.

There was a woman named Betsie ten Boom, who I believe walked in the glory realm all day, every day. You can read about her in the book, *The Hiding Place*, written by Betsie's sister, Corrie ten Boom. The Nazis arrested Betsie and Corrie for hiding Jews in their home during WWII. They were sent to a prison, then a labor and extermination camp. Throughout their time in the camps, they endured unimaginable hardship. Corrie wrote from her perspective, which would be similar to your average Christian's (concerning the injustice), but she also occasionally told us Betsie's.

Betsie would shock Corrie repeatedly with her priorities. When a Nazi guard was beating a woman to death, Corrie lamented, "Oh the poor woman!" Betsie responded, "Yes, may God forgive her!" Betsie, of course, was talking about the *Nazi* woman. When the sisters first received their bunks at their concentration camp, they quickly realized fleas covered the entire room. Corrie was *distressed* by this finding while Betsie *thanked God* for the fleas. Later, both women would find out the guards never entered the bunkhouse because they were afraid of the fleas—allowing the sisters to hold quick bible studies with a smuggled bible inside their sleeping quarters.

While Corrie's thoughts were constantly on the temporary injustice of things, her sister's mind was always somewhere else—on the eternal. In her book, Corrie plainly stated she felt Betsie must have been a different being than the rest of humanity. Towards the end of Betsie's life (she died in the extermination camp), she uttered three prophetic visions to her sister—all of which eventually came to pass. One of these visions showed Corrie running a concentration camp in Germany after the war—but instead of a place to teach hate, it would be a place to teach the Germans how to love again through Christ.

Although Betsie was in a concentration camp, she really wasn't. Her spirit was elsewhere, and she could see far past the current issue into eternal consequence. She knew, even as a guard was beating her, that her pain was temporary, but the guard's damnation would be eternal. So when Corrie rushed over, exclaiming her hatred for the guard, Betsie rebuked her, "Do not hate!" It is almost as jarring as Jesus' rebuke of Peter, "Get behind me, Satan! You are a hindrance to me. For you are not setting your mind on the things of God, but on the things of man (Matthew 16:23)." Corrie, like Peter, was worried about the temporal, but when you walk in the glory of God, none of that stuff matters to you.

If you know highly prophetic people, you have probably come to terms with their fascinating behavior, like Betsie's. You'll be having a normal conversation with them one moment, and the next it is almost as if they've been transported somewhere else. The Lord has their attention, they are hearing or seeing in the Spirit, and they have a mission.

Savannah Ramsey, upon her conversion to Christianity, did not eat for weeks and locked herself in her room, where she experienced angelic visitations and the tangible presence of the Holy Spirit, Who taught her. She lost her job during this time because she failed to go to work—it didn't even cross her mind to go in. Why eat food, and why care about this world so much if you're in the glory of the Lord?

Jesus said He had food we didn't know about—to do the will of His Father (John 4:32). You may be tempted to take His words as a metaphor, but I challenge you to take them literally. Jesus was eating while He ministered to the woman at the well. His spirit *and* His stomach were filled. He told us that if we ate the Bread of Life, we would not hunger or thirst again (John 6:35). In the Old Testament when the Israelites were led into the wilderness, they complained about not having any food. The Lord promised manna from Heaven.

"...in the morning you will see the glory of the Lord, because he has heard your grumbling against him."
- **Exodus 16:7**

The people woke up, and the promised "glory" of the Lord filled them. There is something very tangible about this glory. When Satan tempts Jesus to turn rocks into bread after fasting for forty days and forty nights, Jesus responds with a biblical truth: "Man does not live on bread alone but by every word that comes from the Lord's mouth" (Matthew 4:4).

Friend, maybe what I'm writing to you sounds scrambled and crazy, but I'm trying to reveal a mystery here. As a human with the Spirit of God dwelling inside you, you walk in two worlds. One is this Earth, where God gives you dominion, but the other is in the Spirit, where even the Earth is subjugated. It isn't subjugated by authority or might like demons are when you drive them out with a word. It isn't subjugated by power like when Jesus spoke to the storm, and it ceased. It is subject to the Spirit of God Himself.

"This is the word of the Lord to Zerubbabel: Not by might, nor by power, but by my Spirit, says the Lord of hosts."
- **Zechariah 4:6**

The Earth is filled with the glory of God, and it is humbled by the holiness of Him who sits on the throne in Heaven (Isaiah 6:3). When the Spirit of God comes in this fashion, it is like a cheat code has been applied in a video game. Demons that would have taken three hours of deliverance to see removed are gone in a flash. Healings break out all over churches. Creative miracles occur with ease. Signs and wonders may appear, and entire groups of people may bear witness to them. The hardest of hearts melt like wax.

I want to give you some examples from my life.

One Freedom Night, we gathered in my living room and kitchen to worship the Lord. Partway into worship, I stood up and spoke to everyone, "You don't need a man to lay hands on you to heal you. Heavenly Father can heal you as you sit in your chairs right now. So as we reach out to Him and worship Him, expect to receive what you came for from Him." The worship team continued to play, and a song later, I stood back up and told people to check themselves to see if they noticed any difference in their bodies. A woman spoke up, "There's a difference over here!"

Her friend had come with Ehlers-Danlos Syndrome, and when she walked into my house that night, one of her ribs was popped out of place. During worship, the Lord popped it back in and healed her of EDS permanently. No one laid a hand on her, and no one prayed for her—simply being in the glory of the Lord was more than enough. This woman happened to be a practicing prostitute and drug addict. That bit of kindness from the Lord led to her full repentance, an hour-long deliverance later that night, her being water-baptized, and filled with the Holy Spirit, praise God!

That was my first experience with the glory of the Lord showing up at meetings. Many Freedom Nights later, we were open-air preaching and worshiping in Centennial Park when a man jogging past us stopped and turned toward the worship service. Suddenly, he fell on his knees and then flat on his face out cold. After a long while, he stood back up and continued jogging. The team and I joke about this man sometimes.

We had never seen someone so wacked by the presence of the Lord at one of our meetings without anyone interacting with them. The glory of God was present and struck that man down. I like to believe it was his origin story in the Lord. One day we might hear of a preacher who recounts a time he was in the park, not expecting to meet Jesus, and "bam!"

At another Freedom Night, a woman came who struggled with demonic oppression. Anytime she thought about Jesus, a demonic image would come into her head. No matter what she did, this would not cease. Again, during worship, the glory of the Lord fell on her, and she was delivered from this affliction. She later recalled it was the most powerful experience with God she ever had—and no minister had touched her! No one can even begin to take credit when miracles happen in the glory. All glory goes to Christ, and there's not even a fleshly ability to attempt to take it from Him.

I often tell people to be careful of what they sing and say regarding the Holy Spirit. If you start to ask for Him to come, He may actually show up, and you might not be ready for what He wants to do in your life.

One time, I attended a Randy Clark conference. If you don't know (because I didn't at the time), Randy was the primary speaker at the Toronto Blessing revival for the first few months. I do not mean to denigrate the man, but I wanted to touch on one aspect of the night I experienced as it highlights how the Lord receives all credit in the glory: Randy was among the least engaging speakers I had heard preach before. Many of the hundreds of people who came to listen to him left before the night was over. I felt terrible for those with babysitters on the clock because Randy went on for what felt like hours into the night. I have since understood that perhaps the man was waiting on the Spirit's timing.

Randy gave a few instructions at the end of his sermon that I have subsequently adopted. He said when he calls upon the Holy Spirit, we should all take note. If we began to shake, cry, had heat inside our chests, or became tingly, we should go to the front to be prayed for. As promised, he said a very simple prayer and asked for the Spirit to come. The room got quiet, and not much happened. Randy assured us, "Don't worry, He'll come."

Soon, some people began to cough and move about. Slowly, attendees got out of their seats and walked down to the altar to be prayed for. My wife started to show one of the "signs" and pushed her way to the front. Savannah Ramsey was there, too, and as she recalls and witnesses reported—the Holy Spirit flattened her. People started to scream.

Electricity soon replaced the dullness that permeated the atmosphere. The place looked like a war zone with bodies lying everywhere. Organization went out the window; it became a free-for-all. Tears were flowing out of the eyes of the convicted. There was no escaping the glory of God in that place.

The anointing on that man's life, to call Heaven down to Earth, is a true gift—a gift I want. God isn't looking for sophisticated speakers but yielded vessels.

If you study the Welsh Revival, you'll find an evangelist named Evan Roberts, whom God mightily used to see 100,000 people come to Jesus. Evan wasn't a

particularly great speaker and a lack of preaching typi-
fied the revival itself. But the Spirit was with Evan,
and that anointing made grown men weep and
women quake under the power of God.

An interesting thing about Randy Clark is he used to
be a cessationist Baptist pastor who was miraculously
healed and thus left his denomination in pursuit of the
Spirit. The rest of the night at his meeting reminded
me of something I read in Lonnie Frisbee's book. A
friend of his reported a time at an After Glow meeting
(a believer's meeting held after the leading church service at Calvary Chapel where Lonnie ministered)
where Lonnie asked the Spirit to come, and people began to fly out of their chairs, weep, scream, and fall
out in the Spirit. Lonnie's friend didn't know what to
do, so Lonnie quickly informed him, "Now begins the
work." The ministry team went from one person to
the next, quickly discerning what the Lord wanted to
do and praying for each person.

Going into Randy's meeting, I made a devastating
mistake. I did not come with any expectations out of a
false humility. I have since learned the error of failing
to expect something when I go to worship God.

Leonard Ravenhill was fond of saying (and I have adopted it), "Did you come to hear a sermon *about* Jesus or to *meet* Jesus?" So, while everyone else was being wrecked by the Lord, I meandered about trying to force a similar experience but got nowhere. I hopped in a prayer line where a ministry team person prayed for me, but nothing happened. Conviction settled in about my lack of hunger for the Lord, and soon repentance followed. At that point, I believe I heard the voice of the Lord say, "Talk to Randy."

Talking to Randy seemed like an impossible proposition. First, there were hundreds of people; second, Randy was on the opposite side of the auditorium as I was. By this time, my wife had been slain in the Spirit down front (the first time she had ever experienced that phenomenon). Ethan and I were ministering to those near us to help out an overwhelmed ministry staff at the event (we asked the Lord if we could be released to do that first).

We eventually returned to our group, where we spotted Savannah being carried by friends from our church. They were trying to get her to the front of the auditorium, but God's glory was so heavy that she had no strength left.

The Hebrew word we translate into "glory" is "kavod." It means "weighty" or "heavy." If you've ever wondered why people may "fall out" when the Spirit comes upon them—the weight of glory is one of the reasons. Contrary to popular belief in some Christian circles, falling to the ground under the weight of glory is nothing new. It happened during the Jesus People Movement, Azusa Street, the Great Awakening, etc. In one of John Wesley's journals, he wrote that people "were struck to the ground and lay there groaning" during services. He described this as one of the "outward signs that so often accompanied the inward work of God."

Concerning Azusa Street, Frank Bartleman wrote, "Someone might be speaking. Suddenly, the Spirit would fall upon the congregation. God himself would give the altar call. Men would fall all over the house, like the slain in battle, or rush for the altar en masse [sic.] to seek God. The scene often resembled a forest of fallen trees."

Falling out in the Spirit also happened throughout both the Old and New Testaments of the bible. One noticeable passage is found in the Book of Daniel:

"So I was left alone, gazing at this great vision; I had no strength left, my face turned deathly pale and I was helpless. Then I heard him speaking, and as I listened to him, I fell into a deep sleep, my face to the ground. A hand touched me and set me trembling on my hands and knees."
- Daniel 10:8-10

Paul had a "falling out" experience on the road to Damascus when he first encountered Jesus:

"In this connection, I journeyed to Damascus with the authority and commission of the chief priests. At midday, O king, I saw on the way a light from Heaven, brighter than the sun, that shone around me and those who journeyed with me. And when we had all fallen to the ground, I heard a voice saying to me in the Hebrew language, 'Saul, Saul, why are you persecuting me?'"
- Acts 26:12-14

A whole company of men fell to the ground when Jesus spoke out to them in the garden of Gethsemane:

"Then Jesus, knowing all that would happen to him, came forward and said to them, "Whom do you seek?" They answered him, "Jesus of Nazareth." Jesus said to them, "I am he." Judas, who betrayed him, was standing with them. When Jesus said to them, 'I am he,' they drew back and fell to the ground."
   - **John 18:4-6**

There is something about an authentic encounter with the glory of God that can send our flesh responding in submission to Him. We can't bear the weight, and so sometimes we go down. I want to guard from a few ideas surrounding falling out (or being slain) in the Spirit. First, there is the idea that a person who falls is automatically receiving something from the Lord. While that may be the case, it is not a guarantee, nor does remaining standing mean that God has withheld something from you.

A line of ten people may come to an altar, and half may fall out in the Spirit. That doesn't mean those five

people lying on the ground received and those standing did not. Earlier, I told you about my friend
Jaqualin Pennyman. He's a minister who operates in
one of the most impressive expressions of prophecy I
have witnessed. But he will be the first to tell you that
he has never fallen out in the Spirit while being prayed
for.

Sometimes, people fall out because they are demonized, and that demon makes them go down to avoid
detection. Many ministers will not follow up with
someone once they've gone to the ground, which is a
huge mistake.

I prayed for a young man once, and down he went like
a sack of potatoes. I told two other ministry team
members to sit beside him and ask the Lord for a word
for him. When the young man finally came to, he was
manifesting a demon—heaving and seething. The
team started to drive the demon out, but it would not
budge. I finally made my way back around, and immediately, I heard the word "abuse."

I called back the young man, and I asked him if he
was abused as a child. The word was correct, and after

some inner healing from the Holy Spirit, the young man was able to forgive his abuser, and he was freed from the demon. None of that would have happened if I had seen the man fall and walked on. Discernment plays a role at every level of ministry.

I once saw a man fall out three times in a single revival meeting held by a friend. I was on the ministry team, and at the end of the day, this gentleman rededicated his life to Jesus, and Ethan and I were able to pray for him. He told us the Lord had healed his physical ailments in the meeting, but I discerned that something more needed to be done. We prayed for him, and I saw a vision of him sitting on a couch, drinking alcohol and contemplating suicide. He confirmed he dealt with addiction and suicidality. In the end, the Lord healed the wounds of his heart, and several unclean spirits came out of him. Notice he had fallen out, his body was healed, but his heart was still broken, and he was still demonized even after being touched by the raw power of God.

I once attended a Daniel Kolenda (the current leader of CFAN and an anointed evangelist) impartation breakfast. A woman was in front of me, waiting to have hands laid on her. She was hunched over and unable to lift her head up. Daniel came around and laid his hands on each person, one after the next. Many fell out, including the woman in front of me. Eventually, she came to and stood back up. I went over to her and asked, "Were you healed?" She told me she was not, but she did feel a rush of the Holy Spirit.

This was not a healing service, so I did not expect the ministry team to pray for her healing, but I felt prompted myself. Ethan and I began to minister to the woman, and we found out she used to be about eight or nine inches taller, but her back had collapsed, and she was diagnosed with scoliosis.

Suddenly, I got the word "mom," so I asked her, "Is your relationship with your mom strained?" She chuckled and said, "I know that was a word from God. Yes." We proceeded to pray for inner healing—that the Holy Spirit would bind the wounds in her broken heart received from her mother. I asked her, "Do you think you can forgive your mother now?" She could and did, and that's when we commanded her back to be healed. The woman grew about three inches right before our eyes! She thanked us and left, able to look straight in front of her instead of at her feet on her way out.

Notice, she had fallen out in the Spirit—and maybe the Lord did something in her at that moment—but she wasn't healed. Many people have similar experiences where the power of God hits them emotionally, but they don't perceive a lasting difference. Others feel nothing, and suddenly, their whole world is changed the next day when they start hearing from God for the first time. When a person falls out, it is simply their flesh responding to the Spirit, and not everyone's flesh responds the same. That is why some may shake, others faint, and still some simply say, "I receive it," and walk away forever changed.

As I recalled earlier, there were bodies everywhere at the Randy Clark conference—Savannah's being one of them. Four of us picked her up off the ground and began to carry her to the front, but we were stopped. Somehow, Randy had made his way to the middle of the venue and now stood right before us. He looked at Savannah and said, "At every conference, I ask the Lord, 'Where are the Aimee Mcphersons, the Heidi Bakers, the Kathryn Kuhlmans of this generation...'"

When he mentioned Kuhlman, it was like lightning struck Savannah, and she fell to the floor, shaking and screaming.

I once asked Savannah about this extreme expression, and she responded that Christians have gotten into the habit of saying biblical truths without pondering their implications. For example, we say that God is an all-consuming fire, so why are we surprised that it may feel like we're on fire when we enter His presence? One of the previous times we pulled Savannah off the floor, she couldn't see and kept saying, "He's so bright, He's so bright!" We know God dwells in unapproachable light, so why would we be shocked that our natural eyes couldn't handle that brightness?

Randy then turned to me, and in obedience to the Lord, I began speaking to him. "Hi, Randy, I'm James," I said, extending my hand for a handshake. He didn't say a word but took my hand and immediately began praying over me. Then, he blew in my face, and I went down to the floor. I wasn't on the ground for more than a minute before deciding to stand back up. As I did, I felt something different in my head—a tingling sensation inside. That moment became the catalyst for a vibrant prophetic dream life, something I will share more about later.

What happened to everyone at this meeting? The glory of the Lord came down on us, and each one had a different response according to where we were in our walk with God and our sensitivity to the Spirit. When the glory of God enters the room, things happen. They can't help but happen. The mystery I want to convey here is found in John 17:22, where Jesus prayed to the Father, "The glory that you have given me I have given to them, that they may be one even as we are one..." Jesus has given us His glory—making us glory bearers. As a glory bearer, we should expect the natural to become supernatural all around us.

Peter, a disciple of Jesus, understood this. As he preached, the Spirit of the Lord would fall upon all who listened (Acts 10:44). As Peter went about his business walking down the street, people would be healed by simply touching his shadow (Acts 5:15). This is the spiritual life God is calling all His children into— to bear His glory and His name as we walk about this Earth. Like Betsie ten Boom, may our spiritual eyes be so opened that we forget the temporal and may others question, as Corrie ten Boom did of her sister, "Is she a different sort of being?"

The truth is, if you are a believer, the glory of God is already within you because Jesus asked the Father for it on your behalf. The Lord gives good gifts to His children, especially at the request of His only Son. His glory dwells in you, and at times, you may even witness it manifesting in a tangible way.

After my deliverance experience with Jaqualin, I asked him to teach a workshop on the gift of prophecy at my house. I'll write more about what I saw there because it was mind-blowing, but for this chapter, I want to focus on something that occurred when the class was over. Some people left my home, but many stayed behind to discuss Jesus. At one point in the night, I found myself in the kitchen doing no specific task when I heard a commotion from the living room. I ventured in to investigate and heard people talking about "gold dust."

Now, the only other time I had heard of this phenomenon was when I watched a movie by Darren Wilson called Finger of God. In that film, he documents the appearance of gold dust at a relative's church. Some churches in the past have faked this wonder (I call it a wonder because it genuinely does make you wonder what it is for). One church, apparently, was caught putting gold particles in the HVAC system. I have yet to see such gold flecks appear in the air anywhere, but what I'm about to describe to you I will testify I have seen time and time again (including this very day as I write about it).

Later, I learned more details about what happened before I arrived, but essentially, Jaqualin paused his teaching for a moment and told my wife, "Turn your hands over, and you'll see gold dust on them." She did as he said, and sure enough, her hands were covered in tiny flecks of gold. It resembled golden glitter but appeared to be just beneath the skin. Then, others in the group began examining their hands, and they, too, saw gold dust on their skin. By the time I joined them, I could see gold flecks on my wife's face. Although I checked my own hands, I did not see this sign on them that night.

The next day, Jaqualin led a Freedom Night for us and ministered powerfully "in the glory," as he would say.

Jesus did miracles, ranging from a person being freed from epilepsy to a woman's womb being opened (you can see it pulsating in the recorded video). A group saw a woman's skin rash disappear before their eyes. The prophetic flowed heavily as words of knowledge and wisdom were poured out, and a couple of people gave their lives to Jesus that night. Towards the end of the ministry, several people approached Jaqualin and told him they had gold particles on their bodies. He took time, then, to tell everyone in the room to check themselves. Sure enough, twenty to thirty people come forward with gold dust on their hands or arms. Among this group were firm believers, new believers, and I even saw an unbeliever I know for a fact practiced new age, with the sign all over her skin. It was at this time I saw a few flecks of gold even on my hands, which filled me with great joy!

Soon, this tangible sign of God's glory appeared everywhere. It would cover people at the altar of my church; it would show up in private worship meetings we held at my home. I once even felt compelled to tell a woman I was ministering to over video call to check her hands—and it was there! Gold dust practically follows my friend Ethan wherever he goes.

Once, my cousin was at my house, and the Lord wanted to minister powerfully to her. We were telling her about the things we had been seeing, and I started to try to explain the gold dust to her when I stopped mid-sentence. Something prompted me, so I said, "Actually, turn your hands over and let me just show you." Sure enough, there was gold dust on her hands. She later told me that the sign would appear whenever she prayed, and it has remained with her, manifesting every so often. She was, likewise, freed from suicidality that night and baptized in the Holy Spirit. I'm so proud of her; she is now holding Freedom Nights where she lives.

I once ministered in Montana, and the host evangelist picked me up from the airport. We were discussing things of the Lord when the topic of gold dust came up. He had never experienced it before, but I assured him, "We will probably see it on this trip." Indeed, the moment we stepped into our host church and prayed, gold dust appeared on people's hands. Many of the ministers marveled at this. One of the ministers had it caked all over his hands, large chunks he described as "scales." Usually, I have seen it manifest as tiny specs that can't be manipulated, but early on my wife (of all people!) doubted this golden wonder.

Aly figured the gold dust was probably just makeup (something I verify with people before pointing it out). As she sat in church in the middle of these doubts one morning, a giant piece of gold dust appeared on her palm. It was so large it could be picked up. She knew this was God's way of affirming to her that this sign was from Him. There was no way her makeup could account for it.

Scan the QR code to see an example of gold dust appearing on one of my neighbor's hands.

You may be wondering what on Earth the gold dust could mean and whether you can find it in the bible.

First, I have not found an account of it in scripture. One person told me, "The Old Testament temple was covered in gold. In the New Testament, we are the temple of the Lord, so He also covers us in gold." It is a cool theory, but it doesn't account for the number of unbelievers I have seen this sign appear on.

I do not believe it means anything specific. People want to think that if it appears on them, they are somehow special, but I've concluded that it has nothing to do with the person it appears on and everything to do with the glory of God. It is an expression of Him and *His* glory, not ours.

The sign points you to something greater than yourself—to Jesus. It is a manifestation of His glory that you can see, much like the weight of His glory you can feel. It is more closely related to the manna that fell in the desert that fed grumbling Hebrews. It wasn't about the Hebrews; it was about the Lord. We are not called to chase after the signs but after the one they point to.

With that said, you may be asking, "Lord, if this is real, I want to see it!" I encourage you to take out your phone's light, flip your hands over, and look at your palms under the light right now. I have found the more we talk about the glory of God and acknowledge that He is a wonder-working God, the more His wonders show up in our lives.

Chapter 9
Curiosities of the Spirit

The Holy Spirit is not limited to the gifts outlined in the New Testament, which are commonly referred to as the "nine gifts of the Spirit." These I have covered and will continue to cover. They include the word of knowledge, word of wisdom, faith, gifts of healing, miracles, prophecy, discernment of spirits, tongues, and interpretation of tongues. But, if you flip back to the Old Testament, I can give you an example of a unique anointing (the word "anointing" means to "smear with oil." It means God has clothed a person in the Holy Spirit for a specific task).

"Then the Lord spoke to Moses, saying: "See, I have called by name Bezalel the son of Uri, the son of Hur, of the tribe of Judah. And I have filled him with the Spirit of God, in wisdom, in understanding, in knowledge, and in all manner of workmanship, to design artistic works, to work in gold, in silver, in bronze, in cutting jewels for setting, in

carving wood, and to work in all manner of work-manship.

And I, indeed I, have appointed with him Aholiab the son of Ahisamach, of the tribe of Dan; and I have put wisdom in the hearts of all the gifted artisans, that they may make all that I have commanded you..."
- **Exodus 31: 1-6**

Notice God had called Bezalel, and the Lord had filled him with His Spirit to design and build the Tabernacle (a tent that housed God's presence). This was a unique anointing not found in the New Testament, yet it was from the Lord. Similarly, as you walk with the Holy Spirit, you will find curious changes and abilities arise in your spirit that you may not have a biblical grid for. Let me give you an example from my own life.

From my conception until about 31, I could not remember people's names. Many lament the same issue—they'll meet someone, ask them their name, and not sixty seconds later, they'll forget it again. This deficit was exceedingly embarrassing at family reunions each year, where I'd have to ask for people's names repeatedly. It was just as bad in the realms of business and school. Finally, it hindered the growing call on my life as an evangelist.

My job is to tell people about Jesus, to turn them into disciples, and to see them healed and freed if needed. It is a relational activity, yet I'd make people feel like strangers each time I'd have to ask for their names again before praying for them. This all changed one day when I attended one of my church's young adult nights. Aly and I were speaking that night about relationships as part of a panel discussion, so we greeted people beforehand. We approached a relatively new couple and introduced ourselves. After Felisha and Aaron gave us their *names*, I knew something was true; I knew I'd never forget them.

The Holy Spirit inside me was assuring me of this fact. Immediately, I began to remember people's names even better than my wife, who, historically, was embarrassed by my fault in this area. We'd pray for a server one day and I'd still remember her name several days later, for example. It was incredible! I don't know if the Lord delivered me, fixed my brain, or anointed me with a gift of name remembrance—but it has benefited my pursuit of people for the gospel. I'd estimate my name recall is about 90% better than it used to be. A funny thing about it, though, is I still can't remember people's names I met before the "event" with Felisha and Aaron.

Something about meeting new people now "imprints" on me: if I want to remember people's names from my past, I have to, embarrassingly, ask for their names again to lock into this new gift the Lord gave.

God is interested in your personal life.

"You know when I sit down and when I rise up, you discern my thoughts from afar."
-    **Psalm 139:2**

There is nothing in your life you can't bring to the Holy Spirit.

"...praying at all times in the Spirit, with all prayer and supplication..."
-    **Ephesians 6:18**

My wife and I decided to forgo getting a dog until we could fence in our backyard, which we didn't have the finances or time to complete. One morning I was in my prayer closet praying about something when a vision of a scraggly puppy sitting on a twin-sized bed popped in my head. I had no idea why—dogs were certainly not on my mind.

That afternoon, I received a text message from my wife. In it was a photo of a little scraggly puppy and the request, "Can I bring her home?" The timing was bad to bring a dog into our family by all the world's standards, but I took the question to the Lord because He had given me that vision earlier in the day—a vision that looked very similar to the puppy I was looking at on my phone.

"Lord, is this from you? Should we bring this dog home?" I asked. The response I heard could have only come from God, "It will bring joy to your children." We ended up adopting Ruby, our red heeler, and I have been reminded of God's word concerning the joy she'd produce in our children repeatedly as they've played with her over the past year. We still do not have our backyard entirely fenced in, so Ruby has become a primarily inside dog—something I did not want.

Sometimes, it is easiest to recognize the voice of the Lord when He is saying something your flesh disagrees with. When He tells you to do something that doesn't align with your heart's desires, you can bet that thought didn't originate from your soul. Who knows? Maybe my daughters had been praying for a dog, and the Lord responded by sending me a vision and a word.

My wife once struggled with homeschooling our oldest and decided to ask the Lord for strategy before falling asleep one night. As she was waking up in the morning, she had a dream that turned into a vision. In the vision, the "school area" had moved from our sitting room to our kitchen table. Instead of calling the activity "school," it was now called "Table Time." Instead of the learning being linear, my wife had various activities set up around the table for our daughter to choose from and a checklist of ones she needed to do by the end of the day. Aly was thankful to be given a strategy from the Lord to teach our daughter.

I personally come to the Lord on just about every-thing—right down to where I should eat lunch, as I've mentioned previously. One day, I had finished working a video job in Franklin, TN, when the Lord told me to eat at Carabba's. I did not want heavy Italian food, and I didn't care much for the restaurant personally. These facts helped me understand that the thought must have come from the Lord, not my flesh.

I sat down, ordered my food, and asked for a word for my server—thinking she was the one God sent me there to minister to. At the end of my meal, I asked the server about a word I felt I had for her, but it wasn't accurate. Swing and miss! I then became somewhat despondent, not knowing why I was eating at a place I didn't want to eat at. Why did God send me here?

After paying, I left the building, and that's when I overheard a conversation a man was having with a young woman. He was talking about the evangelist Lonnie Frisbee—someone I admire for the anointing on his life. I knew then that he was the man God wanted me to speak with. I introduced myself and found out he was an evangelist named Mickey Robin-son, who had come to the Lord through a painful recovery from a plane crash. He gave me a copy of his book and prayed for me. The Lord had sent me there not to minister but to be ministered to by someone else.

I was once invited to teach and minister at a conference called Men on Fire. The host said I could also come a day earlier and preach at his church's youth group. This was an incredible opportunity for me, and the Lord had prophesied through several people about how my ministry would impact a young generation. Still, I took the offer to the Lord and heard Him tell me not to go early and to turn that portion of the trip down.

It is hard to turn opportunities like that down when you're a relatively unknown evangelist because they don't come frequently. But my success is based on my obedience to the Lord, so I obeyed. When the day came that I would have flown initially out, I was overloaded with work I needed to wrap up. Had I flown out sooner, there was a chance I wouldn't have been able to take the conference itself or been distracted the entire time there, trying to wrap up work remotely.

Again, the Lord is interested in every aspect of your life, and you can come to Him about the big and the little decisions. If you aren't hearing a word from Him, fall back on scripture. Ask yourself, "Is this decision sinful or against God's written word?" If not, move forward with the plan with a clear conscience. But I do recommend at least inquiring on God and expecting an answer.

One evening at dinner, a young server approached our table in tears. We had already prayed for a couple of other servers who had been either healed or delivered, and word had begun spreading throughout the restaurant about the power of God. One of my pastors gently asked her, "Why did you come over here?" She replied, "Because you told me things about my life you couldn't possibly have known."

This response surprised us, as we hadn't actually spoken to her before. Yet, as we began ministering, the Lord started revealing words of knowledge to us. Suddenly, a glass shattered at her feet—another server had dropped it. Then, a random person interrupted, asking about tea. We quickly recognized these disruptions as an attempt to hinder the woman's freedom, and my pastor prayed against the spirit of chaos in her mind.

When it was my turn, I asked, "Do you, or does anyone close to you, struggle with addiction—specifically opioids?" Her jaw dropped, and with tears in her eyes, she responded in disbelief, "How could you know that?" I knew because the Spirit had shown me an image of the pills. She then revealed that her daughter's father was addicted to opioids—a man she had vowed never to forgive.

But that night, after encountering Jesus, her heart was transformed. She chose to forgive him, and in that moment, she was set free.

What a glorious ending to such an unusual beginning—a woman unknowingly *drawn by a future event* into a divine encounter in the present. Time does not exist in the Spirit—He is unbound.

The longer you walk with Him, the more curiously the Holy Spirit moves in your life. Again, it isn't just about the nine gifts of the Spirit but about an active relationship where you're totally committed to the work of Christ, whether you're awake *or asleep*.

Chapter 10
Dreams

"For God speaks in one way, and in two, though man does not perceive it. In a dream, in a vision of the night, when deep sleep falls on men, while they slumber on their beds, then he opens the ears of men and terrifies them with warnings."

- Job 33:15-16

You most likely have received prophetic dreams from the Lord and have "not perceive[d] it." Many people dream and figure their dreams are sporadic, meaningless images. Have you ever had a dream you woke up from in the middle of the night? Have you had recurring dreams? What about a dream with small details that you're shocked you remember? Has one of your dreams been vivid? Or perhaps you had a fuzzy dream, but somewhere in the middle, there was a portion you recall perfectly? In my experience, these are all signs of a dream being from the Lord.

Where do dreams come from? I postulate they can originate from one of three sources: your soul, Satan, or God. Soulish dreams are typically the result of over-indulgence during your waking hours. When I was in middle school, I would play video games all day some-times, and then I'd dream about playing the games at night. The game captured my mind, and it held me even in sleep. Perhaps you've binge-watched television and then dreamt about the same show at night? Have you ever ruminated on your ambitions all day and then found yourself dreaming about them that even-ing?

If you want to hear from the Lord clearly at night, limit what goes into your eyes. The more space you give the Lord in your imagination, the more easily you'll discern what is from Him and what is from you. The Holy Spirit had me cut out scrolling short-form social media content, and the purpose was to clean up my mind so I could see more clearly. I, likewise, cut out about 90% of television from my diet. I've even cut out reading fiction novels for now. My imagination is precious and necessary to protect if I'm going to see, feel, or hear in the spirit-realm.

Your ears should be guarded. Don't overindulge in music or jingles—anything that will echo in your subconscious. Have you ever woken up singing a song? Have you ever been unable to stop hearing a song in your head? We want to keep our ears open and available for the Lord so when He speaks, we know it is Him and not our soul talking. In today's world, far too many stimuli are killing our ability to interact effectively with our Creator.

Society won't tell you to make your mind sacred; you must decide to do that on your own. I have not perfected guarding my eyes and ears, but with each passing month, I feel the Spirit pulling me deeper into consecration so He can speak louder to me—including through my dreams.

I find a lot of people I minister to suffer from *demonic* dreams. One type is the person dreams about an old sexual partner they used to have, even though they no longer want to. Charismatics call these attachments "soul ties" which they glean from 1 Corinthians 6:15-20.

Another is where the person dreams of sexual fantasies. Others may dream dreadful, never-ending dreams, the same dream night after night. For example, I knew a man who dreamt the same dream for over a month—in it, he was always stuck in the mud, and there were turtles and snakes about. A shared experience I've seen is people waking up in a sleep paralysis state where they can only move their head for a time—often, these people claim they see a "shadowy figure" in their room. Witches have some of the worst night terrors of all, and for the life of me, I don't know why they continue down their dark path when they suffer so horribly from it.

Demons cause such evil dreams (some argue demons can't give you nightmares, but I believe they can as they do intrusive thoughts). The unclean spirit can either be inside the person experiencing the dream or external to them—typically sent by witches to afflict someone. People who are caught in sin (addictions being one of the most prevalent) usually have such nightmares. Sexual sin, such as promiscuity or pornography addiction, typically causes the perverse dreams.

Our Freedom Night team once led a woman to the Lord, who then backslid into her old lifestyle of prostitution about a month later, and upon repentance was delivered again from a demon attacking her at nighttime. She described it as a physical, sexual assault. As incredible as that may sound—she is not the only one to have confided such a thing to me.

People can be freed from these types of dreams and encounters by Jesus! I regularly see God deliver those oppressed in the night. A command I'll often give when praying over someone is, "Whatever spirit is causing nightmares in this person, go now and do not return." Or perhaps I'll say, "Demon causing sleep paralysis, I break you, and I command you to loose this person now."

When it comes to external nightmares, as I mentioned previously, these are typically demonic attacks sent by witches. If you wake in the middle of the night (usually between one and three AM) from a nightmare, and you have not been habitually sinning, you are most likely under attack. If this is the case, follow the pattern of James 4:7, "Submit yourselves therefore to God. Resist the devil, and he will flee from you."

The most important part of that command is submitting ourselves to God. Do not focus so much on the devil or the attack in those moments; that's what the enemy wants. Instead, focus on Jesus. When I minister in new territories, I will often be attacked in my sleep by whatever principality rules there. I'll wake up, maybe I will feel dread, but one thing will be for sure—there are demons in my room. The first thing I do is talk to Jesus, "Jesus, I love you, I submit to you. Thank you that I'm in covenant with you, and your word says no power of darkness can harm me." I will then rebuke the devil, "Every unclean spirit in this room, I command you to leave right now in the name of Jesus and go to the pit!" I might pray for the next little while, asking the Holy Spirit to bring peace, and eventually, I'll go back to sleep. If you submit to Jesus every time Satan attacks, he'll eventually give up because it is a losing strategy as it pushes you deeper into the arms of God.

One of the wildest things about these encounters is the fact I can often feel the presence of these evil spirits coming off my body—it's a tingling sensation that departs me.

Dreams from the Lord are the absolute best, but they also tend to be the least straightforward. God likes to speak in mysteries.

"It is the glory of God to conceal things, but the glory of kings is to search things out."
- **Proverbs 25:2**

In the Old Testament, a prophet named Daniel was skilled at interpreting dreams.

"...Daniel had understanding in all visions and dreams."
- **Daniel 1:17**

The gift on his life to interpret dreams was so substantial that a pagan queen called him in to interpret the dream of a Babylonian king.

"...because an excellent spirit, knowledge, and understanding to interpret dreams, explain riddles, and solve problems were found in this Daniel, whom the king named Belteshazzar. Now let Daniel be called, and he will show the interpretation."
- **Daniel 5:12**

The vast majority of dreams you will have from the Lord are symbolic. There is a tendency for believers to receive a dream from God and then take it literal, but we rarely find that pattern in scripture. Let's take Pharaoh's dream in Genesis 41, for example.

"When two full years had passed, Pharaoh had a dream: He was standing by the Nile, when out of the river there came up seven cows, sleek and fat, and they grazed among the reeds. After them, seven other cows, ugly and gaunt, came up out of the Nile and stood beside those on the riverbank. And the cows that were ugly and gaunt ate up the seven sleek, fat cows. Then Pharaoh woke up."
- **Genesis 41:1-4**

This dream is full of difficult symbolism. Pharaoh sent for all the wise men and magicians in his land to interpret his dream, but none of them could. Why? Because this was a dream from the Lord. The Lord would need to give the interpretation, and He did through Joseph.

Perhaps one night, you have a dream from the Lord, and in it are human characters—people you know personally. In my experience, these people represent something other than themselves. I've dreamt of a friend representing the Church, or my earthly brother representing Jesus.

A disciple once sent me his dream, and in a portion of it, he was with his family upstairs in his home watching TV. His mom then sent him to take his dogs outside to use the bathroom. As he's outside watching his dogs, dozens of turkeys and deer suddenly show up; they are migrating. These animals turn to attack his "little" dog, and he has to fight them off. The dream then goes through several other scenes with various additional animals and dealings with his family.

He asked me to pray about this dream, so I did, and the Lord gave me an interpretation for each character and situation. For example, his family represented his church family, and his mother represented the Holy Spirit sending him on an assignment outside the church. The "little" dog represented his heart and the wild animals were trials and temptations of the world. I heard the phrase "fear of man" and told my friend he must guard his heart while in the world on assignment.

I told him the attacking animals were herbivores, highlighting the world's deceptive nature. It seems harmless, but it is not. The rest of his dream was further warning for him and edification for his church. He wrote back and said this interpretation was affirmed in his spirit.

Previously, I wrote about my neighbor's family revival. A detail I left out was that my wife had been dreaming about Dave and Jaime for almost a year before their salvations. There were three distinct dreams, but we did not have interpretations for them. The night they came to our house to discuss my book, I invited Ethan Sherrer to join. Ethan has a powerful gift of dream interpretation on his life, so he spent an hour in the prayer closet seeking Jesus for interpretations of these dreams.

That night, after dinner, I preached a plain gospel message to my neighbors about salvation by grace and the Lordship Jesus demands of us. I then asked Ethan to share the dreams and interpretations. Each dream was in a different season of the year. One spoke to their marriage, another to their future, etc. It was God revealing His heart (prophecy) to them! As Ethan released the interpretations, I saw the Spirit of God falling upon Dave, and he began to weep (something he had rarely done before). The Spirit was telling him that what Ethan was saying was true. Thus, this was the first time I saw a dream interpretation lead to a person's salvation.

Dreams are inherently prophetic. If you receive dreams from the Lord, understand that He is speaking, and you should listen. He is conveying His heart. Often, He is warning us or making promises to us. When you receive a dream, pray into it or ask someone you trust to hear accurately from the Lord to pray into it. What can be challenging is it often helps to have someone who doesn't know you intimately interpret your dreams because they won't be as biased or tempted to interpret the dream "in their flesh." Sometimes, though, you don't have to interpret a dream. Such dreams could be called "encounters."

"At Gibeon the Lord appeared to Solomon during the night in a dream, and God said, 'Ask for whatever you want me to give you.'"
- **1 Kings 3:5**

In Solomon's dream, the Lord showed up and asked a direct question. Solomon then had an entire conversation with the Lord. At the end of the dream, Solomon was anointed with a discerning heart, and God's favor came upon him for wealth. This would be an example of a dream encounter. I have had a few of these types of dreams.

In college, I dreamt I knew a tornado was headed to where my family and friends were staying. Only I knew about the tornado, so I called and warned them. They left the building, and a tornado struck, but all of them were safe. I felt accomplished and decided to drive home. The day was perfectly sunny; I entered my home, a tornado formed, my house was destroyed, and I was killed. My dream went black, and a "man" came to me, looked me in the eyes, and said, "Those who can see for others often can't see for themselves." I then woke up. I believe the Lord was warning me about a girl I was dating at that time who was not right for me. My family knew it, but I was blinded by "love."

There was a point in my life when I became addicted to caffeine. If I went a morning without it, I would develop a massive headache in the afternoon. One night, I was sleeping, and the Lord came to me. He said, "James, stop drinking caffeine."

"You want me to stop drinking caffeine, Lord?" I replied.

"Yes," came the Lord's affirmation. I then woke up.

That morning, I quit caffeine cold turkey, but I also wrestled with God. I told Him that caffeine use wasn't a sin I could find in the bible. He responded, "It isn't about the caffeine; it is about the addiction. I want you to be free."

The Lord wasn't saying I could never have caffeine, but instead, I should not be a slave to anything other than Him. Similarly, Jesus said we can't be slaves to God and money (Matthew 6:24). It wasn't that we couldn't have money; we couldn't let it rule us in any capacity. To this day, before I drink any caffeine, I ask the Holy Spirit if it is wise for me to have it or not. If I want to use it as a crutch (i.e., energy), He usually tells me it isn't wise. If I want to use it for celebration, He tends to say it is wise. I can't help but think about C.S.

Lewis' rules for drinking alcohol (one of them states to never drink alcohol because you are sad, but only when you are in a good mood).

I recently had a dream where I saw myself in my podcast studio recording an episode on "dream interpretation" with two guests who are gifted in that area. I had recorded that episode a week or so prior to the dream, but in the night-vision I was seeing all three of us in third person view. I heard a voice say, "Since you have honored the gift of dream interpretation, you will now have it." I dreamt many things that night, but this was the only scene I could remember, and I took it as an encounter with the Lord. I immediately began praying into people's dreams to receive the gift in good faith.

An encounter with the Lord can result in impartation, deliverance, healing, salvation, and more. I have a friend who was fervently praying for his buddy one night. In the morning, the buddy called him and said, "I had an incredible dream last night. You were in it; you prayed for me, and I was healed. When I woke up, I was still healed!" Many people have dreams about well-known ministers whom God uses to heal them in their sleep. I've even had people tell me I was in their dreams, praying for their healing. I, myself, dream frequently about healing sick people and driving demons out of others. I once dreamt of being in a large mansion with many rooms. I systematically went to each room and opened the door. Inside was a unique individual who was sick in some fashion. I would pray for them; they would be healed, and then I'd move on to the next room. I can't help but hope these were real-life people who woke up healed around the world.

A woman in our group who went to the Randy Clark meeting with me did not have the same experience as everyone else. She was confused and scared by the sights and sounds. When one of our pastors fell to the ground under the glory of God, this woman thought it was a medical emergency instead of a spiritual experience. That night, she went home and went to sleep. As she slept lightly, the Holy Spirit came upon her all night—teaching her. At one point while sleeping, her husband's hand laid on her forehead (he has no recollection of this), and the woman began to shake uncontrollably in her bed. She couldn't take it for long and pried her husband's hand off her. The shaking ceased. These experiences culminated into a burgeoning prophetic gift in her. She had an encounter with the Lord and received impartation much like Solomon did in the bible.

My sister-in-law gave her life to Jesus because of a dream. Very simply, a voice in the dream told her, "Go to church with Aly." She woke up, called my wife, and came to church with us the next day. She was the type of person who did not want to have borrowed faith. She once told me, "I want to believe, but I don't want to fake it." That Sunday morning, as worship went on in our sanctuary, the Holy Spirit fell on her. She began to weep. The conviction became so overwhelming that she ran out of the church.

While God was *convicting* her, Satan was *condemning* her for her past sins. Fortunately, a woman caught her in the parking lot, brought her back in, and my wife caught up with them. Aly then explained the difference between condemnation and conviction.

Condemnation is where Satan shames you for past sin and tells you there is no forgiveness for it. Conviction is where the Holy Spirit reveals your sin to you but offers a chance to repent and be forgiven.

My sister-in-law went to the bathroom to gather herself, wrestling with what she had just experienced. Sitting in a stall, she argued with God, trying to determine whether she was losing her mind. She even questioned whether she had taken something that could explain what she was feeling—but fortunately, she had not. A battle raged within her between belief and unbelief.

She had recently purchased a silver snake ring that wrapped around her finger. As she sat there staring at it, suddenly, it snapped in half and broke off her hand. In shock, she cursed out loud and finally admitted to the Lord, "You are real."

Moments later, she returned to the sanctuary and gave her life to Jesus that day—experiencing true joy for the first time in her life. And all of it was set into motion by a dream she had, which, in turn, was birthed through intercessory prayer.

Chapter 11
Intercessory Prayer and the Kingdom

In the book of Mark, chapter seven, a Syrophoenician woman comes to Jesus because her daughter is demonized. Jesus has traveled far from His previous ministry location, and one can't help but wonder if He did it simply for this one woman. The woman hunts Him down, most likely because He is a successful and famous exorcist, and in the book of Matthew chapter fifteen, she cries out, "Have mercy on me, O Lord, Son of David; my daughter is severely oppressed by a demon."

Much has been written about Jesus' rebuff, the woman's pagan origins, and the deliverance itself, but I want to point out one simple fact. The woman asked Jesus for mercy on *herself*, yet she was there in place of her daughter. In essence, she offered herself as the intercessor between her daughter and God—she took it personally.

An intercessor is a go-between. Have you ever been bullied, and someone stepped in to protect you? That person was your intercessor. Have you ever been in a lawsuit, or had to file an insurance claim and hired an attorney? Your legal representative acted as your intercessor. When it comes to scripture, we find in the Old Testament there is lament because an intercessor could not be found between God and man.

"If someone sins against a man, God will mediate for him, but if someone sins against the Lord, who can intercede for him?"
- **1 Samuel 2:25**

The wrath of God remained upon sinners, and since God is the Supreme Authority, there wasn't anyone who could mediate between sinners and Him in the Old Testament. There were instances where the Lord would speak between a chosen man of God, such as Moses, and a people, such as the Hebrews—but nothing could satisfy the just wrath of the Lord until Christ's perfect atonement.

"Who is to condemn? Christ Jesus is the one who died—more than that, who was raised—who is at the

right hand of God, who indeed is interceding for us."
-   Romans 8:34

Thus, the ultimate intercessor is Jesus Christ.

Through Him, we are given access to the Father to petition Heaven (Hebrews 4:16). As Christians ("little Christs"), we emulate our Lord in various ways. He healed the sick, so we heal the sick. He preached the gospel, so we preach the gospel. He not only did the "work" of intercession by His sacrifice, though. Jesus also "prayed" intercession for His disciples.

"My prayer is not that you take them [Jesus' disciples] out of the world but that you protect them from the evil one. They are not of the world, even as I am not of it. Sanctify them by the truth; your word is truth. As you sent me into the world, I have sent them into the world. For them I sanctify myself, that they too may be truly sanctified."
-   John 17:15-19

Thus, as His followers, we too should emulate Him in intercessory prayer for others. We were given the right by His sacrifice, and His example provides us with the responsibility of intercession. Intercessory prayer is not a gift of the Spirit listed in scripture. Still, I believe the Lord sets some people apart for violently taking Heaven by force in their prayer closets (Matthew 11:12).

Some seem to easily give way to the Spirit in travailing for others; to travail is to labor in difficulty to birth something. A person might travail for their business to succeed, but a Christian intercessor often travails to see someone come to Christ. My wife had been travailing for her sister to come to Jesus for a month before she had the dream that told her to go to church.

There was one particular moment when the Holy Spirit fell in ecstasy on my wife, and she prayed and wailed for her sister's salvation. It was the Spirit praying through Aly—God's compassion, the love of a Father, using my wife as a conduit for prayer in the Earth. Jesus said we had the power to bind and free things on the Earth, and when we did, they'd be enforced by Heaven (Matthew 18:18). He said the same for forgiving sins (John 20:23). The modern Church has a long way to go in understanding these mysterious powers.

To drive this point home, I need to explain what I call *Kingdom Theology*. No one has influenced my understanding of this perspective more than a man named Greg Hood, so much of what I share here is inspired by his teaching. I only know Greg because God gave me a series of prophetic dreams featuring him, and in the first one, he had wisdom to impart to me.

Through a mutual friend, I was able to meet Greg for breakfast, and we both agreed that God wanted me to grasp this Kingdom perspective.

Jesus did not come to establish a religion—He came to establish His Kingdom. Few truly understood this early on, except perhaps John the Baptist, who declared to Israel that the Messiah would baptize them with the Holy Spirit and fire (Matthew 3:11). The Israelites were expecting a Messiah who would establish an earthly kingdom; a suffering Savior was not in their purview.

But Jesus came to deal with sin so that we could become sons and daughters of God (John 1:12-13)—to be transformed into His likeness. We didn't just need our

sins covered by an Old Testament sacrifice; we needed
them completely removed. We needed to be justified—
just as if I never sinned. This was all part of God's
greater plan to reclaim the Earth from the hands of
Satan.

The Bible calls Satan the "god of this world (2 Cor
4:4)" or the "prince of this world (John 14:30)." In Luke
chapter four it says:

**"And the devil took [Jesus] up and showed him all
the kingdoms of the world in a moment of time, and
said to him, 'To you I will give all this authority and
their glory, for it has been delivered to me, and I
give it to whom I will. If you, then, will worship me,
it will all be yours.'"**
-   **Luke 4:5-7**

Clearly, scripture asserts Satan has been given dominion over the Earth, but it was not always that way. In
the book of Genesis, in the beginning, we find God's
plan for mankind was to rule the Earth.
**"And God said to them, 'Be fruitful and multiply
and fill the earth and subdue it, and have dominion
over the fish of the sea and over the birds of the**

heavens and over every living thing that moves on the earth.'"

- **Genesis 1:28**

The word "dominion" has connotations of authority and rule within a given territory. When we look at the word "kingdom," we see it is a combination of the word "king" and the suffix "-dom." The etymology of "-dom" is "state, province, or jurisdiction." In other words, a kingdom is the territory where a king has jurisdiction or reign. According to the Bible, the kingdom of the Earth was initially given to mankind—that was the intent.

"The heavens are the Lord's heavens,
but the earth he has given to the children of man."
- **Psalm 115:16**

This all means that Adam and his children were given authority in the Earth. To sharpen that point, nothing can happen in the Earth *without* man's consent. That's a bold statement, but if you stick around long enough, I believe I can show you this truth. First, let's talk about the problem.

In the Garden of Eden, there was perfect communion between God and man. Adam was placed over the Earth but under the direction of the Lord. God was in *charge*, but He relinquished *control*. That is one of the reasons why the Tree of Knowledge was available, though forbidden. The Lord expected obedience and warned of the consequence for disobedience. But He did not *control* Adam's behavior. Disobedience was an option. We call this *free will*. Unfortunately, Adam chose disobedience and ate from the tree anyway. The result had unfathomable consequences for mankind—most of them the Church talks about, but one is not often discussed. That is the consequence of turning the dominion of the Earth over to Satan.

Who knows how long Satan had been in rebellion against the Lord before he attempted to usurp the Earth from man? It was that rebellion that earned Satan a swift boot out of Heaven (Luke 10:18). It was that rebellion which Adam and Eve joined in against the rule of their Creator. Instead of submitting their lives to God, they chose to submit to His enemy. Yes, they had dominion over the Earth, but God's rule was supreme over them, and they shirked it. Do you remember when I wrote that nothing can happen in the

Earth without man's consent? When Adam and Eve chose to submit to Satan instead of God, they effectively turned ownership of the Earth over to him (John 12:31, 2 Corinthians 4:4). He didn't take it by force.

Humanity's lords became Satan, sin, and death. Satan can do nothing in the Earth on his own, but because mankind continually sides with him with every sin committed, he has a terrible amount of influence in our affairs. Each king of the world who chooses Satan over God becomes a puppet king in an invisible and dark empire ruled by a hierarchy of demons with Satan at the top. In other words, Satan's kingdom only influences the Earth if it can influence the hearts of men. We turn our right to rule over to our enemy every time we disobey God.

Very rarely does God or Satan do anything in the Earth that isn't done through mankind. When God wanted to call a people His own, He chose Abram and Sarai to do it through. When the Lord brought His people out of slavery in Egypt, He did it by the hand of Moses. When God wanted to punish the sins of those living in the promised land, he did so by the arm of Israel. When the Lord wrapped Himself in flesh and invaded the Earth, He did so through the virgin Mary. When He dealt with sin on the cross, He did through Jesus.

On the flip side, it is the same. When Satan wanted to kill Jesus as a baby, he attempted it through Herod and his armies (Matthew 2:16). When Satan finally had Jesus betrayed, he did so through the man Judas (Luke 22:3). When Satan makes his final stand in Revelation, he does so through the "beast" or "antichrist."

Something about flesh allows spiritual beings to work in the Earth. This is why demons try to inhabit people—if they can gain enough control over a person, they can influence the Earth through that person. The Earth is a warzone, though few of us perceive the battle. Satan's armies are constantly gaining ground in the lives of people. He did so to such a degree once that God had to flood the entire Earth and start over again (Genesis 6). Satan's tactic hasn't changed—his goal is to inhabit the hearts and souls of as much of humanity as possible.

God's response to this attack on the Earth was one of the most amazing things ever. Even today, what the Lord did is nearly impossible for me to conceive. God put *Himself* in mankind. Man was given dominion but gave it to Satan. Jesus came to take back what was stolen and to set the world in proper order again—God as supreme, and man exercising His will in obedience to Him. You will not find anywhere in the Bible where Jesus says He came to create a new religion. You will, however, find constant references to a Kingdom Jesus brought to Earth.

"And proclaim as you go, saying, 'The kingdom of heaven is at hand.'"
> - **Matthew 10:17**

"...but he said to them, 'I must preach the good news of the kingdom of God to the other towns as well, for I was sent for this purpose.'"
> - **Luke 4:43**

"Jesus answered, 'My kingdom is not of this world. If my kingdom were of this world, my servants would have been fighting, that I might not be

delivered over to the Jews. But my kingdom is not from the world.'"

- John 18:36

-

"Being asked by the Pharisees when the kingdom of God would come, he answered them, 'The kingdom of God is not coming in ways that can be observed, nor will they say, 'Look, here it is!' or 'There!' for behold, the kingdom of God is in the midst of you.'"

- Luke 17:20-21

It might be better to translate this last verse as saying, "...behold, the kingdom of God is within you." Jesus was constantly pointing us to spiritual truths. As humans living in a three-dimensional and physical world, we are preoccupied with naturalism to our detriment. A human being is not merely physical; we can walk in both the spiritual and physical realms simultaneously. As Christians, we are both on Earth and "seated in heavenly realms (Ephesians 2:6)."

The Kingdom of God is not a physical kingdom that can be seen; rather it is a spiritual kingdom invading the Earth, and it started when the Spirit of God conceived a Baby in the womb of Mary. Jesus was the first to invade and set things right—He was the image of redeemed humanity. He embodied what mankind was meant to be before sin, and He is the example of who we are called to become. In the same way Satan's strategy is to put *unclean spirits* inside of men—God's strategy is to put the *Holy Spirit* inside of men.

The Kingdom of God is truly brought to the Earth when a person is filled with the Holy Spirit. Because of Christ's sacrifice, man can become the temple of the Lord. The Old Testament temple was a foreshadow, as the very presence of God rested in the Holy of Holies (the innermost chamber) where the ark dwelt.

This room was untouched by humans except once a year when the high priest entered with the sin-goat (scapegoat) to have the people's sins placed upon it (Leviticus 16:20–22). Even then, tradition says the high priest had a rope tied to his ankle with a bell on it, just in case he should be killed in the holy presence of the Lord. The holiness of God is devastating to humanity. In 1 Samuel 6:19, we see 72 people are killed by looking at the Ark of the Covenant. We find Uzzah is struck down for reaching out to touch the ark in 2 Samuel 6:7. The holiness of God is like the fire of our Sun—

one does not get near it for fear of burning up. Humankind is not made of the right sort of material to stand in the presence of the Lord and live.

That is why we must die in Christ and be born again. Jesus said we would be "born of the Spirit (John 3)." Because of Christ's atonement, we can become vessels capable of being filled with New Wine (Matthew 9). We must become new wineskins by our faith in Christ before being filled with the Holy Spirit. Without the blood of Jesus, the Spirit could not dwell in us. We would "burst;" we would die. Jesus has made us into "new creations," though (2 Cor 5:17), so we can receive the Spirit and not only stand in the presence of God but possess His presence *inside* of us. What a grand mystery, and what an almost unbelievable concept!

An *individual* who is filled with the Spirit of God, we call a Christian. But the *totality of true believers* is called the Church, and this now brings me back to the incredible power of intercessory prayer. As I previously mentioned, the word for "Church" in Greek is "ekklesia," which is an assembly of citizens called for political purposes. The Church is the part of the

Kingdom of God which *now* exercises authority in the Earth.

"And I [Jesus] tell you, you are Peter, and on this rock I will build my church, and the gates of hell shall not prevail against it. I will give you the keys of the kingdom of Heaven, and whatever you bind on earth shall be bound in Heaven, and whatever you loose on earth shall be loosed in Heaven."

- **Matthew 16:18-19**

Jesus built His ekklesia and declared hell could not prevail against it. In other words, the Church has authority in the Earth now as Christ has built it, and He has delegated that authority to it. The "keys" to the Kingdom were given to us, which means the Kingdom of Heaven is open to us, and we are free to call upon it in any way we deem necessary to advance that Kingdom in the Earth.

Heaven backs up the works and word of the Church of Christ, and Satan can't do anything about it unless, again, like Adam, we let him.

Thus, as a believer, when you pray for someone else, you do so from a position of authority within that Church. The Bible declares, "But you are a chosen race, a royal priesthood, a holy nation, a people for his own possession, that you may proclaim the excellencies of him who called you out of darkness into his marvelous light (1 Peter 2:9)."

Peter isn't writing to a physical nation, but the Church itself which is connected by the Holy Spirit of God, with Christ as its Head (leader and source).

The number one problem the Church faces today is that it does not know who it is. We are the executive branch of the Kingdom of God. We execute the will of our Heavenly Father on Earth because He has placed His Seal upon us.

"In him you also, when you heard the word of truth, the gospel of your salvation, and believed in him, were sealed with the promised Holy Spirit, who is the guarantee of our inheritance until we acquire possession of it, to the praise of his glory."
   - **Ephesians 1:13-14**

A "seal" is a marking that a king would place upon things He owns; those things are part of, or an extension of, his kingdom. For example, a signet ring pressed into wax may create a seal mark. In the book of Revelation, we read about the "mark of the beast," which is a counterfeit seal of the kingdom of darkness—meaning those who take that mark have pledged allegiance to that kingdom. In the Church's case, the "Seal" is the Holy Spirit of God. He is the authentication of the power and authority of the Church. Jesus cast out demons by the power of the Holy Spirit—and it's that same Spirit who now empowers the Church to do likewise. In fact, Jesus said that deliverance is a clear sign that the Kingdom of God has come.

"But if it is by the Spirit of God that I drive out demons, then the kingdom of God has come upon you."
- **Matthew 12:28**

Deliverance is an act of intercession. In some sense, the Church is stepping between the person and the power of darkness and declaring, "You can't have this soul." Driving a demon out is displacing the present kingdom of darkness and pouring in the Kingdom of

God. I will dedicate a future chapter on deliverance ministry, but for now, I want to hammer home this simple point: people are waiting on the Church to get it together and start interceding for this dark world.

Again, God uses *people* to affect change in the Earth. In the Old Testament, He used Israel. In these last days, He is using the Church. We should be diligently praying for the lost—asking the Lord to remove the veil from a blind and deaf generation so it can hear the word of God and be *moved* by it.

Too many believers take on the mindset that this life is about being as comfortable as possible until they die and make it to Heaven. Others are watching the world burn and hoping it continues to be plunged into deeper darkness so it might force the Father's hand to send Jesus again and end things. Contrary to these positions, Jesus has established His kingdom in the Earth, though invisible, and asked us to pray it in: **"Your kingdom come, your will be done, on earth as it is in heaven."**
   - **Matthew 6:10**

The Church must wake up! Our slumber is allowing the lost to perish. Our inability to recognize the power of our prayers results from a deep spell the enemy has sent against us. We must learn to kneel again, with folded hands, and usher in the Kingdom of God as Christ has directed us. We must learn to partner with the Holy Spirit to see that same Kingdom manifest in the lives of the lost so some might be saved. Awaken Church! Grab hold of your mantel of responsibility as God's governing authority to push back the gates of hell.

You are the calvary Jesus has sent; now draw your sword, and make sure there is blood on it each day before you go to sleep—for the "Kingdom of God has suffered violence, and the violent take it by force (Matthew 11:12)." Be like the Syrophoenician woman or the persistent widow (Luke 18), who though opposed did not give in, and were rewarded for their faith and tenacity.

Chapter 12
Called into Ministry

I never wanted to go into ministry full-time primarily because I thought that meant I'd need to be a pastor. To clarify, a pastor has a position in the church of shepherding people. That involves a great deal of heartache: dealing with complaints, balancing opinions and perspectives of the congregation, and making sure the "sheep" are fed and taken care of spiritually (just to name a few things they do).

When I envisioned pastoral ministry, I always pictured myself in a small office with a large wooden desk, harsh Walmart-style overhead lighting, and a married couple sitting across from me—on the brink of divorce. Not because of infidelity, but over some minor disagreement. The wife would be complaining about the husband, the husband would be complaining about the wife, and they'd both be asking me whether God would permit their divorce.

A good pastor would take their feelings into account, counsel them extensively, and, if all went well, guide them through reconciliation over the course of a year, if they were lucky.

I never thought I'd be able to do that. Instead, I imagined myself looking them in the eyes and telling those sinners they had better repent now or go to hell. I would tell the man to get his life together and nail it to the cross because if he didn't, God wasn't going to answer his prayers anymore (1 Peter 3:7). I would tell the woman that she needed to have a *come to Jesus* moment—dying to herself and submitting to her husband, not out of love for him, but out of love for the Lord (Ephesians 5:22). Finally, I would send them both home with little business cards that said, "God hates divorce," instructing them never to utter that word to one another again (Malachi 2:16).

Jokes aside, I just could never see myself fulfilling the role in the church that's carved out for taking care of believers. Thankfully, at least for now (one day I suspect I may move into pastoralship, should I mature), God agrees with me. Instead, the Lord showed me there are at least five official roles one can take on within a church (apostle, prophet, evangelist, pastor, teacher) found in Ephesians 4. Much of the charismatic church has turned these designations into titles rather than job descriptions. It is why you'll find people calling themselves "apostle so and so" who have never planted a church in their life. You will find people call themselves, "prophet so and so" who may have the gift of prophecy, but are in no way doing the job of a prophet within a local church. God set me apart to be an evangelist within the body of Christ, but that is what I *do*, not who I am. If I were to stop bringing the good news to people—the very essence of what an evangelist does—I would no longer be an evangelist. It would be just as odd as someone calling themselves a "swimmer" on their business card, yet never being seen in the water.

On the flip side, mainstream conservative churches have done a massive disservice to the body of Christ by excluding many of its functions. As the evangelist Lonnie Frisbee quipped in one of his books, "You know the five fold ministry? Pastor, pastor, pastor, pastor, and pastor." Some of these churches might have a teacher (they still call them a "teaching pastor"). Very few, if any, have apostles, prophets, and evangelists. The point of these five offices in the church is found in Ephesians 4:

"So Christ himself gave the apostles, the prophets, the evangelists, the pastors and teachers, to equip his people for works of service, so that the body of Christ may be built up."
- **Ephesians 4:11-12**

The purpose of all five is to "equip people" so that "the body...may be built up." I'd argue a church is not fully functioning, nor capable of fully equipping the saints, if it is operating without some of these roles. Similarly, those with strong prophetic gifts or apostolic bents, who are not part of a local church, are incapable of equipping the saints in any meaningful way—because they are disconnected on a personal and corporate level.

There is a vicious circle here. Going back to Lonnie Frisbee, he was an evangelist with an incredible gift of prophecy upon his life. His work kick-started movements like the Calvary Chapel and Vineyard church growth, as well as the Jesus People movement in the 60s and 70s. Many pastors failed to properly use his role within their churches. Even Chuck Smith, who initially took him under his wing at Calvary Chapel, warned Lonnie at one point that if another person "fell out" in the Spirit at a service, Lonnie would be kicked out of the ministry (Chuck's children attest to this fact). Ministry team would literally be holding people up as Lonnie prophesied over them to keep them from falling to the ground.

Many pastors were jealous of the gifting upon Lonnie's life and could not understand how such a broken individual could move in such power. Which brings me to the flip side—pastors may find it hard to work with evangelists, but evangelists can also find it hard to work with pastors. Lonnie carried pain from his childhood and a spirit of rejection. He took correction and rebuke from pastorship as personal attacks. Instead of sticking it out and conforming to what his headship required of him, he would simply move onto the next ministry.

His gifting was constantly exploited or misunderstood by *pastors*, but at the same time *he* would never humble himself to receive the inner healing and correction he needed.

I see the same pattern today from the prophetic community. Many of today's churches quench moves of the Holy Spirit, which has driven prophets out of them. Simultaneously, these prophets tend to carry massive chips on their shoulders when it comes to the Bride of Christ. One can become so convinced of their hearing from the Lord that they fail to take into account all the safeguards in scripture that tell us to "test the spirits." Such people scorn headship instead of leaning into it.

There is an entire movement right now that seeks to do away with any notion of "headship" within the church (that is, a person you *willingly* submit to, whom you trust to rebuke and speak into your life). The fruit of this movement has been disastrous. It doesn't help that a great deal of our church leaders aren't leading the type of life Paul said they should, in scripture, either. Thus is the current vicious cycle we find ourselves in, and it has created very few churches firing on all five cylinders.

In my case, it took the majority of my life to realize that there is a role within the church that is outward-facing. An evangelist isn't called to care for believers—

he is sent to seek unbelievers. I love telling people about Jesus. I love seeing their eyes light up after witnessing a miracle or well up with tears after receiving inner healing. Jesus is so kind and so generous, and I have the privilege not only of telling people about Him but also of showing them His love in a tangible way.

So one day, I knelt in my prayer closet and asked God three questions. "Will I always run my companies?" I asked.

The Lord responded, "No."

Naturally, my next question followed: "What am I supposed to do?"

"Preach," the Lord replied.

"How am I supposed to make money?" I asked.

With mystery, God answered, "It will be obvious."

Thus, God revealed to me that I was to enter full-time ministry. The idea no longer unsettled me, as I now understood He was calling me to be an evangelist, not a pastor. However, the journey to get there would prove to be tumultuous.

I had spent roughly eighteen years of my life developing a skillset in video production. Twelve of those years were working in the industries of commercial production, animation, and reality television. The final three years, I was finally making good money producing scripted content. During this time, my family was well taken care of as we were taking home about $150,000 per year before taxes. Yet, within the span of roughly a month and a half, I lost almost every client.

To this day my wife and I debate about the cause of this. Her theory is we would never have gone into full-time ministry if our business was still lucrative, so she calls its collapse our "whale," like Jonah's, to get us where God wanted us to be. In opposition, I argue Satan destroyed our business in a bid to crush our part-time ministry so I'd need to find a full-time job, or ramp up my work hours in order to rebuild.

Whatever the case, we entered dire straits precisely
when I started to feel God pull me into full-time ministry the hardest.

One Sunday morning I was kneeling at the altar when
the Lord spoke to me, "Satan desires to sift you." The
next few weeks were the worst of my life as I kept
hearing a voice that sounded like God's, but put fear
into my heart. It would tell me things like, "I'm going
to take your daughter's life when you go into ministry." The sound of it was so familiar, but the content
was never what I wanted to hear. Fear gripped my wife
during this time too. It didn't help that dozens of people approached us, called us, or messaged us, to tell us
that God had put us on their hearts to pray for us.
Why were we needing so much prayer? What was
about to happen to us? One man was genuinely dis-
turbed by whatever the Lord had told him concerning
us, and was interceding on our behalf constantly.

I can't fully describe the amount of spiritual warfare
going on in our home and minds during this time. It
was as if God took His hand off us and allowed Satan
to test our resolve. I leaned heavily into godly men—
bringing them things I was hearing and asking for

wisdom. One day I called my buddy Glen and laid out the word I heard concerning my daughter. He reassured me that it did not sound like the voice of the Lord based on scripture. It is sad, but I already knew that. I just needed someone else to echo it because the voice was so convincing.

I have since seen many Christians fall by the wayside as they endure similar testing. New believers, without a firm scriptural foundation, get very excited upon hearing the voice of the Lord for the first time. Inevitably they begin to hear other voices, too, and fail to "test the spirits" as John 4 tells us to do. Pride ends up being their downfall, and I have seen some completely forsake the gospel as they follow the voices they hear, unrestrained. The first signs of this have routinely been an obsession with government conspiracy theories, and strangely, Judaism and its rituals and holidays.

One of the most prominent examples I know is a student from Bethel in Redding, California, who was featured in the documentary *Finger of God*. He operated in extraordinary power through the Spirit of God as a prophetic evangelist. Angelic visitations were not uncommon for him to experience, but one day "beings" came and delivered a different gospel message. He called these beings "aliens." The man believed what he was told, forsook the gospel, and was formally denounced at his church after his mentor first tried to reason with him. To my knowledge, he has still not repented.

It is imperative new believers, especially those gifted with prophecy, have a firm biblical foundation for their faith. They should also be part of a local church and discipled. If you are not in a church, I highly recommend it. If you are not being discipled, I also encourage you to approach someone you know and respect, and ask them to disciple you. Notice, I went to someone like that to help me through this period of my life. I submitted to the biblical wisdom he highlighted, over the voice I was hearing.

Another deception I have found people can fall into is looking for "omens." An omen is just a pagan coincidence, but far too often Christians look for these signs instead of calling on the Lord. God may be speaking to us through a prophetic sign, but again we must test everything. Learn from this passage in Deuteronomy:

"If a prophet or a dreamer of dreams arises among you and gives you a sign or a wonder, and the sign or wonder that he tells you comes to pass, and if he says, 'Let us go after other gods,' which you have not known, 'and let us serve them,' you shall not listen to the words of that prophet or that dreamer of dreams. For the Lord your God is testing you, to know whether you love the Lord your God with all your heart and with all your soul. You shall walk after the Lord your God and fear him and keep his commandments and obey his voice, and you shall serve him and hold fast to him."

- Deuteronomy 13:1-4

Understand that the prophet in this passage is able to not only predict an omen, but it comes to pass. Satan can conjure tricks. Two magicians in Egypt were able to turn their staffs into snakes (Exodus 7:11-12). Too often, believers can be led astray by shiny things and sensual feeling. Simply because you see, hear, or feel something spectacular does not mean it is from the Lord. Satan may be sifting you, and God might be testing you. He wants to know if you are going to listen to His word, or be led astray by something or someone else. When in doubt, fall back on the written word of God found in the bible.

This time of testing in my life came to a head one night as I laid in bed with my wife and we jointly decided to transition into full-time ministry. We had no idea how we'd pay our bills, and very little concept concerning the execution of our ministry. But I had heard from the Lord, and the only thing left was for me to step out in faith and push through the dark curtain that Satan had used to smother me. That night, I sent a text to a few close family members, sharing the news and asking for their support. The next day was my family reunion where word spread quickly.

Aly and I heard two of the same stories back to back: One person told us that God had revealed our calling into ministry to him two months earlier—and that he was to sow into us financially, ultimately becoming our largest donor. Likewise, another person shared that God had told her long ago, and she became our very first donor.

Aly and I have occasionally posted ways for people to support our ministry, but we've never had to personally ask anyone else to sponsor us. Instead, the Holy Spirit continues to press us upon people's hearts to donate. We'll get "random" donations here and there that cover the various expenses which crop up.

Many people sow into us out of their lack, and some out of their abundance—but always in obedience to what the Spirit has told them to do. I thank God for taking care of us through His Church! That dark season in our lives lifted immediately, but it wouldn't be our last bout of spiritual warfare. In fact, things only intensified.

Chapter 13
Witches

My formal education rarely touched on the subject of witches, briefly addressing it only in the context of the Salem Witch Trials. Most of Western society, heavily influenced by a worldview that prioritizes empirical science and material explanations (naturalism), tends to dismiss the existence of the spirit-realm. The Western church too often behaves as though the spiritual world does not exist despite its professed belief in it. If you were to ask the average Christian in America about their views on witchcraft, they likely haven't given the matter much thought. Some of the more traditional believers might dismiss it as make-believe.

Have you noticed that the term "superstition" seems to have fallen out of common use? When I was a child, we referred to things like lucky rabbit's feet and four-leaf clovers as superstitions. Today, however, there is a burgeoning market for items like crystals, angel numbers, tarot cards, and other metaphysical merchandise. The concept of "manifestation" has gained widespread acceptance—the idea of attempting to create or achieve something through focused thought (such as wealth). Faith in the authenticity of psychics, Reiki healers, and the belief in spiritual energy residing in physical objects, is on the rise. Many of these practices and beliefs fall under the broad umbrella of "New Age" philosophy, yet they are, in fact, a fusion of ancient pagan belief systems that have been around for a long time.

If you venture online, you may find the #witchtok hashtag, a popular trend on TikTok where users share videos related to modern witchcraft. This hashtag has amassed tens of billions of views, featuring clips that teach people how to cast spells and hexes, utilize voodoo, perform rituals, harness energy, and manipulate metaphysical items to achieve their goals.

No one in the present generation seems to be condemning these things as superstitions. The witches themselves swear by the practices. The Church is either blind to it or has incorporated New Age into itself (the most common being the Enneagram personality test, which was created through automatic writing, whereby an author channels a demon for inspiration).

As of writing this book, an increasing number of celebrities have publicly embraced New Age practices or witchcraft. For example, Vanessa Hudgens documented her journey into the dark supernatural, while singer Lorde has openly identified as a witch. Tom Brady's ex-wife, Gisele Bündchen, reportedly performed rituals before his football games. Similarly, Lana Del Rey encouraged her fans to perform a "mass hex" against U.S. president Donald Trump. Madonna has participated in American Indian smudge ceremonies, and Paris Jackson has even formed her own coven. Others, like Katy Perry, use crystals to attract relationships. Ariana Grande identifies as a witch and tarot card practitioner. Adele and Sam Smith also use crystals, claiming they help with anxiety, while Mary-Kate Olsen sages her home. Actress Heather Graham has been linked to a witch coven.

These are just a few of the many public figures embracing New Age practices, signaling their growing acceptance in mainstream culture. There are bound to be hundreds more. The number isn't the point; it is how *accepted* these practices have become.

The materialist West is slowly waking up to the spirit-realm, and it is not all bad. I have found witches to be more open to the Holy Spirit's workings than atheists and the religious. A person dabbling in New Age is far more likely to let me pray for their healing than someone who has been a member of the Church of Christ their whole life.

In October 2023, Ethan Sherrer and I rented a booth at a paranormal investigation expo in Nashville, TN. The majority of vendors there were practicing witches. Across from our booth was a bone divinator who would toss dead animal bones on a table, "read" them, and then accurately tell clients things about themselves she could not have known by natural means. Other booths featured tarot card readers, healing crystal stands, demonic artwork, etc.

Ethan and I knew that if we wore Jesus t-shirts, no one would stop by our table. Thus, we attended posing as New Agers, setting up a large, vibrantly colored, psychedelic-looking sign that stated in bold words, "Free Healing Services." The sign then listed several ailments people might be suffering from, such as pain inside their body, depression, or panic attacks. Leading up to this day, we and our intercessors prayed heavily. We interceded for those who would stop by our booth, and Ethan saw, in a vision, a whole company of angels that would be going with us. Our intercessor (to protect her I'll leave her name out) covered us in prayer almost daily.

Walking into the vendor facility was like stepping into Ephesus—an ancient city notorious for its marketplace of sorcery. We set up our booth under the name "The World's Last Night," which is the name of my podcast and sounds like something New Agers would use. For clarification, I derived the name from the titular C.S. Lewis essay that I highly recommend one reads.

Ethan and I sat on one side of a white card table—microphones and go-pros at the ready—and we left two empty chairs across from us. It wasn't long before we received our first curious ghost hunter—a middle-aged man with severe nerve damage. He was electrocuted by 40,000 volts in a restaurant accident, which almost took his life, and he had been unable to feel his hands, the left side of his body, and the majority of his face for nine years. The man reported having gone through over five years of rehabilitation, only for doctors to give up and declare his nerves had regenerated all they could. He wasn't allowed to cook anymore because he could not distinguish hot from cold, which resulted in his hands burning.

I asked if we could take his hands, and we each grabbed one. Then we waited. I had thought a great deal about how I was going to pray for people in such a hostile environment. I concluded I would simply take Jesus at his word, "…they will lay hands on the sick, and they will recover (Mark 16:18)." I wasn't going to say much of anything, just hold their hand and wait for the Holy Spirit to come. I had also made up my mind not to utter the name of Jesus until after the person was healed—that way, I could introduce the person to Him first, hopefully in a light they had not encountered before. After the person was healed, I'd share the gospel message and explain that the Person who healed them was Jesus.

As we took the man's hands, I said, "You let me know if you feel anything tingly, okay?" After a while, he reported his face started feeling like "needles." I told the sensation to increase and then commanded every nerve in his body to regenerate. The air was cold in the facility, and I had not brought a jacket. On the other hand, Ethan was sitting nice and cozy in his hoodie. Looking back, God had to have played some role in me leaving a jacket behind because, at that moment, the man withdrew his hands and asked, "How are you hot and he's cold?" To which I replied, "You can feel in your hands?" He was flabbergasted. Hilariously, he then asked me for a business card—thinking we were some medical professionals selling healing. That's when I revealed that Jesus had healed him, not me, and we shared the gospel.

Scan the QR code to watch a video recording of this man's healing.

Another man showed up to our booth. This one was younger, quite tall and skinny. He was nervous to sit down, but eventually consented. "I have walked past your booth at least three times. I knew I needed to talk to you guys, but every time, I would get too nervous and keep on walking," he candidly stated.

He asked what kind of healing we did, so I gave him the answer I had come up with weeks before, "We practice what we call Divine Healing." The thing about New Agers is their mind will be opened or closed depending on the branding they are presented. If I call the things dwelling within them "demons," they will reject it immediately. But if I were to state, "You are afflicted by a spirit," they would be more open. I am saying the same thing, but I am also "[becoming] all things to all people, that by all means I might save some (1 Cor 9:22)."

Satisfied with my response, the thin man began to share a story. As a child, his mother recalled a pivotal moment when his grandfather picked him up and whispered something into his ear. From that point on, the boy was different. He began experiencing premonitions, and strange spiritual occurrences became a regular part of his life.

One day, he played a prank on his mother and, speaking in the third person, said, "We really scared her good!" His fascination with the supernatural led him to become a ghost hunter, deeply invested in all things spiritual—except for Jesus. If you haven't guessed by now, his grandfather was a practicing warlock, the male counterpart of a witch.

As this man continued to divulge family secrets concerning the occult, he shook uncontrollably. He felt compelled to continue talking to us and explained the real reason he was sitting at our table. In a dream of his, he and three buddies were in their small town when a bus pulled up. They hopped on the bus, delighted to find three beautiful women onboard: a blonde, a redhead, and a brunette.

Pairing off, they arrived at a cabin in the woods where his friends and their women went on ahead of him. As he entered with the blonde woman, he saw his friends were massacred. Suddenly, the blonde woman he was with transformed into a hideous creature and pounced on him to sexually abuse him. He tried running away and fell onto the forest floor outside, where he crawled through the leaves. The creature clawed him deeply.

When he finally woke up from this nightmare, he found himself on the floor of his room, crawling and in pain. There was no discernable difference between his nightmare and real life, which terrified him.

The man told us, "I don't believe in Christianity, but I suspect these women were succubi. I don't know what else to call them."

A *succubus*—or its "male" counterpart, an *incubus*—is a demon assigned to afflict people at night. They are known for causing lustful and violent dreams, and when I pray for someone struggling with sleep paralysis, I often rebuke this entity. Our tall friend suffered from all three issues.

Ethan then asked him, "Do you see a shadowy figure in your room wearing a hat when you're in sleep paralysis?" The man immediately responded, "Yes. Once, he even flipped the lights on and off, and I couldn't do anything about it."

Interestingly, witches tend to report dreaming about the same types of demons. For instance, I've heard an unusual number of witches describe encounters with a demon they call the "Green Man." A brewing company in Asheville, NC, is even named after this entity, highlighting how occult themes have subtly woven themselves into mainstream culture. Spiritual symbols and references are often embraced without a full understanding of their origins.

Of course, this ghost hunter dealt with a plethora of other demonic oppression issues, but there was a matter of his heart to fix first. I felt like he did not want rid of the powers these demons afforded him (such as premonitions), and so I told him he'd need to desire to be rid of the spirits even if the powers went too. He thought about it for a while and told us the powers were great because they made him unique, but when the spirits got bad, they got really bad.

We told him we'd make them leave; as Ethan took the man's hand, he was immediately emptied out. This great peace fell upon our friend—something he'd later describe as "warmth in [his] chakras," and I'd correct it as it being his "spirit." The concept of chakras comes from Hinduism and Buddhism. They are supposed "energy centers" in the human body that must be "opened" to achieve cosmic or spiritual awareness.

When New Agers do this, they open themselves to evil spirits.

Scan the QR code to listen to our encounter with this ghost hunter.

Now, typically, when you're doing deliverance on a person who has dabbled in witchcraft or the occult, it may take some time. There will often be wild manifestations and maybe even demons talking out of the person. But with this man, the only manifestation was the spirits rushing in his stomach and then ceasing the moment Ethan touched his hand. I call this the overwhelming and dominating power of the Spirit of God. One might say it is a result of perfect faith, but I believe God gave us a special grace at this festival because every witch, occultist, or ghost hunter who came to our booth to be prayed for was healed and delivered. In fact, three witches told us they would throw away their tarot cards and start going to church because of their miraculous encounter with Jesus.

There are different levels and motivations for witchcraft, though. Like all cults, the people at the bottom don't realize the depth of darkness in the organization until they rank up, and by then, it is too late for them to get out unscathed. In other cases, those consorting with demons enjoy it and seek that darkness as it gives them power and a sense of purpose. This rabbit hole goes deeper than most readers would care to know, becoming far darker than the Western Church can stomach. I will dip you in smoothly here.

As you may know, my wife and I used to host Freedom Night at our home. We had to overcome many logistical issues, such as parking, hiring childcare, and setting up systems to ensure our family (specifically our two young daughters) was physically safe. We'd welcome active drug addicts, prostitutes, and the heavily demonized each month. What started as a worship night with close friends ended up becoming 60 or so people encountering Jesus on a level they didn't know was possible, and with that came demons growling out of some and contorting others.

I remember my five-year-old walking onto our back deck once where a woman was groaning on all fours as a demon manifested. She asked her mom, "What is happening to her?" My wife graciously explained that sometimes, when Jesus is freeing someone, it can look like that. Ella shrugged her shoulders and accepted her mom's explanation.

One fateful Freedom Night, a church hungry for a move of the Spirit, but with leadership that refused to allow Him, came with fourteen representatives. The woman who invited them had been to many previous Freedom Nights and had experienced her own miracle as we prayed for brand new kidneys (both were in failure), and "coincidentally," within a week, she received them via organ donation after waiting for years and years.

One of the women who came was on staff at the church, and as I was praying for her deliverance that night, a word popped into my head—"witchcraft." In obedience, I stated, "I break all witchcraft off this woman," and immediately, she fell backward onto the couch, manifesting. She was freed! I heard another word from the Lord, "Someone in her church has been cursing the staff." I later spoke to the lady who brought these fourteen to our home, and she confirmed the church staff knew they were being cursed.

At the night's end, as we were praying for someone's healing, I spotted a crying woman. I approached her and asked, "Are you okay? Has someone prayed for you yet?" Her body language was off, and the way she snapped out of crying so quickly was jarring to me, but I still didn't suspect anything other than she may be a bit strange.

"Oh, I'm just crying because I want to see that person healed they are praying for," she replied.

We had some solid ministers praying for the woman she referenced, so I asked again, "She'll be okay. Do you need prayer for anything yourself?" Immediately, the woman jumped into accusation, raising her voice so those around could hear, "Why were you praying in tongues over me earlier?" I had no recollection of praying in tongues over the woman at all, so I asked for more information. "I was over by the dog bowl," she stated, "You came behind me and prayed in IS-LAMIC!"

I pretty simultaneously replied with three things: First, that "Islamic" wasn't a language but a religion. Second, I did not remember praying over her that night, though I apologized if she was offended. Third, I explained the gift of tongues, thinking she was simply unfamiliar. We ended the little conversation, and I believed in my heart that this was the witch who had been cursing the staff of "her" church.

Accusing someone of being a witch, especially when they claim to be a Christian, should not be done rashly or without careful discernment. What if you are wrong? How are you any better than those quick to judge at the Salem Witch Trials? I mostly sat on my suspicions, but I did tell that same woman who had invited her church about them.

Over the next several weeks, my family was being attacked roughly every other night by demons. I'd wake up with palpable dread in the room—rebuking these entities and commanding them to leave. One night, I woke up, and the Holy Spirit told me, "There is a spirit of sickness coming onto your wife; pray!" So I prayed, and as I did, my wife woke up and began to feel very ill. The illness lifted almost immediately after rebuking it. Like clockwork, these attacks kept coming.

Often, my children would have nightmares in the middle of the night, and they'd come down to wake my wife and me up. This would, obviously, cause us to lose sleep. Compounding this treatment for weeks left us battered but not broken. I chalked these attacks up simply to the fact I was an evangelist, and it probably came with the territory.

One Saturday morning, I scheduled a Spiritual Warfare class where we invited people from our church, and those who knew me from other churches, to attend. I taught for five hours on the spirit-realm, healing, and deliverance. During the lunch break, I showed a video compilation of miraculous healings and deliverances that I had recorded. You could imagine what this did to the sixty people that attended. Many of them began to manifest, some so heavily they had to be taken to the back hallway to be delivered by a small team. One of the videos I showed had demons yelling out of a former New Ager who was also afflicted by a Satanist she met in her church (though she didn't know the woman was a Satanist at the time).

A former witch in the audience ran to the back of the room upon seeing this woman being delivered and began to argue with the small ministry team, saying, "He's a liar! That woman wasn't a witch!" Of course, this was a demon in the lady speaking out. Demons in this room were terrified by having to sit through an entire course dedicated to teaching Christians how to destroy them.

There was one woman who came, though, who was later reported to me as having excused herself for a moment. A ministry team leader told me, "She looked very ill but was suppressing it." This was the same woman who had come to Freedom Night at my home about a month prior; the one I felt God told me was cursing the staff of her church. At the end of the Spiritual Warfare course, I invited people up for impartation.

Now, impartation is the practice of laying hands on someone and asking the Lord to impart whatever power or gifts He desires onto the person (Romans 1:11, 2 Timothy 1:6). I have seen countless people receive the gift of tongues through this practice—others visions and dreams. Paul gave us an example of this in 1 Timothy 4:14 when he told his disciple, "Do not neglect the gift you have, which was given you by prophecy when the council of elders laid their hands on you."

A line formed, and we began to pray for impartation. Several people fell out in the spirit. One man, seeking the gift of tongues, told us that he denied the Holy Spirit and lived as a cessationist his whole life. He was afraid he had cursed himself by saying the gift of tongues was not for today or for him, but that if it was real, he wanted it. We laid hands on his stomach, and fire filled his belly. He fell to his knees and coughed violently as an evil spirit left him. The spirit was a religious spirit that came in through his agreement of cessationism, but God was gracious to free him as he humbled himself!

The very last person to come through the impartation line was the woman I suspected was a witch. As I looked at her, my eyes were drawn to a cross necklace with a strange shape carved into it. I turned to one of the other ministers, Savannah, and asked, "Are you discerning anything about this necklace?"

She replied, "Yes, let's take it off."

The woman explained where she got it from and agreed to remove it. As Ethan reached his hand out to hold onto it for her, she snapped at him, "No! I will hold it in my pocket!" Have you ever seen Lord of the Rings and the scene where Bilbo Baggins undergoes a sudden demonic manifestation, desperately clinging to his ring? That's pretty much what we saw in the spirit. Having lost her necklace, the woman was no longer desirous to be prayed for.

I heard the Lord say, "She's trying to pollute the altar." At that, I walked away. I left her there with the other ministers. Perhaps I should have confronted her, but again, society's polite ways concerning accusation kept me from saying anything. Later, I asked Savannah if the Lord gave her discernment concerning the woman. Revelation hit her, and she said, "Wolf. She's a wolf. Definitely in a coven."

A couple of days later, my wife received a phone call from our friend who had initially invited those fourteen members of her church to Freedom Night. She told Aly, "You know the woman James thought may be a witch? The leaders of my church told me today to not let her pray for me because they had discerned she was, in fact, a witch."

What's impressive about this story is that two different ministries sniffed out the same wolf in sheep's clothing around the same time. What's sad is it took us that long to do anything about it. The witch had been attending that church for two years undetected!

After receiving that call and confirmation, I went into the secret place and cried out into the spirit-realm, "Any unclean spirit that was sent to torment my family from the witch called 'X,' I command you to leave and never return. I break all of her magic over this place and come out of any agreement I made with her. I take back my pity." I then began to bless the witch, calling Heaven to save her from her sin (Luke 6:28).

That evening, my whole family slept like babies, and those attacks in the night ceased.

What was the mistake I made to allow this woman's curse to come upon my family? God only knows the whole truth, but from reading an account of a former Satanist who used to do the same work, I believe the first mistake was welcoming this wolf into my home.

"For many deceivers have gone out into the world, those who do not confess the coming of Jesus Christ in the flesh. Such a one is the deceiver and the antichrist. Watch yourselves, so that you may not lose what we have worked for, but may win a full reward. Everyone who goes on ahead and does not abide in the teaching of Christ, does not have God. Whoever abides in the teaching has both the Father and the Son. If anyone comes to you and does not bring this teaching, do not receive him into your house or give him any greeting, for whoever greets him takes part in his wicked works."
- **2 John 7-11**

My second mistake was showing pity to the woman for her tears (which were obviously fake). I should not have even given her my emotions that night. My third mistake was not rebuking her the moment the Lord gave me the word about her but allowing her to remain in my home and attend my Spiritual Warfare class. All three of these mistakes were ways I, spiritually speaking, permitted this woman to afflict my family and me.

You may be wondering about the justice of this all—how could I have known she was a witch to begin with not to welcome her? In this case, I believe the church she attended failed me. The other thirteen with her should have been more discerning and not counted her as a sister in Christ. I don't blame them, though, because even with the revelation I had, I failed to act. I believe the modern church is ill-prepared to deal with these types of witches, unfortunately. We all need our spiritual senses sharpened.

One way witches gain access to your life is by giving you gifts. I've been offered all sorts of things—even jewelry. The rule for my team and I is we do not accept gifts from anyone while on the mission field. Witches like to give cursed articles of clothing, food, jewelry, and lotions—anything that you will keep with you at all times or put in/apply to your body. They also seek tokens from you, such as strands of your hair, to put on their altars to mark you for demonic attacks.

Notice, these witches do not care about who you are— this one cursed my small children with nightmares. A New Ager may tinker with crystals, a witch may delve into spells, but then you get to occultists, and they are entirely sold out to the devil and know it. The Satanic gospel story has every element of the Christian gospel story except one—Satan has his followers believing Jesus stayed dead. It is Christianity without the resurrection, and without that, Satan looks like he won. These occultists genuinely think they're following the "true god," who they perceive as the devil, and they have been deceived about the extent of his power. One of the greatest witnesses the church can give such people is a demonstration of the power of God.

There's a story in the book *He Came to Set the Captives Free* by Rebecca Brown where an ex-Satanist recalls the first time she suspected Satan wasn't telling her cult the whole truth. Several of her cult members were tasked to murder a minister and his family. They met up physically to do this and then astral projected to the minister's home.

Astral projection is the practice of disassociating your spirit from your body and traveling in the spirit-realm (or astral plane). Whether this is an innate human ability or a person always needs an evil spirit to accomplish it, I do not know. Witches who practice astral projection can do so at varying lengths of time. They can travel around the world in no time at all and can manipulate physical objects. This is a counterfeit of what Paul may have experienced (and thus we can too, by the Spirit) in 2 Corinthians 12.

A pastor David Bryan has stated Anton Lavey (the creator of the Church of Satan) died while astral projecting because he could not return to his body. God directed David's church to pray for Anton's "silver cord" to be severed. There is only one reference to this in the Bible:

"...and desire fails, because man is going to his eternal home, and the mourners go about the streets— before the silver cord is snapped, or the golden bowl is broken, or the pitcher is shattered at the fountain,

or the wheel broken at the cistern, and the dust re-
turns to the earth as it was, and the spirit returns to
God who gave it. Vanity of vanities, says the
Preacher; all is vanity."

- Ecclesiastes 12:5-18

In essence, David's church was praying for God to
take Anton's life if you read this verse in context. David, though, will say the "silver cord" is the *demon* a
witch uses to astral project, connecting the person's
spirit to their body. Other "seers," such as Micah
Turnbo, will attest silver cords exist and can be seen
extending from the body to the spirit.

As the ex-Satanist and her cult were astral projecting
to destroy the minister and his family, they came upon
extremely tall angels in the spirit-realm. Later, they'd
dub these "link angels" because they were linked together such that the Satanists could not get into the
minister's home. No matter what they tried, nothing
would harm the angels—who would simply laugh at
the weary Satanists in return. One of the angels bent
down and spoke to the now ex Satanist, "When are
you going to give your life to Jesus?" This was the first
time the Satanist thought perhaps Satan had been

lying to her about his power. Eventually, this woman would become a Christian, but not without terrible suffering placed upon her by her former cult and Satan himself.

The problem is, most of our churches do not display a level of power that would convince an occultist that, maybe, just maybe, they are on the weaker team. Heavily demonized occultists can perform incredible false miracles such as stopping bullets, transmogrifying animals, cursing people with sickness and blindness, astral projection, pushing thoughts into other's minds, and much more. Meanwhile, your average churchgoer doesn't even have faith to see Jesus heal a headache miraculously through them. Thank God for the blood of Jesus!

Witches tend to be terribly afflicted themselves. The first thing they lose is their sleep. There truly is no rest for the wicked, as many suffer from insomnia, sleep paralysis, and nightmares. The ones that have delved into spell work or serving Satan himself will start their days at midnight. These agents of darkness will barter with demons by offering sacrifices—just as pagan peoples have done throughout human history.

More significant sacrifices for them include babies, virgins, and pastors. After that, they turn to animals, eventually working their way down to insects and other objects. Blood is a valuable commodity in the Earth. When the first people sinned, God immediately sacrificed animals to cover them (Genesis 3:21). The Old Testament sacrificial system, likewise, used animal blood to atone for sin. Satan has a perverted version of this. All demons want to be worshiped; their kingdom is built on competition and pride. If they can get humans to worship them and, better yet, offer them sacrifices, they are pleased with themselves.

Occultists in Western society evade detection of human sacrifice by sacrificing their members or kidnapping the homeless for rituals. To get babies, often a woman in the cult will have a child at home, not report it at a hospital, and offer it to the cult. Welcome to the very dark end of witchcraft that the church couldn't stomach, but note it was prevalent throughout all of the history of Israel.

"And the people of Israel did secretly against the Lord their God things that were not right. They built for themselves high places in all their towns,

from watchtower to fortified city. They set up for themselves pillars and Asherim on every high hill and under every green tree, and there they made offerings on all the high places, as the nations did whom the Lord carried away before them. And they did wicked things, provoking the Lord to anger, and they served idols...And they burned their sons and their daughters as offerings and used divination and omens and sold themselves to do evil in the sight of the Lord, provoking him to anger."

- 2 Kings 17:9-17

Not only were Israel's neighbors practicing such evil, including human sacrifice, but Israel itself, at many points, adopted the same abominations and was punished because of them. We live in a society where some mothers, often in moments of deep pain or pressure, choose abortion—unaware that similar actions are openly embraced by Satanists. While many are unknowingly sacrificing their children to Satan, Satanists do so intentionally.

As of 2024, the Satanic Temple is seeking to make abortion a religiously protected right since it administers abortions in ritual. The truth is the most heinous of witchcraft is done in the West every single day, but the Church is blind to it.

As a minister, the tricky part for me is walking the fine line between trying to save the souls of witches who attack my family, and rebuking them. Jesus clearly said we are to bless those who curse us (Luke 6:28, Romans 12:14). Yet, some Christians pray that the curses they receive will be returned to the one who sent them. I don't see any biblical evidence to say such a prayer, even though we have the power to do it. Just as a witch can curse, a Christian can curse, and Heaven will back up their words. We have the power to bind, and we have the power to loose, as Paul shows us in Acts 13:

"They traveled through the whole island until they came to Paphos. There they met a Jewish sorcerer and false prophet named Bar-Jesus, who was an attendant of the proconsul, Sergius Paulus. The proconsul, an intelligent man, sent for Barnabas and Saul because he wanted to hear the word of God. But Elymas, the sorcerer (for that is what his name means), opposed them and tried to turn the proconsul from the faith. Then Saul, who was also called

Paul, filled with the Holy Spirit, looked straight at Elymas and said, 'You are a child of the devil and an enemy of everything that is right! You are full of all kinds of deceit and trickery. Will you never stop perverting the right ways of the Lord? Now the hand of the Lord is against you. You are going to be blind for a time, not even able to see the light of the sun.'

Immediately, mist and darkness came over him, and he groped about, seeking someone to lead him by the hand. When the proconsul saw what had happened, he believed, for he was amazed at the teaching about the Lord."
- Acts 13:6-12

I once prayed for a man with a detaching retina to be healed, and the Lord re-attached the retina (I have the before and after scans to prove it). I do believe if God has given us that kind of power, then we can also command a person's retina to detach, and it will be. I have cursed many places (businesses that sell witchcraft material, places of idol worship), but never a person. The evangelist in me has difficulty with what Paul did in this passage, though it may have led to the man's repentance. I often pray for my adversaries to be humbled so they may turn to the Lord—perhaps Paul took a more direct approach.

Scan the QR code to see before and after scans of the previously mentioned eye.

I have a friend who tells a story about a witch cursing him. He began to pray for the witch's salvation relentlessly. I don't know what exactly was happening to her, but I suspect she was having angelic visitations, and maybe the Spirit of God was putting the fear of the Lord in her. She later messaged my friend, "Please stop praying for me to be saved!" in desperation. One of the prayers I pray is that witches won't be able to use their demonic powers.

Did you know that God has given you the power to drive out every evil spirit from a witch, but there is no power in hell they may possess that can drive the Holy Spirit from you? In a head-to-head match, the witch will lose if she comes up against a Christian with the slightest understanding of who they are in Christ. That's why they use deceit and look for areas of compromise in the Chrisitan's life they can exploit.

Perhaps you have heard the term "monitoring spirit?" A monitoring spirit is a demon sent to spy on someone. This demon reports information to the witch that may be used to destroy the person.

I highly recommend watching an interview with a man named James Kawalya that can be found online. James used to be a high-ranking Satanist in Africa, groomed from before the time he was born, married to an elderly witch at his birth, taken into occultism by a false arm of the Christian church, abused and broken repeatedly in his youth, and finally unleashed on college campuses to recruit others into Satanism.

There was a time in his life when a small prayer covenant in a backwoods church in Africa had a tremendous impact on the spirit-realm. James' cult feared that if the prayer covenant (these women were praying six hours per day for ninety days straight) were to be finished, it would cause seventy years of church revival. The Satanists convened to discuss how to destroy the covenant. They had already tried using their demonic powers and sending agents to simply murder the women, but all of their agents were either killed or converted. James was tasked with breaking the covenant and was given massive binders of information. In these binders were all the details they had gathered on each person within the covenant.

James meticulously analyzed each one and eventually identified two points of weakness—a character flaw in one of the women that could be exploited and a vulnerability in the church's pastor that could be leveraged. With this knowledge, he sent undercover Satanist women to infiltrate the church and work their way into the prayer covenant itself.

These women manipulated the pastor by offering large donations to his church while secretly cursing his baby with an affliction that kept her awake all night. As a result, the exhausted pastor was unable to find the rest he needed to pray in the secret place each morning. Meanwhile, they sowed division by exploiting the unresolved unforgiveness in the targeted woman, stirring up past wounds. In the end, James' cult successfully disrupted and ultimately broke the prayer covenant.

Notice how he went about doing this, though. He didn't show up and square off with his demons versus the Holy Spirit. Instead, he took intelligence gathered by monitoring spirits, searched it for weaknesses within the church, infiltrated the church with trained witches, exploited the weaknesses and disobedience, and finally won. It wasn't the power of darkness that overcame; it was its deceit, paired with the disobedience of the believers. The original tight-knit group came to blows the day before their covenant was supposed to end, and James testified that all they needed to do was humble themselves, forgive one another, and show up for the final day. But their pride wouldn't allow that.

In another account, James spoke of an evangelist who once traveled to his country in Africa and could not be stopped in the spirit-realm. He described how every word the evangelist spoke lingered in the spirit-realm for weeks, carrying such weight that his entire cult was ordered to evacuate the territory to avoid conversion. They were instructed not to return until several weeks after the evangelist had left. The power God had given this man was immense, rendering him untouchable by the agents of darkness.

So what did the cult do? Unable to attack the evangelist directly, they conducted research and discovered that his divine protection stemmed from a devoted team of intercessors who prayed for him day and night. Realizing this, they shifted their strategy—not by targeting the evangelist, but by working to turn some of his intercessors against him. Their efforts succeeded, and although the evangelist continued to make some progress in the nation, his impact eventually faded.

Satan is not omnipresent, nor omniscient. He can't be everywhere at once or know everything, so he has a network of demons collecting information on target-rich environments worldwide. If you are in ministry, chances are good that witches and demons are assigned to you, and you need to be aware of their schemes (2 Cor 2:11). One of their goals is to destroy a ministry's funding, which has been a primary attack on my work, personally.

Once, in the span of a few weeks, my family went through a nightmare of property destruction. First, a lawnmower fell apart, and then our other lawnmower (gifted to us by a ministry friend) broke. Suddenly, black mold was discovered behind our shower wall, requiring the entire thing to be gutted and replaced. Then, our hot tub, which my parents donated to us to baptize people, stopped working. Our family room TV then broke. My smoker broke, and then the dishwasher sprung a leak, requiring the whole thing to be replaced. Again, these things happened in just a few weeks and cost us all our savings to fix.

One night, my wife and I retreated to our basement guest bedroom to try to watch a documentary on a little TV we had there. We got a few minutes into the documentary when the volume suddenly turned down. "Strange," I thought while walking over to manually turn the volume back up because this TV didn't have a remote anymore. The volume slowly crept back down again. Believe it or not, I did have the thought a witch might be astral projecting, doing this to us, but I was too afraid of looking like a nut to speak out about it. I tried restarting the TV, unplugging it, and plugging it back in; the same thing would happen each time. But it was sporadic, not like a machine was turning the volume down at a constant rate, but as if a person was clicking it down. My wife and I resigned and went to sleep.

Strange occurrences became a regular part of our lives during this time. One night, about five minutes after we had crawled into bed, my child's CD player randomly turned on and began playing music in the living room. It was unsettling, but I initially dismissed it, thinking perhaps the CD player had been left on pause for too long and had simply resumed on its own. However, when I tested this theory later, I found that the CD player did not behave that way—it would remain paused indefinitely unless manually restarted.

Another night, our smoke alarm suddenly went off, even though there was no smoke, power surge, or other apparent trigger. The alarms weren't battery-powered, and there was no dust buildup that could have caused a false alarm.

I recalled a story from *He Came to Set the Captives Free,* in which an ex-Satanist described how, out of spite, she would astral project into the home of a nurse who had annoyed her and unplug his refrigerator. Looking back, I now believe there was a deliberate effort by a coven to drain our finances through property destruction. Another common tactic they use to attack finances and ministries is by cursing people with sickness.

When Citipointe took over the church I currently attend in Nashville, God gave someone on staff revelation that a Satanist was on the worship team—left over from the previous church. The moment this man was found out, he left and never returned. Simultaneously, the church grounds became contested as Satanists would stand in the corner of our parking lot and curse us. Signs of ritual sacrifice were found, and pentagrams were drawn on the parking lot as well. The entire church leadership, including lay leaders like my wife and I, were sick for months and months before we caught the revelation that it was a concerted attack by a coven to destroy us. The intercessory prayer team went into action, and the sickness lifted.

Still, Satanists routinely try to infiltrate our church. They'll send people who are overtly cultists, and also people who blend in with your average church goer. One time they sent a young man who demanded he be allowed to move a chair to the very back of the auditorium. We suspect this guy was there to act as a "chalice" - a home for demons to find after leaving people being delivered in the church.

As an evangelist, I encounter an incredible amount of people who do witchcraft but claim Christianity. Many of these people are ignorant that things like tarot cards, healing crystals, saging their home, and visiting reiki healers, are witchcraft. Such Christians are demonized and in pain due to their idolatry. Thus, one day, I decided to write a post on social media outlining many of these practices and why Christians should avoid them. This post was picked up by a coven of witches and warlocks and shared for ridicule. They commented many blasphemous things. I shrugged all of this off and went to sleep for the night.

Sometime in the early hours of the morning, I woke up with severe pain in one of my testicles. I had never felt such a thing in my life and didn't know what to do, so I hopped online to type in my symptoms. The issue that came up was "testicular torsion." The moment I read there was a likelihood of needing surgery, I became gripped by fear. Praying against the pain, I managed to fall back asleep but woke up again in agony. I could barely walk. My wife and I decided to go to the ER as the pain began to radiate into my side.

While blazing down the interstate, a man I had baptized and was discipling reached out to me. He said God had put me on his mind to pray for and that he had been on his knees on the floor of his auto mechanic shop crying out for me under the unction of the Holy Spirit. He said the Lord revealed to him that my testicle was twisted, so he prayed for it to untwist over the phone, and I felt it do so in my body, which offered great relief.

By the time we got to the hospital, I wasn't in as much pain. My wife and I sat in the car trying to decide whether it was worth going in or not due to the medical bills we'd incur. I was leaning toward not going in, but by this point, my wife thought I may have a kidney stone. I called some of our highly prophetic friends and asked them to consult the Lord. One of the women on the phone eventually said, "I see a monitoring spirit," which she promptly rebuked. Aly and I ultimately decided to enter the ER, where they did multiple tests and diagnosed me with a hydrocele, but they could not find a cause. This eventually became a pattern in diagnosing my issue. I visited a specialist, and although the pain in my side looked like a kidney stone, my kidneys were clear. In fact, I ended up with symptoms for about five different issues, but not enough symptoms of a single issue to narrow anything down. We wasted a ton of money on the medical system in this way.

A few days into my torment, I was out with my family at the DMV but couldn't bring myself to go inside. The pain was unbearable. I hobbled down a long road while my wife dealt with our passports, crying out to God, "Is healing only for other people, or me too?" As tears fell down my cheeks, I heard the voice of the Lord, "Healing is for you too." Finally, my wife and children returned, and we hopped into the car. The pain became more severe in my side as we drove home. Words can't describe it well enough other than to say I thought I was going to die.

By the time we got to the house, I was sweating pro-fusely, crying, and angry. I closed the door to my bed-room, laid on my bed, and writhed in pain. Suddenly, in my anger, I yelled for my wife, "Aly!" She came into the room where I pleaded with her, "Put your hand right here on my side and tell a demon to get out of me!"

My wife did as I demanded. As she prayed, my side be-came extremely hot; sweat poured out all over my body. Aly continued praying while I called Ethan and told him what was happening. He took over the deliv-erance from Aly. At the same time as all of this, I had one of my intercessors praying for me, whom I had texted. These three people stayed on it while I contin-ued to relay to them what I felt in my body. Eventually, I began to cough so violently that my wife became worried. Again, another spasm of coughing came over me, and my head felt like it was on fire. Finally, the pain left, and I could feel something collecting in my stomach. The area became tingly, and pressure built, but there was no pain. Looking back, I believe the Lord was gathering all of the excess gas (for several days, I was also burping all the time) and fluid in my body to the center and then making it dissipate.

Just as fast as it all started, everything ended. My hair was soaked; the sheets needed to be changed from all my perspiration, but I had no pain in my body. I stood up, asked for food, and took a shower. All was perfect in my life again until about a week later. I was sitting on the couch, eating popcorn and watching a Christmas movie with my family, when that pain suddenly came back in my side. I ran to the bathroom and began to rebuke it, telling that spirit it had no right to my body. Still, it gained entry. Again, for the next few days, I battled and endured torture in my body. I remember asking God, "Why? Why can this thing do this to me?"

The answer I received was more of a memory or thought and also a place of shame for me. When you're a healing evangelist, you get bombarded with daily messages to pray for people to be healed. The people who come to you can often be very frustrating to work with, as many seek a quick fix to their lives but do not desire holiness. About half of the people who reach out to me online for deliverance are not planted in a church, nor do they want to be. They typically shun the idea of headship or submission to a pastor.

Some people seem to spend their entire day running from one healing minister to the next, seeking prayer and not finding deliverance. Or, if they do find deliverance, they don't hold onto it for long. In my frustration with these encounters, I became selective about who I prayed healing for and how many times I'd give them an audience.

I drew a warm bath and laid in it—indeed, the only setting I found marginal relief from my pain. There, I repented of choosing who I would pray for and how many times I'd go to bat for them despite disappointment. The Lord reminded me that the gift of healing upon my life was just that—a gift. I did not have a right to horde it but was tasked to "freely give" it (Matthew 10:8). I then asked my wife to pray for my deliverance again. She did, I coughed violently, and the pain went away in an instant.

A week or so later, that spirit returned for a third time. Pressure began to build in my side, but it was not painful. I contacted one of my intercessors and asked her to consult the Lord on my behalf. She responded, "I hear the Lord saying you must stand firm." Thus, for the rest of that day, I stood firm in my freedom,

and by nightfall, the pressure never amounted to anything more. It was completely gone the following day,
and I have been free ever since by the grace of my
Lord. I am convinced those spirits of sickness were
sent to torment me by the witches I had angered.

Months later, some ministry friends of mine reached
out, asking me to pray for their son, who was at the
ER with suspected testicular torsion. I immediately
recognized this as a similar attack and called it out
over the phone—demanding that spirit of witchcraft to
leave the boy. His pain then vanished, and the hospital
discharged him.

On another occasion, my entire household had amo-
rous dreams about forbidden people. I won't get into
details about what our roommate dreamt, but I will
tell you that my wife and I had dreams about past love
interests. In my dream, I was trying to convince a girl
I once knew to let me take her on a date. In my wife's
dream, she was with a guy she had dated in high
school. A disciple of mine, about a week after our
household endured these temptations of the heart, had
taboo sexual dreams. These dreams would have made
sense if the four of us had been living in sin. But we

had all been living consecrated lives for some time by this point. One night, our roommate came out about her dream, asking for advice because of how confusing it was. I then divulged my dream, and then my wife told us hers. We knew instantly this was witchcraft. It was a concerted effort to draw us into sinful desire—ultimately failing. Together, we rebuked the witchcraft and any unclean spirits with an assignment to give us dreams, and we have been free from them ever since.

Again, it is not that witches have more power than believers; it is the fact they are deceptive. I believe many Christians are afflicted by Satan and are unaware because it has never crossed their mind that they were externally under attack. We do not teach much about spiritual warfare in the West, and our churches are paying the price for it.

About a month after I was delivered from the spirit of torment in my body, my wife revealed something unexpected to me. One night, she asked, "Do you ever feel like the veil between life and death is very thin?" Aly is not esoteric in the least, so this strange question caught me off guard.

I told her I had no idea what she was talking about, so she elaborated. "I've been dealing with this feeling where it seems like my spirit is floating out of my body, as if I could cross over to death at any moment." Still taken aback, I asked, "How long has this been happening?"

We traced the timeline, and suddenly, something clicked. "So it started around the same time I was dealing with that pain in my body?" I asked. She nodded in agreement. I realized this was likely a different form of witchcraft specifically tailored for my wife. At that time, between the two of us, I tended to walk more frequently in healing (thus, pain in my body), while my wife operated more regularly in the prophetic (seeing and feeling in the spirit-realm).

I told my wife we should consult the Holy Spirit regarding the issue, so I began praying.

Almost immediately, I had a vision of a goat-headed demon resembling a Baphomet. "Oh, I know what it is," I said. I shared what I had seen, rolled over in bed, placed my hand on her, and began to rebuke the demon tormenting her. As I prayed, Aly began to experience a panic attack and had a vision. She screamed, "It has wings! It has wings!" I commanded the demon to go to hell and prayed in tongues over her. After a few minutes of rebuking, the atmosphere calmed. I then asked my wife, "How do you feel?"

"Heavy," she replied.

I couldn't discern if that was a good thing or not, so I began to probe, "Heavy as in the glory of God is upon you? Or heavy as in demonic oppression?"

"No," she answered, "I feel my normal weight again. I'm not floating out of my body anymore."

Just as in my own experience, this entity returned once more to torment my wife. She endured it silently for a time, but the night she finally told me, Jesus drove it out of her again—and she has been free ever since.

Chapter 14
Asheville

My wife and I celebrated our seventh anniversary by visiting the Biltmore in Asheville, NC, in June 2023. We tried to visit the city on two prior occasions—the first time was thwarted by a freak snowstorm, and the second by the COVID pandemic. Finally, we were on our way and looking forward to seeing a new town.

Our estate tour was a wonderful experience—we enjoyed the gardens even more than the Biltmore home. The food in Asheville is some of the best we've ever eaten, but as we ventured from restaurant to restaurant and shop to shop, something felt off. Upon entering the city center, my wife recalls that the spiritual atmosphere felt "thick." Every store we visited had witchcraft paraphernalia. Vendors were selling crystals, tarot cards, dream catchers, sound bathing bowls, etc.

I attended a Todd White Power + Love conference in Mississippi about a year later, where a prophetic man named Jeremiah Johnson spoke. He told an anecdote about a family vacation to the mountains of North Carolina. As he drove into Asheville, he recalled immediately sensing witchcraft and said, "There must be a large coven here." Asheville is home to one of the largest witch covens in America. It is an epicenter for New Agers who believe ley lines (alleged invisible spiritual lines of power that run through the Earth) intersect downtown. Diagonally across from the First Baptist Church resides a pagan temple dedicated to worshiping the "divine feminine." There are roughly seven metaphysical shops in a city of only 100,000 people; these shops sell witchcraft paraphernalia used in demonic rituals and pursuits. That is serious demand!

While eating at one restaurant, I noticed our server was wearing a crucifix necklace with a dead skeleton on it. I asked him why he chose to wear it, and his answer was, "I thought it looked cool, and I hate Christianity." Delving deeper into the topic, he revealed to me that his parents were once on the verge of separating and tried going to church to see if it could save their marriage. It, unfortunately, did not.

The vast majority of people who disbelieve in God or are hostile to Christianity are that way because of pain in their heart. The militant atheist will tell you his/her reasons are purely rational, but having debated hundreds of them, I can assure you they never are. Atheism is a learned trait. If we look at cultures all around the world that developed independently of one another, we find each seeking the face of the "Divine," though ignorant of how to reach it. On this topic I recommend the book *The Everlasting Man* by G.K. Chesterton.

Children are born knowing there is more to the world than what they can touch and see—that belief must be stripped out of them through experience to form an atheist.

These experiences often stem from *disappointment* in the so-called *good things of life.* When fame, money, sex, and a host of other fleeting pleasures fail to bring lasting joy, a person can easily become cynical. That disappointment can then turn to anger—especially when they seek fulfillment in the Church but fail to find life there (*what a rebuke!*)

As C.S. Lewis once said, *"I was at this time living, like so many Atheists or Antitheists, in a whirl of contradictions. I maintained that God did not exist. I was also very angry with God for not existing. I was equally angry with Him for creating a world."*

His influence, G.K. Chesterton, offered this insight on pessimism: *"Pessimism is not in being tired of evil but in being tired of good. Despair does not lie in being weary of suffering, but in being weary of joy. It is when for some reason or other good things in a society no longer work that the society begins to decline; when its food does not feed, when its cures do not cure, when its blessings refuse to bless."*

A significant portion of atheists and agnostics I have ministered to grew up in the Church, mainly from a Catholic background. They have seen the fruit of religion and decided in their hearts they want nothing of it. This can make it challenging to evangelize such people, but again, Jesus didn't come to establish a religion; He came to bring a Kingdom. Jaded people don't need more rules and regulations; they need an authentic encounter with Jesus. They need cures that cure.

I ministered to one such atheist on one of my visits to
Asheville. He was a college student from Russia with a
questioning yet open mind. At that time, Russia was at
war with Ukraine, and although this man was Russian,
he was raising money for Ukraine. He said to me,
"Putin is an evil man; why doesn't God just kill him?"

This was a funny question to receive from an atheist,
but I answered him in earnest, "God loves Putin. Yes,
Putin's sins have made him an enemy of the Lord, but
God loves His enemies and wants them to repent. He
is having mercy on Putin out of an abundance of patience. But if Putin does not repent, he will have to
pay for all of his atrocities in hell."

I then shared the gospel message of salvation with the
young atheist and challenged him, "If I were to show
you a miracle right now, would that give you at least
one evidence point to suggest God existed?"

The man replied, "If you prayed for me, and something changed in me, I would believe. That would be
enough for me." What an amazing opportunity! I
wasn't going to waste it, so I asked him, "Do you have
any pain in your body?" He was healthy. I then asked,

"Do you deal with anxiety or depression?" He admitted to me that he dealt with depression. I rebuked the spirit of depression in him, and in a moment, he felt the power of God displace the thing! I then asked if I could put my hand on his chest, and at this point, he was more than willing to receive. I prayed the peace of God would come and fill him, and for the first time, I saw him smile. That is how you convert an atheist—with a demonstration of the power of God where the blessings do bless.

Driving home from Asheville after our first visit to celebrate our anniversary, I lamented how everyone we met was oppressed. My wife and I may have met a single closeted Christian in the city, but the rest were in severe depression and darkness. We were talking about how the Church needed to do something there when my wife suggested, "Why don't you?"

Over the next half hour, the Holy Spirit of God filled that vehicle. Lightning began to course through my arms to the edge of pain. Immediately, a multi-step plan was downloaded into my brain for a mission trip to Asheville—a city a local pastor told me was nicknamed the "Wiccan capital of the East Coast." It was a town ruled by Satan and unbelief, but the Lord told me something I would never forget. "They are crying out for Me," He said.

Upon entering our church that Sunday, Savannah Ramsey saw me kneeling at the altar, receiving what she described as "coded messages" into my mind. Later, she shared the interpretation with me—that the Lord had given me a strategy uniquely tailored to my personality. This served as confirmation that what had happened to me in the vehicle was indeed from the Lord!

Savannah also had a brief meeting with my wife, during which she saw "Springtime" all around her. She remarked that we were not the same people who had left on our anniversary trip and said we had "walked through the looking glass, like Alice." My wife, whom I call a *signs person*, was completely floored, as we had made an unplanned stop in Knoxville on our way home and visited a store called Alice in Appalachia, which was themed after *Alice in Wonderland*. Shortly after returning from that trip, I was called into full-time ministry.

The plan for taking Asheville was simple, and I believe God gave it to us as a blueprint for rending a territory from principalities. First, we would need to find local churches that preached orthodoxy (biblical Christianity) and were Spirit-filled. These would be the congregations we sent converts to. It isn't good to lead a person to Jesus and fail to help them down the road of discipleship!

Second, we would need a team of missionaries dedicated to sanctification and *walking in miracles* (a phrase I use to describe someone seeing the miraculous happen around them).

Third, we would need housing for this team. Fourth, we would spend several days street evangelizing in the city before we held Freedom Night events. We needed not just to have one event but a series of them. Fifth, we would need permitting to host these events. And sixth, probably the most vital, we would need to pray for the city for months before going.

God immediately brought a team together, and everyone was shocked that we jumped through the extreme red-tape-laden Asheville event-permitting process. It turned out there was a couple in our little church that owned three rental homes in Asheville, and they had been seeking God to use them for His glory; these were donated to the mission team, and the owners joined us! We decided to spend a week in the city—several days of street evangelism in teams as the Spirit led us, followed by three Freedom Night events downtown. An intercessory prayer team quickly came together, consisting of people from all across America. Six of us entered into a prayer covenant in preparation for the mission trip. We committed to spending at least thirty minutes in prayer each day for Asheville, maintaining this dedication for ninety consecutive days.

Unfortunately, we did not fulfill this commitment perfectly. I missed one day of prayer because Freedom Night lasted until 1:30 a.m., and that was when I finally prayed. Another intercessor became too sick to pray one day, and a third person also missed a day.

Overall, this was one of the most challenging acts of discipline I have undertaken to date. I'm grateful I did it, but if I were to do it again, I would need to make more careful preparations. One of the biggest challenges was finding enough things to pray about for ninety consecutive days. Eventually, I realized the importance of praying in tongues for a significant portion of the time and leaving space to simply sit and listen to God.

As each intercessor did this, visions and words of knowledge began to flow. The Lord revealed six different principalities which ruled the region. We called on God's angels and Spirit daily to wage war over the city. Ethan and I both received prophecies about the city becoming flooded. Initially, we thought these were symbolic, but after hurricane Helene swept through and decimated the area later in the year, the Holy Spirit reminded me to look back on our list of words for Asheville, and the prediction was there.

I believe the flood was both literal and symbolic of an outpouring of the Holy Spirit upon the city, resulting in widespread revival, not just in Asheville but throughout the Eastern Seaboard. That flood decimated the art district. I have vivid memories of entering a store there where every fourth or fifth painting was of a demon. There are many artists in Asheville, and many of them channel spirits for their craft.

Finding Spirit-filled orthodox churches was a much more difficult feat than the rest of the objectives. The Church there is either dormant/religious, infested with New Age, or righteous but without much influence. Fortunately, the people who hooked our team up with lodging also connected me with a solid local associate pastor I will call Joshua. I made several trips to Asheville before our mission trip to meet with various pastors, but the first trip was to grab coffee at a shop on the river with Joshua. Before leaving to meet him, as I was packing my suitcase, the Holy Spirit said, "Take an extra pair of clothes." I obeyed—telling my wife, "God told me to take extra clothes; I might be staying longer than we expected."

I was filled with joy on the drive up, made it to our appointment in time, and noticed two women in line at the coffee place. These women were dressed in hipster fashion and were in a relationship with one another. God's love for them filled my heart, and I knew that the Lord had finally broken me of some of my prejudices toward the demographic of people I'd meet repeatedly in Asheville (political progressives). Between 10% and 15% of Asheville self-identifies as LGBT, which is almost triple the national average of 4% to

5%. Like witchcraft, the LGBT lifestyle is advertised in every store you enter.

I couldn't minister to the women, but when Joshua finally arrived and was in line to grab a drink, I looked into the shop's corner and saw a young blonde man, and I knew in my heart that the Lord had a gift for him. I approached and told him I believed God had something for him, and I invited this man to join Joshua and I at a table. I guess the Lord was drawing him, and he sat with us.

I began sharing with Joshua the word I had received from the Lord for Ashveille, and many accurate words of knowledge for him personally. Eventually, I turned to the blonde man beside me and began to discern what the Lord wanted me to do for him. He needed deliverance, so we prayed, but he was not freed. I then asked him, "Have you been water baptized?" He had not, so I told him, "The Lord told me to bring an extra pair of clothes with me, and I now believe it was so I could baptize you." The man was elated, and he also had an extra pair of clothes in his car. So we waded into the river while Joshua filmed, and I baptized that man (the first person I *ever* baptized). When he came out of the water, he felt the demon leave him; his eyes brightened, and the warmth of the Holy Spirit filled him.

A woman once prophesied over me, "You will baptize people, and they will be delivered in the water." I have seen it over and over again. No one can tell me baptism is just symbolic. It is symbolic in many ways, but it is also spiritual. God does something inside the believer. I've had the privilege of baptizing many who were delivered or filled with the Spirit the moment they came out. Others will start manifesting, and we can deal with the demons promptly. Water baptism is a powerful act and grace from God. If you have not been water baptized, I urge you to be like the Ethiopian eunuch Philip ministered to in the book of Acts, and get to it (Acts 8:36).

Joshua told me later, "When you baptized that man, I heard it was the 'first fruit' of your mission trip; I will tell my senior pastor." I then spent another day in the city. That night, I tried ministering to the man behind the counter at my hotel. I asked him if he needed a miracle in his life, but he was hesitant to reveal anything to me. Later, I learned it was because he worried

I was a New Ager. As it turned out, he was a believer, but his wife and he were trying to escape the city. All of his neighbors were miserable, he said. He was aware of the darkness and gloom that haunts Asheville, and he couldn't take it anymore. I told him to hold on and that Jesus was coming.

As we conversed, a food delivery driver began to stomp her feet and groan in the lobby. She was supposed to deliver some food, but could not contact the customer. No one was coming to get it and she feared she'd be stuck—having wasted precious time to earn money. As I looked at her, the Holy Spirit said, "Give her $50." She trudged out the front door, now on the phone with customer service, to figure out what to do with the order. I told the man behind the counter, "God just told me to give that woman some money," and I followed her out the door.

After she hung up, more irritable than before, I approached her and asked, "Do you have a Venmo or Paypal or Cash app profile I can send some money to you on?" She said she did not, became frustrated with me, and marched off into the parking lot to her car. In a desperate bid, I yelled after her, "God told me to give you $5o!" The woman stopped dead in her tracks and returned to me, telling me what a blessing that would be. It turned out her roommate had a Venmo, and I could be obedient to the Lord that way. But God was not done with this driver.

He gave me a word for her, which got her to sit down and converse with me. Jesus ended up healing her knee, which had been broken for a very long time, and He also delivered her from several evil spirits. The Lord then baptized her in the Holy Spirit, and I saw an irritable woman turn into serenity. She asked what she could do for me, and I told her my request, "Will you please go into the hotel and tell the man behind the counter what the Lord just did for you?"

She gladly witnessed to him! I then connected her with Joshua's church, which she began to attend regularly. The church and one of my donors pitched in to help her with housing needs. That's the Church on fire! The woman was healed, delivered, discipled, and physically cared for.

The next day, in the evening, I went to a Kava bar with Joshua. If you don't know, Kava tea is a depressant that some people drink, which can eventually become a coping mechanism for anxiety and stress. I kid you not; this establishment was one of the most demonic venues I had ever been in. Idols of false gods were everywhere. Paintings of demons dotted the walls and bar area. The spiritual atmosphere was darkness and malaise. Joshua introduced me to a tattooed man who worked there and loved Jesus but could not bring himself to make Him his Lord. The tatted guy told me how he once angered his warlock roommate.

After that, an abscess appeared on his chest that would not heal. I told him about the power of the Holy Spirit and delivered a word from the Lord, "Quit your job." He told me I was the third "source" to give him that word. I explained, "The atmosphere of this place is apathy, and it is keeping you from following Jesus wholeheartedly." I then heard another voice. A demon spoke to me, "You have no power here." I began to laugh on the inside because I knew all the demonic powers in that bar would have to watch this man get delivered. I went to pray for him, and the power of God struck him immediately. Evil spirits fled, and I asked the Lord to heal him; his pain left. Joshua would tell me months later, "Remember the guy in the Kava bar who you told to quit his job? The very next day, he left."

During my visits to Asheville, the Lord graced me with unbelievable faith. The sign gifts are truly available to authenticate the message of God. It is almost as if the further away from religion one gets into the darker areas of the world, the more readily the Spirit of God moves. I believe He is desperate to draw children in and will lavish ministers with power who dare to seek the lost.

The warfare our team endured from that trip was intense. For months, we waged spiritual war against incursions by our enemy into our homes. These attacks mostly came in the form of fear during the night-time, but they also came for our finances. Some coven in Asheville must have been activated and assigned to us. Obviously, the principalities in the region feared what the Spirit was doing.

I visited several other times and brought two additional churches on-board to partner with our mission. One of these churches, now three total, supplied a worship team for our largest event, while another did so for our other events. The third church was more reticent, but they did advertise the gatherings and many of their members came to our meetings.

It was amazing to hear the same words come from these pastors separately. One told me that "you can't come into Asheville guns blazing" against the principalities there, or you'll die—much like a pastor he knew previously. Multiple pastors told me there was hardly any unity among the churches in Asheville. Each church was afraid to support one another's endeavors for fear of losing adherents to the other churches. Joshua's church had only 50 people then, and the other two were not much larger.

A successful church in Asheville, having been there for over a decade, was roughly only 100 members strong. The third church that partnered with us invited me to tour their building, after which I prophesied over the head pastor. I saw him standing before a large crowd and the word was clear, "Your church is about to explode." Sure enough, it eventually did.

One day, in heaven, pastors who worked hard to reach the lost and sustain their churches will be rewarded.

Some things will also be revealed to them that they did not know on Earth. Nameless intercessors, who faithfully covered them in prayer with tears for years, were pivotal to the success of their endeavors. I believe entire ministries are birthed in the prayer closets of random believers around the globe who choose to submit themselves to intense prayer and fasting at the behest of the Spirit. My ministry is undoubtedly the result of such people—many long dead.

April of 2024 came around, and the night before our missionaries would venture to Asheville, Aly and I had our first angelic visitation. I woke up in the middle of the night, groggy, and asking the Lord, "Why am I not having any prophetic dreams?" It was a strange question to ask, but for some reason, I did. Then I opened my eyes, and before me was a luminescent being. It was two-dimensional, plastered on the wall at the foot of my bed. I had heard my neighbors were graced with a similar visitation months prior, and I immediately recognized this as an angel by their description. For months, the only things I'd seen in our room at night were demons. Now that an angel had appeared, I didn't know what to do. I was frozen in bed, not out of fear, but just not wanting the creature to leave. I also wondered if what I was seeing wasn't just caused by a light coming in through the window. The angel had an almost hourglass appearance and was brighter than bright. I thought, "Maybe it is headlights from the road?" But it didn't move an inch, and the angle of the road didn't allow for that theory. Suddenly, the angel left. The moment it went, I was even more convinced I had seen an angel for the first time in my life.

Then, a second one appeared. This one was shorter than the first. I reached over to grab my wife's hand. She then woke up and thought, "Maybe I'll see an angel like my neighbor did." Opening her eyes, there at the foot of the bed was what she hoped to see. We both lay there in complete silence as our minds raced. Then, just as quickly as the first, this angel disappeared. My wife exclaimed, "James, did you see the angel!" We spent the next hour trying to figure out if there would be any natural cause for what we witnessed, and there wasn't. I found it difficult to fall asleep again that night, popping my eyes open every so often to see if another would appear. Finally, I understood the significance. The Lord had sent His angels to protect us; we were guarded.

Our team loaded up in multiple vehicles the next day, drove 4.5 hours to Asheville, and moved into our donated accommodations. We had a loose plan based on the words God had given us, but most of our trip featured rapidly changing circumstances based on what we felt the Spirit was conveying. About a month before arriving, the Lord had told my wife that our team needed to eat at a specific restaurant. So, on the first afternoon, we obeyed. We would break into twos and threes throughout this trip to accomplish effective street evangelism. Feeling led to split from the main group, my friend Joel Cosand and I began to walk down the street this restaurant was situated on. It was an older part of town dotted with retail sprawl and hipster-inspired restaurants.

Joel and I started a conversation as we walked, but I quickly cut it short by saying, "I believe those people are ripe." A homeless couple was walking our way, and their lives were about to be interrupted by the power of God. The man had a broken body—the result of a car wreck. He was also majorly addicted to fentanyl. The woman was injured and heavily demonized but had given her life to Jesus about a month prior. The Lord healed the woman's body first, and then she was set free from demonic bondage and baptized in the Spirit. Jesus healed one of the man's injuries, and then we worked with him for a while (feeding him truth about his life) and finally drove a demon of addiction out of him. He contorted for a bit and was finally freed.

Joel and I traveled down the road—cursing a metaphysical store as we passed it. Eventually, we found an older, unbelieving "hippie" couple; Jesus healed the man's hand, which allowed us to share the gospel with him. Our days and nights in Asheville were spent doing the same work Jesus' seventy-two disciples did in Luke 10. We sought out the lost and broken, and we brought good news and a demonstration of the power of God.

One evening, our team booked three ten-minute time slots back to back at the Kava bar for its open mic night. Our time on stage wouldn't begin until extremely late, so our group sat in the bar watching as a menagerie of pain took the stage to express itself through various types of people. One was a relatively older gentleman dressed as a woman who was obviously suffering from a neurological disorder as his body shook. He played his guitar and sang a song about how envious he was of women. His heart's most resounding cry was to be female.

Another man went up and delivered the most demonic monologue you could think of. Take a bit of every religion, including Christianity, put it into a blender, and that's this man's belief system. He called himself a blasphemous name, spoke in demonic tongues from the stage, and openly performed rituals throughout his act.

There are a couple of responses Christians can have in such a scenario. One of our members stormed out to compose herself. My wife went around laying hands on each of us. I was praying in tongues under my breath and rebuking the curses coming from the stage. Jaqualin, though, chose best. He entered the presence of the Lord through meditation.

Finally, our group's block was called up. Weeks prior, I spoke to the Lord about what I planned to do on Kava bar night. I told Him I wanted to call our act "Divine Healing with Ethan and James!" The plan was to ask volunteers from the audience who were in pain to come up, and we'd see Jesus heal them. I believe the Lord laughed in delight at my idea and thought it would be great fun.

Ethan and I took the stage, where I explained we practiced *Divine Healing* and needed audience participants who were currently in pain to come up. I didn't know it then, but since the open mic was being live-streamed, two of our intercessors were watching online, praying for people to come up on stage, interceding for their healing, and interceding for Ethan and me the whole time!

Finally, a gentleman took the stage and told us he was unable to turn his head to one side. There was pain, but also a limitation, which made him a perfect example to demonstrate the power of God on. Ethan and I each took his hands and we told the pain to leave and the neck to be healed. Just like at the witch festival, we did not use the name of Jesus out loud when saying these things. The man was able to turn his neck, and all of his pain left. The crowd cheered and clapped (mostly our own group of people).

A woman in the audience then raised her hand to volunteer but said all of her pain was mental. Ethan and I told her, "We deal in that area too. Come on up, sister." The woman came to the stage and revealed the root cause of her issues was a custody battle she was currently in. She admitted to dealing with anxiety, a heaviness in her chest, and panic attacks. I asked her, "Do you want rid of your panic attacks?" She responded, "Sure," I told her that would be "easy." I then spoke to the spirit causing her panic attacks, and commanded it to leave. I told her I wanted to say "good things" over her. "Peace," I proclaimed. "I'm going to believe you'll feel peace washing over you starting from the top of your head on down." In the end, when I asked her what she felt, she said, "I don't know if it is you or the kratom, but I feel good!"

We were now running out of time for our 10-minute act, so a man rushed up on stage. He had been dealing with severe pain throughout his body, anxiety, and panic attacks. Ethan and I took his hands and rebuked the spirit of sickness in his body. The young man flipped his head back and probably would have fallen backward if we weren't holding onto him. When it was all over, his pain was gone entirely, and he felt like a new man.

Scan the QR code to see Ethan's and my Divine Healing "act" at this bar.

Do you know what happened in that bar when we rebuked the pain in this man? What may look simple from a natural perspective was not simple at all on a spiritual level. The man had a demon in him, and it had been there for a very long time. When we told it to leave, this entity of immense power had to—because Jesus lives in us. Something was ripped out of this man's body against its will because of the cross. Jesus' blood was sufficient for our healing and freedom, but simply because something has been purchased doesn't mean it has been applied. I can have a bank account full of money, but it is useless if I don't swipe my debit card. The Holy Spirit applied the freedom purchased for this man by Jesus—and suddenly, he was healed.

In Colossians, Paul writes, "And having disarmed the powers and authorities, [Jesus] made a public spectacle of them, triumphing over them by the cross." Jesus not only disarmed the powers of darkness, but He humiliated them, too. Similarly, in this bar were witches and demonic powers that were forced to watch a display of the Spirit's dominance.

At the end of our act, Ethan and I shared the gospel and told everyone in the bar that Jesus had healed three people, not us. Many were offended, some livid, at least one was grateful, and others were confused. Our team overheard people questioning, "Did they have something on their hands? Like a chemical?" Even when presented with a miracle, very few will believe.

Following our timeslot on healing, Jaqualin took the stage and began to give "heart print readings." He was able to prophesy accurately over three volunteers from the crowd, including a woman who practiced witchcraft. Jaqualin then concluded by telling the crowd that a true God named Jesus sees their coming, going, rising, and sleeping, and is always near them when they call out to Him. Finally, pastor Joshua used his ten-minute slot to share the story of the prodigal son and preach the gospel.

What our team did was the essence of evangelism—we went where all the lost people were, demonstrated the power of God, and shared the good news of Jesus with them. Without Divine intervention, such people will never step foot in a church. Thus, the Church has to go to them.

There are hundreds of stories from our time in Asheville. I estimate we impacted at least 500 people for the gospel; about thirty gave their lives to Jesus, a dozen or so were water baptized, and probably eighty were baptized in the Holy Spirit. There were hundreds of deliverances and miraculous healings.

There were many encounters with witches and those hostile to the gospel message. One witch, dressed eclectically with her teeth filed into fangs and offering tarot card readings on a sidewalk in downtown

Asheville, cursed at us and made a massive scene about "being harassed." About five seconds into our conversation, her demons told her we were Christians. I tried to tell her that God wasn't angry at her but loved her, to no avail. Savannah joined us on our trip to Asheville and had an encounter with a woman who identified herself as a "high priestess." When she shared this, the Holy Spirit rose up in Sav, and she boldly declared, "I have a High Priest." Immediately, the pagan priestess became visibly unsettled and anxious.

Meanwhile, hostility toward us escalated. Some people threw water bottles at our worship team, while a car repeatedly drove past our outdoor meeting, hurling water balloons at our sound equipment. Witches cursed every member of our team to some degree. At our first outdoor worship meeting, Ethan and I lined up all of the ministers and prayed for them one after another. When we came to one woman on the team, Ethan got a word about "witchcraft." The moment he spoke that word, the woman dropped to the ground, screaming and weeping. Others on the team became ill after leaving the Kava bar, and I myself saw a rotating menagerie of monsters anytime I'd close my eyes that night. Our team prayed and praised the Lord through all these issues—eventually, the afflictions lifted.

I believe Asheville will one day be an incubator for sending evangelists out all over the world. In our team's mind, the deciding factor will be whether the local Church there unifies, or not.

Chapter 15
Somebody Gave Me Fire

"On the count of three, I command every unclean spirit to leave this girl," I said to demons that had tormented a young lady since childhood. Her dad had brought her down to the altar of my church.

Previously, the Lord had opened this father's partially deaf ear after praying twice for it. That same night, his friend regained his eyesight and was freed from afflicting spirits. Now, his teenage daughter stood before me, manifesting a spirit of fear. The Lord had already revealed to me the root issue through a vision. I saw her climbing a staircase, and the interpretation came quickly, "You're a perfectionist—always striving and putting a great burden upon yourself. This fear came in from a young age as you've always worried about your future." She nodded in amazement while tears began to roll down her cheeks.

She admitted her current fear was whether she would get into a good college or not. I told her Jesus would free her, but she needed to repent for indulging this familiar spirit. She did.

"One, two, three," I spoke calmly and then snapped my fingers. The moment I snapped, the girl collapsed to the floor like a sack of potatoes. She didn't fall backward, but her legs gave out on her as the fear vacated. Days later, her dad texted me, "[My daughter] has not been able to stop talking about Sunday, praise God." That girl is still free months later.

While in Asheville, our mission team was invited one Sunday to take over an outdoor meeting of small churches in a nearby town. One of the pastors had come to a Freedom Night in Knoxville, where I preached about the glory of God. Gold dust appeared on people's hands that evening; many were laid out on the floor under the Spirit, and the pastor himself received healing for his knee.

Now, I was standing in front of a group of churches that were formerly cessationist and hungry for the Holy Spirit. Another pastor at this meeting told me, "Each of us paid a heavy cost when we decided to stop quenching the Spirit in our churches. We lost half our congregations almost immediately. We've since adopted a motto, 'Christ over congregation.'"

These pastors hoped that our team would bring the fire of God. I preached on the Kingdom of God and Jesus' strategy for taking ground in the Earth.

I then introduced the third person of the Trinity to these churches and, beginning with the children, called them forward to be baptized in power. Fire from heaven fell on our assembly as people received the Spirit. Some fell out, multitudes were healed, and gifts were imparted. I got a word that one woman had been desiring the gift of tongues. I told her to put her hand on her stomach and close her eyes. My wife and I touched her hand, and within a few seconds, the woman began ecstatically praying in tongues!

One woman came up with a severely broken knee. Some of our team members were praying for her healing when I came over. Eventually, I asked to put my hand on her knee, and the moment I did, it began to shake uncontrollably. I repeated this several times, and with each repetition, her joint healed a little more.

In the end, I sat on the stage and marveled at what the Lord had done. One of the pastors then approached and knelt in front of me. He said, "The Lord said you had a word for me." I, in fact, didn't have anything at the time. "Can I have your hand and see if I can hear anything?" I responded. I took his hand, and the Lord began to speak with imagery I could understand—scenes from the *Lord of the Rings* movies. I saw how this man was like Gandalf; he was wise and filled with power, and he was being used to raise an army to fight against the forces of Mordor.

I saw that he had a teaching gift, and his role was to equip the church. I then saw Saruman, a dark wizard and one of Gandalf's nemesis in the movie. At about that time, my friend Ethan walked over, touched the pastor on the head, and said, "I break witchcraft off you." Immediately, the pastor fell to the ground, convulsing and weeping as he was delivered from an evil spirit. When he finally returned, he confessed, "Everything you said was spot on. I gave up my church a little bit ago and handed it to one of my sons. I am now spending my time teaching and training pastors in various churches to raise them as an army for the Lord."

One time, Ethan and I were invited by some evangelist friends to seek the lost in downtown Murfreesboro, TN. As we walked around the square, mostly finding religious folk who wouldn't let us pray for them, I felt drawn to another part of the city. It was in that space we came upon a woman who was homeless and hobbling. I asked about her disability, and she told us her femur was shattered, which caused immense pain. We had her sit down on a stone wall, and I got her consent to place my hand on her femur.

Immediately, she felt the power of God shoot through her leg, and upon me commanding her bones to come back together, we both felt them move. She stood up to test and was completely healed. This allowed us to share the gospel with her, and Jesus baptized her in the Holy Spirit and fire after Ethan led her through inner healing and forgiveness.

One Freedom Night we were ministering in Centennial Park in Nashville, TN. A homeless man, bent over in severe pain, dragged his leg in a roundabout fashion to our meeting. Many on the team had been praying for him for a while, and whenever they did, his body would respond by moving around aimlessly. Naturally, we all thought this was a demon manifesting, so we tried to drive it out, but nothing would leave him. Eventually, I stopped the deliverance and talked more with the man. It turned out he had fallen on the Parthenon steps and landed on his side—which caused the injury. "So you just need your hips healed?" I asked. One side was 3-4 inches higher than the other.

We took him to the stage and had him sit down. I then spoke, "In the name of Jesus, I command these hips to move! Right now, pop into place!" A small crowd watched the man's hips move, and the gentleman exclaimed, "I felt them rotate!" He then stood up and walked normally! His back was still in severe pain, so we sat him back down. Touching the muscles in his back, they felt like stone. His body was clearly trying to compensate for how he had been walking. Ethan then commanded his back to be healed and his muscles to relax. They did, and Jesus restored this man's health!

In the winter of early 2024, I was invited to minister at a church held at a barn wedding event venue in Alexandria, TN. This is a part of the state dominated by religion and cessationism, but the venue's owners were a

Spirit-filled and highly prophetic couple from Australia.

The week prior, I came down with influenza for the first time in my life. It was a miserable time of isolation in my basement, filled with unabating fever and chills. Ethan, also, had been struggling with sickness for weeks up until that point. I broke isolation a day before the ministry engagement. The fever and chills had left, but my body was still exhausted, and my psychological state was not great from the loneliness. Ethan felt well enough to make our ministry trip, so we hopped in a car and drove over an hour through the dark to take on one of our first opportunities to preach in a church.

Having not eaten much in the last week, we were both pretty starved, so we stopped by a fast food restaurant to not be late, stuffed ourselves, and began to regret it immediately. We made it to the venue just in time for me to find the bathroom—a space I'd visit at least two more times before going up to preach. Needless to say, our flesh was weak, but the Spirit was willing.

God had told me weeks before to preach on forgiveness, so I went through the parable of the unforgiving servant. The church was comprised of about
30-40 people, so once I was done preaching, we invited them to come up one by one to be prayed for in
the presence of all. My goal was to make a spectacle of
the power of God in the heart of this religious community. Thus, I started by asking anyone in the group
with physical pain to come up first.

The head pastor raised his hand and came up with a
knee issue. We prayed several times, but he wasn't
healed. An excellent start for demonstration, huh?
The pastor took his seat, and then a woman presented
a more severe issue. We took her hands, and the fire of
God fell on her—she was immediately healed. Now
that's more like it! I kid you not; every person who
came up after that woman was healed—that we could
test. It didn't matter how tame or severe of an issue
they wrestled with; God met them.

I was hearing testimonies from the pastors for weeks
of people healed from things like arthritis and neurop-
athy. An encounter that stands out from that service
was a middle-aged woman who was dealing with

severe trauma and pain in her heart. I took her hands and prayed, "Holy Spirit, I ask that you will come and do what only you can—will you bind this woman's heart up?" I then blew on her, and she crumpled to her knees, where she began to cry out and weep for the next ten minutes as some other women in the church surrounded her. I believe God siphoned out all of that trauma and healed her heart.

Somewhere in the middle of praying for everyone, I noticed a woman who looked like she was hyperventilating. I motioned for her to come up, and we tried talking to her, but the fire of God was on her, and a demon was manifesting heavily. All we understood was she had severe pain throughout her midsection; there was no diagnosis, and it would come and go. Ethan and I began to command the demon to come out of her. She doubled over and stretched out, but the spirit wouldn't leave. I stopped the deliverance and asked her, "Did you listen to my sermon on forgiveness? Is there anyone you need to forgive?" She responded, "There's no one." I told her to sit back down and that we would pray for her again at the end of the service.

Keeping my word, I brought her back up later, and I invited the prophetic pastors to join us. We asked the Holy Spirit for a word from God as to why this evil spirit wouldn't leave. The pastor with the bad knee spoke up, "I see you, and I see two people, and you're in an argument with them." Immediately, the afflicted woman cried and confessed, "That's my brother and sister-in-law. I sinned against them, and they mistreated me." She forgave them and asked the Lord to forgive her. I told the demon to leave, and she was immediately healed.

One of the last people to receive healing was a much older fellow with metal rods in his back. I commanded the metal to melt and asked the Lord to rebuild the man's spine. All of his pain left, and all of his mobility came back. Months later, I was invited back to the church, and that man came up to me, testifying about how he was still healed but now had a new issue elsewhere in his body. The Lord healed that issue, too. At that follow-up meeting, a man with drop-foot due to underdevelopment was immediately healed and went on a hiking trip the next day to test it out—reporting no issues at all. When I laid hands on this man's foot, a prophetic seer said he saw lightning shoot from his toes to the top of his calf.

Interestingly, while Ethan and I were ministering for the first time at the barn church, our sickness symptoms completely left us. The moment we hopped back in the car to head home, it all came roaring back. And do you remember the church pastor with his knee issue? Well, he woke up a couple of days later, and his knee was completely healed. I had never seen God's grace and power for healing flow so profoundly in a service before that night.

As I mentioned in my previous book, Jesus promised we would do the same works He did and even greater ones than those (John 14:12). Keep in mind that Jesus raised the dead and multiplied fish. Christians are often limited by their imagination when it comes to miracles, and because of this, I challenge churches to start feeding children's imagination early on. My daughters find it strange when someone is not healed after praying for them, while many adults, fat on theology, can't imagine God healing a headache. Reading testimonies is the best way to expand my imagination for the Lord.

I have a friend whose meetings are becoming famous for dental miracles and people receiving arches in their flat feet. Reading about such things gives me the confidence to believe for them in the people I pray for. Recently, I saw a woman with flat feet from birth receive a slight arch in her foot after Ethan and I prayed for her—she was likewise healed from lymphedema. I have also seen a person immediately cured of a painful toothache.

Your imagination is contested ground, and Satan will try to corrupt it. Romans 1:30 states humanity is filled with "inventors of evil." To invent something, we must *imagine* it first. Lately, the Lord has urged me to read about Christian martyrs. One thing that stands out to me about their plight is how the ones murdering them invented many ways to make their torment last as long as possible. A lion might kill dispassionately, but humans have the capacity for malice. I delve deep into this topic, considering the suffering of Jesus, in a booklet of mine called *Unreasonable Brutality*. One way many Christians were executed in Europe was by being hanged, drawn, and quartered. When I first read that, I wondered how so many things could happen to a human at one time—wouldn't the hanging simply kill them? It turns out they would hang the believer until he (women were typically spared this type of death) *almost* died, then they would save their life only to "draw" them, which was the process of disemboweling the martyr while he was still alive. The bowels, and sometimes the genitals, would then be burned in front of the man. This phase of the torment would eventually kill the person, and then his body would be "quartered"—cut into four pieces.

Someone invented this form of depravity, and I guarantee you it was inspired by an evil spirit inside their imagination. I've talked to several people who see pornographic images while they try to worship God or pray for others. Still, some have told me they hear blasphemous thoughts when they think of the Lord. Satan can certainly captivate our imagination, but it wasn't meant to be his. As one friend told me, "Your imagination belongs to God."

In the hands of an ardent believer, imagination is deadly to the kingdom of darkness. If one can imagine something, they are very close to having faith for it to occur. I remember the first time I prayed for metal to melt in a person, and it did. Many people would not think to even ask for such a thing, but I did because I had seen another minister do it. Now, I find metal melting frequently. I have a video of a man with a titanium and ceramic shoulder replaced by one made of flesh and bone. As I tell the metal in his body to get out, it becomes extremely hot. When he goes to test his shoulder, he begins to freak out because even the clicking it once made has gone. That is the fire of God.

Scan the QR code to watch Jesus heal this man's shoulder.

I have another video of myself and a fellow minister praying for a young woman with a broken shoulder. I actually "met" her in the comment section of an Instagram post where she was talking about her spiritual brokenness, and I offered to set up a video call to pray for her. She was a teenager with a traumatic history, and as she walked the road of her neighborhood, we preached the gospel to her.

Eventually, she sat down on the sidewalk, and the Lord siphoned that trauma out of her heart. Jesus then delivered her as she gagged up on the road. Joggers offered to help—seeing a medical issue where she was actually being freed from spiritual torment. Finally, I asked if she had any pain in her body, and she told us her shoulder had been wrecked from accidents and physical abuse. Speaking to her shoulder, I commanded it to pop into place. In that moment, the Holy Spirit supernaturally yanked her arm backward; the woman exclaimed, "Oh!" then, with a bewildered look on her face, she told us a large lump in her shoulder had disappeared. That is the fire of God.

Scan the QR code to see the fire of God restore this woman's shoulder.

One Sunday morning, I was worshiping Jesus at the altar on my knees when I had a radical encounter. Suddenly, I was in God's throne room, and before me was the Father on His throne. I could not see His face—pure light emanated from where it would be—but I could see His white flowing robe. I began to weep and put my face to the ground to learn reverence for a King. He then told me to stand.

I complained to Him, "I am unworthy."

"I will make you stand," He responded.

Strength came, and I stood.

He said, "I will send you."

"I will go to the nations," I responded.

The Lord then put something in my mouth, and fire came out of it. The encounter then ended. I knew then this vision was about God empowering me to preach. Two months prior, I was at that same altar worshiping Jesus when a vision of me preaching from the stage entered my mind. In the vision, I began my sermon by asking God to send His Holy Spirit. I saw literal fire from heaven come down in a massive pillar and spread out over everyone in the auditorium, burning above their heads. I then asked the Father to send angels, and a massive multitude came down from the ceiling and stood among the audience. Heaven invaded my church.

It would be many more months before my head pastor asked me to preach a sermon for Salvation Sunday (an excuse to invite lost friends and family because you know the message will be evangelistic). I am not on staff at my church and am a very unknown evangelist, so this was a great honor and opportunity. I asked God what I should preach, and He pointed me to an author and preacher named Leonard Ravenhill. I picked up his book titled Why Revival Tarries, and by the end of the second chapter, I became a mess of tears under heavy conviction. When asked at a wedding around that time, "Why do you think our church has not seen revival?" I admitted to my friend, "I am the reason."

How could I expect others to be hungry for something I, by my actions, did not show a hunger for? One of the main things in that book that convicted me was when Ravenhill exclaimed a preacher who didn't spend at least two hours a day in the secret place was worthless to preach.

The Lord then told me to read Ezekial chapters 9-16, where God condemns Israel for its idolatry, witchcraft, and double-mindedness. Even though the leadership of my church had been spurring us toward holiness and revival, the church itself was carrying too much baggage. This is the message the Lord wanted me to preach—one of great conviction filled with hard truths. Yet, it was Salvation Sunday, so I ended up preaching two messages to the chagrin of some but to the cheers of many others. The first message was straight gospel. I told people from the start that they would feel the Lord calling them to the altar at any point during the sermon, and if they did—to come down. You could see the Lord resting on the place from the beginning. Later, a man would tell me I could have done the altar call after the first few sentences, and people would have come.

How is that possible? Because God doesn't need polished or sophisticated speakers—He's simply looking for willing, surrendered vessels to let His Spirit flow through. That day, six people gave their lives to Jesus. One of them came forward before the altar call was even given, trembling and weeping under the power of the Lord.

I ended up going overtime. My pastor officially dismissed the service, but he graciously allowed me to continue preaching. About a hundred people chose to stay, hungry to hear what the Lord truly wanted to release that day. In the month leading up to that sermon, God had taken me through a deep season of repentance and pruning. So by the time I stood up to speak, I had already felt everything the crowd would feel.

I told them, "If you're feeling convicted, it is because I've been convicted myself for months." The Lord poured His glory into me for weeks, and then, in one service, He poured it onto a people desperate for gentle rebuke.

I exclaimed to them, "Miracles happen because of the mercy and grace of God. They are not a benchmark for success. You have not arrived because you're seeing people healed, and delivered, and set free, and saved, and literally—I don't know if you've seen it the past four weeks—physical manifestations of the glory of God found in gold dust on people's hands has been appearing. That doesn't mean you've arrived because it's all the grace of God. This is the grace of God! Now, the grace of God is there to make you repent. It's not, 'I've repented, now here's the grace of God. Here's all the good stuff.' He's drawing you into something deeper! He's drawing you into something deeper, and too many of us are holding onto this baggage that Jesus came and crucified upon a cross, and we're sitting here trying to keep it alive. You're trying to keep the old corpse alive! And you have hidden sin, and you won't forgive your neighbor; you won't forgive those who abused you growing up. You won't do the basic tenets of what Jesus preached that the body of Christ should do, and like in Ezekiel's day, Jesus can come and take His lampstand from our house at any moment."

After receiving this rebuke, dozens of people came down to the altar and asked the Lord to set them on fire for Kingdom work. This, too, was the fire of God.

Scan the QR code to watch the first sermon I ever gave at Citipointe Church Nashville.

So, what do I mean when I use the phrase "fire of God?" I am speaking directly about the Holy Spirit's interaction with the physical realm. At Pentecost, in Acts 2, the bible records that split tongues of fire came and rested upon the heads of those waiting in the upper room for the promised Holy Spirit.

Immediately, these disciples of Jesus were clothed in power to do the miraculous in the Earth. Most of them set about preaching the gospel, and as they preached, the Spirit fell on crowds who were cut to the core and responded to Jesus (Acts 2:37). These disciples likewise healed the sick, drove out demons, raised the dead, and performed many other signs and wonders as demonstrations of the Spirit.

One man named Simon in Acts 8 tried to purchase the power of the Holy Spirit. Peter sharply rebuked him and told him to repent from bitterness and sin. When I read this passage, I want to give Simon the benefit of the doubt, but I presume Peter knew the man's heart best and told him to ask the Lord to forgive him for the "intent of [his] heart." Not everyone uses the fire of God for righteous ends. In the gospels, two of Jesus' disciples wanted to use the fire of God to burn up their enemies (Luke 9:54).

Many ministers use their supernatural power for monetary gain or fame. I've seen others use the prophetic gifting to manipulate people's relationships. Since the gifts of the Spirit are given without repentance (Romans 11:29), they are not revoked simply because a person's character becomes corrupt. This is why many ministers today can call down the fire of God while secretly cheating on their spouses or indulging in other hidden sins. Surely, they will face their reward in the afterlife when Jesus tells them, "I never knew you (Matthew 7:22)." However, because they did not receive the fire of God based on personal merit, they likewise will not lose their gift due to personal failure. At some point or another, I believe all of us have grieved God by perverting the gifts He has placed upon our lives.

After one has received the Holy Spirit, they need to ask themselves, "What am I going to do with the Gift God has given me?" Your options as a believer are to bury and quench the Holy Spirit or partner with Him to advance the Kingdom of God in the Earth.

Savannah Ramsey once sent me a video that showed a little girl holding a sparkler. Text on the screen said,

"Two types of reactions to the baptism of the Holy Spirit Fire!" The young girl twirled the sparkler around, playing and enjoying its light. Suddenly, a young boy runs into the frame behind her, carrying his sparkler like a torch and screaming, "Somebody gave me fire!" The boy is gone just as fast as he appeared. I laughed very hard at that video and replied to Sav, "I aspire to be that kid." She responded, "lol you are."

Scan the QR code to watch this hilarious video first posted on TikTok by @brittiniechristine.

If God has given you fire from heaven that can force demons out of addicts, heal broken bodies, and touch the souls of people so they come to Christ, are you going to use that fire? I challenge you to be like that little boy—run and scream about the One who gave you fire, and then go and set this world ablaze to His glory.

Chapter 16
Believer's Oppression

My church has started to take every person we water baptize to the chapel immediately after. There, a team of ministers will prophesy over, deliver, heal, and baptize in the Spirit, each new believer. One time, we only had one woman to pray for. There were three ministers, including myself, and as I began to pray for the convert, she fell to the ground and began to breathe heavily. A demon manifested itself, and it looked like she was hyperventilating. We told the demon to leave the woman as usual, but it wasn't budging. The manifestations intensified, so I took a risk and spoke directly to the demon. "What is your name?" I asked. The demon spoke out of the woman between labored breathing, "Trauma!"

"Trauma, do you have a right to be in this woman?" I followed up.

"Yes!" it responded.

"What is your right?"

"She wants me!" it yelled out in a deep voice.

I thought about it for a moment and decided the devil was lying. "She doesn't want you; she just got water baptized and has made Christ her Lord. You have no right to be in her; now, in the name of Jesus, get out!" I commanded. After more coaxing, the demon finally left, and the three of us saw gold dust settle on this woman from head to toe. That was the first experience those fellow ministers had dealing with a demon speaking out of someone.

If you've experienced something similar, then you know that Christians can be demonically oppressed. This was a woman who had made Jesus her Lord, been water baptized, and then delivered of at least one demon. Trust me when I tell you, I've seen hundreds, if not thousands, of demons leave Christian believers of every stripe.

A doctrine snuck into the Church that stated Christians could not be demonically oppressed. I don't know when it came in, and I don't know if any denomination has formalized it, but I do know two things. One, it is a doctrine of demons (1 Timothy 4). What better way for Satan to gain access to our lives than to make us believe it is an impossibility? And, two, it is not derived from scripture.

When challenged, most people who believe this doctrine cannot tell you where they read about it in scripture. Some will bring up a single verse—"In Him you also, when you heard the word of truth, the gospel of your salvation, and believed in Him, were sealed with the promised Holy Spirit...(Ephesians 1:13)."

They will argue that the word "sealed" in this passage refers to a closing up. It is actually referring to a signet or a seal of authentication and ownership. It isn't saying we are sealed like a Ziplock bag, but rather that God has placed His mark of ownership on us by His Spirit as a king would place a signet in lieu of signing his name.

Notice this verse says nothing about demons, nor does it say a Christian can not be demonically oppressed. Nowhere in the bible will you find such a statement being made. In general, I find that people are simply uncomfortable with the notion Satan can oppress a Christian; thus, they cling to this doctrine because it makes them feel safer—rather than having a rigorous scriptural basis for their belief.

In contrast, I can give you four biblical examples of believers being oppressed by Satan. I'll start with the most convincing example. In 2 Corinthians 12, Paul wrote, "...a thorn was given me in the flesh, a messenger of Satan to harass me, to keep me from becoming conceited."

Paul was a mighty man of God. If anyone could be declared a Christian, it would be the man who was among the first to be called one (Acts 11:26). The word "messenger" in the original Greek is "angelos," which is typically translated into "angel" throughout the majority of the New Testament. Since Satan is sending this angel, though, we recognize it is actually a demon.

In Matthew 25:41, Jesus proclaims those judged for damnation will be told, "Depart from me, you cursed, into the eternal fire prepared for the devil and his angels." The word "angel" in this passage is simply the *plural* form of angelos. In both cases, scripture shows Satan has authority over these beings, and traditionally, we interpret them to be demons (or fallen angels).

Some scholars interpret this passage as a demon assigned to make his ministry difficult. Others interpret it as a physical ailment because it is described as being in his flesh. Either way, this Christian is clearly being oppressed by a demon in some fashion.

The second example is Judas. Judas was one of Jesus' twelve apostles. Not only was he a follower of Christ, but he drove out demons and healed the sick (Matthew 10:8). Jesus likewise stated in Matthew 19:28-30 that Judas would sit on a throne to judge the twelve tribes of Israel when Christ returned. Despite his nearness to Jesus, the call on his life, and the power God gave him, Judas ended up betraying his Master.

Why? If you carefully read the gospels, you'll find iniquity was the gateway Satan used to enter him. In John 12:6, the author explains why Judas was upset that a year's worth of wages was spent on washing and anointing Jesus' feet. Judas claimed it was because he cared about the poor, but in actuality, "he said this, not because he cared about the poor, but because he was a thief, and having charge of the moneybag he used to help himself to what was put into it."

Judas' greed created a foothold for Satan to climb deeper into his heart, and we're explicitly told in Luke 22:3 that Satan entered Judas. Immediately, Judas struck a deal with religious leaders. He would betray Jesus but wanted money in return. Thirty silver pieces was the price, and Judas fulfilled his obligation for it (Matthew 26:15-16). Many Christians become oppressed by Satan in similar fashion.

One of the reasons God desires His children to live holy lives is to keep us from the bondage of sin. I have ministered to dozens of Christian pornography addicts who are demonized because of their lust. It is through their habitual sin that Satan gained a foothold in their lives, and suddenly, they were enslaved.

"Do not let the sun go down while you are still angry, and do not give the devil a foothold. Anyone who has been stealing must steal no longer, but must work, doing something useful with their own

hands, that they may have something to share with those in need."
- **Ephesians 4:27-28**

Paul constantly calls Christians to forsake their sin. It is through one's unrighteous anger that Satan gains power in our lives. It is through our stealing, slander, gossip, idolatry, you name it! Sin is an open door whether you are a Christian or not. If one drinks too much alcohol, they will get drunk even if they believe in Jesus. In the same way Christians can still get drunk and sick; we can still be demonically oppressed. Remember, when Peter wrote, "Be sober-minded; be watchful. Your adversary, the devil prowls around like a roaring lion, seeking someone to devour," he was writing to the Church—not unbelievers (1 Peter 5:8). The onus is on us to keep guard over our hearts lest the devil try to steal them.

Again, Paul wrote in 2 Corinthians 2:9-11, "Anyone whom you forgive, I also forgive. Indeed, what I have forgiven, if I have forgiven anything, has been for your sake in the presence of Christ, so that we would not be outwitted by Satan, for we are not ignorant of his designs." I will go into unforgiveness in a future chapter, but presently, I want to highlight how Paul is warning Christians that Satan is scheming for them—and through sin, it is insinuated he might have them.

The third example from scripture is Peter. This one is not as solid as the other two, but the anecdote is challenging to understand outside of the framework of demonic oppression in some form. In Matthew 16, Jesus tells the disciples that He must be murdered, and Peter rebukes his Master for saying such a thing. Jesus' response sounds harsh, "But he turned and said to Peter, 'Get behind me, Satan! You are a hindrance to me. For you are not setting your mind on the things of God, but on the things of man.'"

The most extreme interpretation of this passage would be Satan had entered Peter and was trying to persuade Jesus not to go to the cross. The lightest rendering of the text would state Peter's mindset was aligned with Satan's and not God's. So, at the very least, this is proof-text that Satan can influence a believer's mind.

The fourth example is Job in the Old Testament. Although not a Christian, I would argue that had Jesus lived during his time, Job would have believed. Job is described as a righteous and very blessed man. Satan claims the only reason Job loves God is because God protects him, so the Lord removes that protection little by little (Job 1:10-11). Throughout the story, Satan manages to cause a storm that kills Job's children, he causes Job's livestock to be stolen, and even causes sickness to afflict Job's body. What this story reveals is that Satan truly does steal, kill, and destroy—and that he can afflict a righteous man in many ways.

Aside from there being no biblical passage stating believers can't be demonically afflicted, and at least a few passages that show examples to the contrary—the doctrine itself has horrendous practical implications. Many believers *know* they are demonized. Perhaps they suffer from sleep paralysis and see a "dark figure" in their room at night. Maybe they hear blasphemous thoughts in their head whenever the topic of God comes up. Or perhaps they suffer from bursts of anger that they know are irrational but can't control.

Whatever the affliction, I meet many Christians who are positive they need Jesus to deliver them. If we apply the doctrine that such people can't be demonized because they are believers, we end up with one of two dystopian outcomes. On the one hand, the person may come to believe they are not actually saved because, again, they know they are demonized. On the other hand, the person may never get free from demonic oppression because the Church claims they can't be demonized. One hand offers insecurity; the other leaves them in torment.

You may protest, "But James, how is it theologically possible for demons to be in the same vessel as the Holy Spirit? Scripture asks, 'What fellowship does darkness have with light (2 Corinthians 6:14)?'"

You are not alone in asking this question as many traditional believers wrestle with the same perplexation.

To help, let me give you an analogy from the Old Testament. Many authors, such as Alexander Pagani, have better presented this theory, but I'll do my best to summarize it. The Tabernacle Moses built was comprised of three main sections. The outside was called the Outer Court, where any ceremonially clean Israelite may enter to bring their sacrifices to the Lord. Inside the tent was the Holy Place, where only the priests may enter. Further inside was the Holy of

Holies, where the manifest presence of God was, and only the high priest could enter this room once a year to offer atonement for the unknown sins of the people.

It is traditionally held the high priest would have a rope tied around his ankle, so if he died in the presence of God, the other priests could drag his body out. Being in the presence of the Lord was a dangerous business due to His holiness. It was in the Holy of Holies where the Ark of the Covenant (an ornate box) was housed. Many stories in the Old Testament exist about the Ark's effect on war and provision when others are in its presence. One such story is when the Philistines captured the Ark and decided to take it to the temple of their demon-god Dagon.

The following day, the Philistines found the statue of Dagon had fallen before the Ark. They set it back up, but the next morning after that, it fell again and shattered into many pieces (1 Samuel 5). The message was clear—demons submit to the presence of God.

We know God is Triune—God the Father, God the Son, and God the Spirit. Humans seem to be made up of three similar parts. We have our soul, including our will, emotions, and mind. Then there is our body. Finally, we have a spirit. Jesus said when we put our faith in Him that the Father and He would make their home inside of us (John 14:23). Further, Paul wrote in 1 Corinthians 6:19-20, "Do you not know that your body is a temple of the Holy Spirit within you, whom you have from God? You are not your own, for you were bought with a price. So glorify God in your body."

It is clear that whereas the Lord manifested His presence in the Holy of Holies in the Old Testament, He now does so in Christian believers. We are the new Tabernacle in a sense.

In 1 Corinthians 6:17, Paul wrote, "But he who is joined to the Lord becomes one spirit with him." And again, in Hebrews 10:14, we read, "For by one sacrifice he has made perfect forever those who are being made holy." Finally, in 1 Corinthians 15:42-44, Paul argued, "So will it be with the resurrection of the dead. The body that is sown is perishable, it is raised imperishable; it is sown in dishonor, it is raised in glory; it is sown in weakness, it is raised in power; it is sown a natural body, it is raised a spiritual body."

When we combine these biblical truths, we come to understand a mystery. How is it that we may be *perfected* by Jesus' sacrifice but still need to be made *holy*? Why are our spirits joined with God, but our bodies are perishable and sown in dishonor? We seem to be awaiting a day of transformation when our Earthly body will be put off, and we will be given a glorified one in its stead.

"But our citizenship is in heaven. And we eagerly await a Savior from there, the Lord Jesus Christ, who, by the power that enables him to bring everything under his control, will transform our lowly bodies so that they will be like his glorious body."
-   Philippians 3:20-21

This day will come when Jesus returns, but until then, we seem to possess corruptibility in at least two areas of our life. The first is most apparent—our bodies are decaying and susceptible to sickness. The second is less obvious because fewer people can readily see it— but our souls seem corruptible, too. Christians still struggle with anger issues, depression, fear, laziness, and all the other afflictions nonbelievers go through. Where we digress seems to mostly be in our spirits—

something promised to be preserved even through death. I believe it is our spirits that are perfected, and it is our souls that are being made holy, as referenced in Hebrews 10.

If we are new tabernacles of God, perhaps the old one reflects us somehow. If that were the case, then surely the Outer Court would be our bodies—the thing that touches the world most. The Holy Place would be our soul—a more private space that mostly we and God seem to be privy to unless we allow the outside world to affect it through trauma or sin. Finally, the Holy of Holies would be our spirits—an area of our being made perfect by Christ, joined seamlessly with the Father, and a space that even we have difficulty measuring, understanding, leveraging, or entering.

Just like Dagon, I believe demons can't coexist with the Holy Spirit, and that is why our spirit—which is joined with the Spirit of God—is completely preserved by Christ. Yet, as we've discussed, humans possess souls and bodies. These are the areas of possible demonic influence in the believer's life. It is why Paul could write, "Be angry, and do not sin (Ephesians 4:26)." Anger is an emotion, making it part of the soul, but it can be corrupted to the point of sin. I have seen many people, including Christians, delivered of an evil spirit that caused irrational anger. Similarly, I have witnessed many Christians freed from spirits of sickness (infirmity) in their bodies—these range from auto-immune disorders to arthritis to cancer.

The notion that a believer can be demonized is only a hard pill to swallow until you see someone you know without a shadow of a doubt is saved, freed. Then, see about a hundred more cases, and you'll turn your back on that doctrine forever. It doesn't seem to reflect scripture, and it certainly doesn't reflect reality.

Chapter 17
Drive Them Out

Being an evangelist is not for the squeamish. I have heard just about everything when it comes to people's interactions with trauma and the demonic. I've ministered to men and women who were repeatedly raped (even as children). I've ministered to an ex-gang member who saw and participated in brutal and heinous crimes. I once did deliverance on a young man who was kidnapped by a cult as a child, where he endured Satanic ritual abuse. I've had women tell me they've had sex with demons, and one told me she made a deal with Satan to serve him in exchange for being able to orgasm (this woman came to three Freedom Nights in a row and was finally delivered at the end of the last one). I've ministered to a suburban young mom struggling with homicidal ideation, and during her deliverance, a demon screamed out of her that its name was "murder."

Men have told me about the highly perverted types of pornography they were addicted to and the demonic reasons behind such deviance from normal sexual function. During one deliverance session, I saw a young woman's face supernaturally turn into an old woman's—wrinkled and angry. Demons have yelled at me, cursed at me, spoken in demonic tongues, mocked heavenly tongues, laughed at me, growled, and even hit me during deliverance sessions. Although I avoid them, I have had several conversations with demons through those they possessed in order to discern their assignments, entry paths, and ways to drive them out. From what I'm told about parts of the world where paganism and witchcraft are more prevalent—I haven't seen anything yet. Still, I believe I have enough experience in deliverance ministry to teach about it, so I will.

If we want to believe the mythos surrounding Satan (which I do), then we know he was once a great angel in heaven serving the Lord. He was, perhaps, the mightiest angel created because even Michael, the archangel in Jude 1:9, refused to slander him personally. Desiring to be God, Satan led a rebellion with a third of the angels. The Lord told His loyal angels to wage war. So heaven overcame the devil who was flung to the Earth like lightning (Luke 10:18). Still desiring to rule and jealous of the domain of Adam, Satan deceived the first king and queen of humanity, and the world was plunged into darkness.

"What pagans sacrifice they offer to demons and not to God. I do not want you to be participants with demons. You cannot drink the cup of the Lord and the cup of demons. You cannot partake of the table of the Lord and the table of demons."
- **1 Corinthians 10:20-21**

One must understand the reason God wanted the Israelites to be separated from pagan peoples was because they were in partnership with Satan. The worshippers of Molech sacrificed their babies to him (Leviticus 18:21), and the worshippers of Baal did the same (Jeremiah 19:5). Those who worshipped Asherah committed unspeakable ritualistic sex acts with cult prostitutes (Hosea 4:13-14). False gods like Chemosh, Dagon, and Bel were invoked using divination, a practice explicitly condemned by God (Deuteronomy 18:10-15). The number of pagan deities in the world is estimated to be tens of thousands on the low end and millions on the higher end when Hinduism is considered.

"They sacrificed to demons that were no gods, to gods they had never known, to new gods that had come recently, whom your fathers had never dreaded."
- **Deuteronomy 32:17**

Most of the Western Church seems to have ignored that these are real entities we read about in the Bible. They are not "false gods" because they don't exist. Rather, they are supernatural beings who have illegally set themselves up for worship. If we recall the first commandment, "You shall have no other gods before me," within it lies a truth—that other gods (lowercase "g") exist. To be sure, this biblical truth is different from polytheism.

There is not a pantheon of gods equal to the one true God. Rather, these false deities are powerful but created. Now, some Christians believe demons are separate from fallen angels. They come to this conclusion from the book of Enoch, which portrays demons as the spirits of the Nephilim, now chained to the Earth (1 Enoch 15:8-12). The book of Enoch is not biblical canon nor considered sacred by Jews. God only knows what the demonic hierarchy truly looks like—what the principalities, powers, rulers of the darkness of this world, and spiritual wickedness in high places genuinely look like. As believers, we just know our job is to oppose them (Ephesians 6:12).

The physical realm is now dominated by a dark kingdom—one which the Israelites found difficult to continually oppose due to their heart's fickle loyalty to God. However, Jesus came into the world, and the darkness could not overcome Him (John 1). The Kingdom of God hatched a plan to remove Satan from the Earth while saving as many of God's image bearers as possible. Jesus was the perfect solution because He came to deal with sin itself—sanctifying people and divorcing them from demon gods by writing His laws upon their hearts (Hebrews 8:10). Even still, all of humanity wrestles with the demonic and needs the active work of the Spirit to deliver them.

The only example of deliverance we have in the Old Testament is found in the book of Samuel:

"And whenever the harmful spirit from God was upon Saul, David took the lyre and played it with

his hand. So Saul was refreshed and was well, and the harmful spirit departed from him."
- 1 Samuel 16:23

Saul was the first king of Israel, but due to his disobedience, he became demonically oppressed. The spirit would torment Saul, and he only found relief when David played the lyre for him. This scripture states that the harmful spirit departed from Saul, but many argue that the manifestations or torment simply stopped for a time, and Saul remained oppressed. Either way, it is an interesting anecdote of man trying to deal with the demonic in the Old Testament.

The New Testament is an entirely different story. Jesus routinely drove demons out of people (a third of the miracles He performed). As I mentioned earlier, in Matthew 12:28, Jesus said, "But if it is by the Spirit of God that I cast out demons, then the kingdom of God has come upon you." This is a significant statement because it indicates deliverance is proof of God's kingdom in the Earth; one kingdom is now displacing another. Satan was beaten in heaven, and He is now being beaten in the physical realm.

Jesus gave the power to drive demons out to His followers. In Luke, chapter 10, we find seventy-two disciples returned to Jesus, proclaiming that even the demons submitted to them in His name. Jesus responded, "Behold, I have given you authority to tread on serpents and scorpions, and over all the power of the enemy, and nothing shall hurt you."

Again, in the book of Mark, chapter 16, Jesus states, "And these signs will accompany those who believe: in my name they will cast out demons."

It is plain to see the Lord has not only given authority over demons to Christians, but He expects His followers to be doing the work of deliverance actively. Jesus said the gates of hell would not prevail against His Church (Matthew 16:18). In other words, we're on the *offense*, assaying hell to save souls from it.

Something Dutch Sheets once wrote (I'll summarize) is the Church has two options. Option one is to do the work of Jesus in the Earth. Option two is to waste the cross. Let's not waste the cross. Jesus is worthy to receive the treasure He paid dearly for—and His Church practicing deliverance is a way to get Him that treasure.

In Matthew 15, Jesus referred to deliverance as the "children's bread." He is making an obvious metaphor, but it is interesting He would use something as important as daily food for kids to symbolize freedom from demonic oppression. If you've been delivered yourself or have done several deliverances with desperate people, you'll know the feeling of freedom. People's eyes grow brighter, their soul feels lighter, their breathing becomes easier, and their sleep deeper. There's a sweetness to the Holy Spirit removing oppression—no matter how grizzly the reality may look on the outside.

The first thing you should know about deliverance is how key *consecration* can be. In the Bible, we only have two examples of failed deliverances. In one case, Jesus clearly states the issue was with the ministers' lack of faith—and that the specific type of demon they were dealing with would only come out through prayer and fasting (Matthew 17:21). Faith comes by hearing the word (rhema) of the Lord (Romans 10:17). One hears the word of the Lord through prayer and fasting. It is in the secret place that our faith grows, and the Lord consecrates us. We become tools set aside to be used by the Lord to bring Him glory. Developing consistency and patterns is crucial. Just as a sinner develops consistency in his/her sin, a believer must do the same in righteousness. When Jesus told the demon to leave that His disciples couldn't drive out, it went. Jesus didn't take a break to pray and fast before doing that because He lived a *consistent* life of prayer and fasting. As deliverance ministers, we must also live the life of Christ.

When demons start talking out of a person, you will want to know who you are in Jesus. They will often try to undermine your credibility or identity. If you live a life of connectedness with the Lord, the evil spirit will fail in trying to compromise your confidence.

The second failed deliverance found in the Bible is the story of the seven sons of Sceva.

"And God was doing extraordinary miracles by the hands of Paul, so that even handkerchiefs or aprons that had touched his skin were carried away to the sick, and their diseases left them and the evil spirits

came out of them. Then some of the itinerant Jewish exorcists undertook to invoke the name of the Lord Jesus over those who had evil spirits, saying, 'I adjure you by the Jesus whom Paul proclaims.' Seven sons of a Jewish high priest named Sceva were doing this. But the evil spirit answered them, "Jesus I know, and Paul I recognize, but who are you?" And the man in whom was the evil spirit leaped on them, mastered all of them and overpowered them, so that they fled out of that house naked and wounded. And this became known to all the residents of Ephesus, both Jews and Greeks. And fear fell upon them all, and the name of the Lord Jesus was extolled."

- Acts 19:11-17

Something the revivalist Leonard Ravenhill loved about this passage was the fact this demon knew of Paul; his reputation had made it to the demonic realm. Ravenhill thought it a great honor! The part of this passage that stands out to me is the question the demon asks, "...but who are *you*?" It is a question we should ask ourselves before we let a demon present it.

Do you know who you are in Jesus? Is Jesus your Lord, or just your Savior? I do not suggest attempting deliverance ministry if you have not submitted your life to Christ. If you do not regularly sit with Jesus to firmly understand your identity in Him, create that habit first. When a demon challenges, "Who are you?" you'll want to be able to confidently retort, "I am a son/daughter of God." The vast majority of bluffs demons make are quickly rebuked by the son or daughter of God who, just hours before, was sitting in His presence having a conversation with Him.

Never have I encountered more verbose demons than the ones my team and I drove out of an older woman I'll call Cynthia. Cynthia came to us with physical pain, and she wanted healed. What we thought would be a simple prayer turned out to be thirteen hours worth of deliverance over the course of three sessions, where we drove out at least 130 demons.

Cynthia was dedicated to Satan as a baby by her mother, who was a witch. Throughout her young adult life, she practiced idolatry and New Age ignorantly. She participated in tarot card readings, visited psychics, had reiki healing sessions, opened chakras, practiced yoga, and more. To make matters worse, when she finally gave her life to Jesus in her later years, she unknowingly befriended a Satanist in her Catholic church. This witch was posing as a Christian believer, and through their "friendship," she cursed Cynthia. For the purpose of this book, I'll call the Satanist Laura.

As our team prayed for Cynthia, the presence of the Holy Spirit would come upon her strong, making her demons manifest heavily. Some would easily be driven out, but others would come to the surface and stick. Our conversations with these demons were wild (many I have recorded on video). One particularly stubborn demon told me it would be destroyed if it left her. It admitted failure in the kingdom of Satan would subject it to Satan's discipline. I told it to face the consequences of its failure, and we eventually drove it out of Cynthia. Another demon called itself Shiva and plainly stated it had entered when Cynthia opened a chakra near her midsection.

Not so coincidentally, this area of her body was subject to shifting pain that banded around her. Once Shiva had left, the pain also left. In the middle of our first session with Cynthia, my friend Ethan had to leave. He later texted me he heard the Lord say, "Rebuke Shakti." Neither of us had heard that name before, but in obedience, I called Shakti out of the woman. Sure enough, a demon by that name manifested and told me it entered her when a yoga master had laid hands on her. I later looked this demon up and found a local yoga studio actually named after it.

Many of these spirits would manifest and accuse Cynthia. For example, one yelled out to me, "She has a gay son! She has a gay son!" Another screamed, "She hasn't forgiven her mom!" Indeed, Satan has earned the name "accuser of the brethren (Revelation 12:10)." I led Cynthia through a great deal of inner healing and forgiveness over the 13 hours. When it came to the accusation about her son, I explained to her (and the demon) that such an accusation had no bearing on Cynthia's soul. She believed her son's choices were her fault and had to forgive herself.

Deliverance is not so much about driving darkness out as it is about pouring light in. The best way to get demons to manifest in a person is to love them and speak life into their souls. I've been in rooms where all

I'll do is explain the gospel, and suddenly, a person will become nervous, hot, and eager to leave because a demon is manifesting inside of them. That's the power of the word of God.

A woman once came to my house to be healed of cancer. Now, if you read my previous book, then you know I believe cancer is usually an evil spirit. I sat on my closet floor about 15 minutes before the woman arrived and asked the Lord if He had a word for her. "Dig up a root of bitterness," He commanded me. At this time in my life, I questioned whether or not a person would need to forgive to be healed in some instances. This was the first time I saw that for delivering believers, specifically, it can be the case.

The woman came with her family, and we all sat on my couch. After small talk, I told her pointedly, "The Lord told me to dig up a root of bitterness, so I have to ask, are you bitter?" She stared at me momentarily and then candidly admitted, "I am bitter. I am bitter." Jesus then told me about how she had felt rejected her entire life, and we worked through the Spirit to heal those wounds. Finally, I pulled out my Bible and read scripture to her concerning forgiveness. I didn't even get to finish the passage when she screamed from across the room, "What did you just do!" She had felt a wind blow through her soul and began to weep. The conviction of the Lord fell upon her; she repented and was delivered. Again, the light of God was enough to displace demonic darkness.

I remember a breakthrough moment for Cynthia when the Lord told me she doubted her salvation. I brought this up with her, and she confirmed it. The way I dismantled that lie was by quoting scripture. Demons had been telling her that, given her condition, she was not saved. God's promise about the free gift of salvation spoke a better word. She later told me she received major breakthrough the moment she believed in the assuredness of her salvation. Satan is called the father of lies, and many oppressed people are that way because they've believed him (John 8:44). I've seen people free from both oppression and sickness the moment they changed their mind (repented) on a lie they were holding onto.

On our second deliverance session with Cynthia, a demon manifested that would not leave. Eventually, it just stared darkly at us. "Cynthia, come back," I beckoned. Now, in my experience, when I want to end a deliverance, I can call the person back by name, and the demonic manifestations will always stop. Remember this because it can be key to safely preserve a person, and it is also helpful to be able to speak to the person in order to minister more before continuing the deliverance. Oddly, in this one instance, Cynthia did not come back. The demon stared at me and finally piped up, "I'm not a demon; I am Laura!"

A couple of months before this deliverance, a prophetic man messaged me online to tell me I needed to read a book, I have mentioned previously, titled *He Came to Set the Captives Free* by Rebecca Brown. After it arrived in the mail, I sat it before me along with another book I wanted to read, and I consulted the Holy Spirit, "Which one should I read?" He highlighted *He Came to Set the Captives Free*, so I read it.

There are things in that book I wish I had never read, but only because they were hard pills to swallow. The work is actually co-written by an ex-Satanist turned Christian who was a bride of Satan operating in a powerful cult. Her insights into the dark realm of Satan worship were rough on the heart but important for the mind. I recommend that mature believers read this book to grow their understanding of spiritual warfare.

The moment the Satanist Laura revealed herself, the Holy Spirit reminded me of a passage I read in *He Came to Set the Captives Free*. The author recalled a time of intense spiritual warfare when witches astral projected into her home, causing mayhem. She wrote a passage about dealing with this phenomenon and ominously stated that witches have been known to astral project into *people* to make them do or say certain things.

"I'm not a demon; I am Laura!" the witch growled through Cynthia.

Immediately, the two ministers with me were taken back, but I tried not to miss a beat since the Spirit had prepared me.

"Oh, I know what's going on. Laura, you have no right to this woman. Get out of her now," I demanded.

"I have a piece of Cynthia's hair on my altar." She responded.

"Laura, you should give up serving Satan. Jesus loves you. Repent and put your faith in Him."

"Satan gives me power. I can levitate!" she snarled.

I proceeded to share the gospel with her, as the author of *He Came to Set the Captives Free* suggested. Laura continued to assert Satan was worthy to be served because of what he afforded her. She bragged about the ways she had cursed Cynthia through gifts.

Eventually, I realized no one ever taught me how to get rid of a witch astral projecting into someone I was doing deliverance on. Turning from Laura to the Lord, I prayed, "Father, I ask that you break whatever magic this is." Cynthia came to the forefront briefly, then Laura took over again and spoke a few words. Finally, Cynthia was back for good. She was unnerved by the ordeal, asking, "How can she do that?" The truth is that the witch *cursed* Cynthia in several ways over a long period.

One night, Ethan and I were ministering in Centennial Park (Nashville) when a woman came up to be baptized in the Spirit. Ethan got a word of knowledge for her and briefly discussed it. I stared off past the woman, fixated on what the Spirit was telling me. Ethan finished, and turning to me, he asked, "Do you have anything else, James?"

"Yeah," I said, as one waking from a daydream. Turning to the woman, I stated plainly, "I see a curse on your family." The moment the words left my mouth, the woman stumbled backward onto the lawn, manifesting several demons. We walked through inner healing with her, and she renounced the witchcraft her ancestors had participated in.

It is negligent to discuss deliverance ministry without mentioning curses. Curses in the Old Testament are connected to sin.

"However, if you do not obey the Lord your God and do not carefully follow all his commands and decrees I am giving you today, all these curses will come on you and overtake you: You will be cursed in the city and cursed in the country. Your basket and your kneading trough will be cursed.

The fruit of your womb will be cursed, and the crops of your land, and the calves of your herds and the lambs of your flocks.

You will be cursed when you come in and cursed when you go out.

The Lord will send on you curses, confusion and rebuke in everything you put your hand to, until you are destroyed and come to sudden ruin because of the evil you have done in forsaking him."
- Deuteronomy 28:15-20

"The Levites shall recite to all the people of Israel in a loud voice:

"Cursed is anyone who makes an idol—a thing detestable to the Lord, the work of skilled hands—and sets it up in secret."

Then all the people shall say, "Amen!"
"Cursed is anyone who dishonors their father or mother."

Then all the people shall say, "Amen!"

"Cursed is anyone who moves their neighbor's boundary stone."

Then all the people shall say, "Amen!"

"Cursed is anyone who leads the blind astray on the road."

Then all the people shall say, "Amen!"

"Cursed is anyone who withholds justice from the foreigner, the fatherless or the widow."

Then all the people shall say, 'Amen!'"
- Deuteronomy 27:14-19

I've never heard a pastor give a sermon on verses like these. Very few preachers want to talk about the consequences of our sin concerning the spirit-realm. They may preach that if we sin, we won't prosper in life, but they rarely talk about curses as obligatory spiritual realities with supernatural enforcement. A curse is like a warrant, open contract, or mark put on someone, which allows the demonic realm to enforce punishment or afflict them.

In Revelation, some people take on the "mark of the beast," pledging their allegiance to Satan's camp. In the world, believers who refuse to take this mark are heavily persecuted. But in the spirit-realm, those who do take this mark are tormented:

"So the first angel went and poured out his bowl on the earth, and harmful and painful sores came upon the people who bore the mark of the beast and worshiped its image."
- **Revelation 16:2**

"And another angel, a third, followed them, saying with a loud voice, 'If anyone worships the beast and its image and receives a mark on his forehead or on his hand, he also will drink the wine of God's wrath, poured full strength into the cup of his anger, and he will be tormented with fire and sulfur in the presence of the holy angels and in the presence of the Lamb."
- **Revelation 14:9-10**

There are cursed people walking this Earth who do not even know it. I once ministered to a cancer patient whose entire family of females (mom, sisters, aunts) had all passed away from the same awful disease. This is an example of a generational curse passed down through the bloodline. Unfortunately, many of our ancestors worshipped demons and made oaths with them. Like Cynthia, whose mom dedicated her to Satan as a child, some of these oaths were to have their descendants likewise belong to demons.

Ethan and I once ministered to a teenage girl who was struggling with depression. As we rebuked that spirit, a demon manifested in her—stretching and heaving as we commanded it to leave. She got free from some things, but one nasty spirit bent her over and would not leave her. I stopped the deliverance and asked her, "Are there people in your family who have done witchcraft?" It turned out she was from Nigeria, and her close relative was some sort of priest to a demon god there. In fact, her last name was the name of that demon. She later told me her plan to change her name to rewrite her family legacy.

We can't see curses in the physical realm, but demons can undoubtedly see such marks in the spirit-realm. They take these as signs of agreement and legal right to afflict torment. There is good news, though. First, the Bible declares, "Like a sparrow in its flitting, like a swallow in its flying, a curse that is causeless does not alight (Proverbs 26:2)."

Most curses come upon people because of their sin or agreements with Satan. If those aren't in place (the cause), a curse won't land. Second, the Bible also declares, "Christ redeemed us from the curse of the law by becoming a curse for us—for it is written, 'Cursed is everyone who is hanged on a tree (Galatians 3:13).'"

Jesus is the curse breaker. He took care of them on the cross by nullifying sin and fulfilling the law. Many Christians are walking around under curses they don't need to carry because of the freedom Jesus procured through the atonement.

Likewise, believers are born of the Spirit and not of the will of man. They are made new in Christ and not subject to their lineage (John 1:13).

This leads to an intriguing observation in deliverance ministry: many demons remain in people illegally simply because no one has taken the initiative to cast them out. I have ministered to countless individuals who recently surrendered their lives to Jesus. However, the ministers who led them in prayer or baptized them neglected to expel the demons, still oppressing them. Part of the cross's redemptive work is wasted without someone applying God's power for deliverance. Early Christian leaders recognized this and made exorcism integral to the baptismal process.

For instance, around 200 AD, Tertullian—a prolific writer and priest—documented in his work *De Baptismo*: *"When we are going to enter the water, but a little before, in the church and under the hand of the presiding minister, we solemnly profess that we renounce the devil, his pomp, and his angels."*

This renunciation would have been accompanied by trained ministers offering prayers of exorcism for the individual about to be baptized.

Hippolytus, one of the most significant theologians of the 3rd century, described in *The Apostolic Tradition* the practice surrounding baptism: *"A deacon shall hold the Oil of Exorcism and stand on the left. Another deacon shall hold the Oil of Thanksgiving and stand on the right. When the elder takes hold of each of them who are to receive baptism, he shall tell each of them to renounce, saying, 'I renounce you Satan, all your services, and all your works.' After he has said this, he shall anoint each with the Oil of Exorcism, saying, 'Let every evil spirit depart from you.'"*

In the mid-to-late 4th century, Saint Cyril of Jerusalem wrote in his *Catechetical Lectures*: *"You were anointed with the oil of exorcism, which you received from the top of your head to your feet, to be delivered from every power of the enemy. Every evil spirit fled from you, unable to endure the virtue of that anointing. It was not by a mere application of oil, but by the name of God and by the presence of the Holy Spirit that the whole power of the adversary was consumed."*

This "oil of exorcism" was applied before water baptism.

In the 7th-8th century, one of the earliest Western liturgical texts, the *Gelasian Sacramentary*, included specific prayers for exorcism within the baptismal rite. One such prayer read: *"I adjure you, unclean spirit, in the name of the Father, and of the Son, and of the Holy Spirit, that you depart and leave this servant of God, whom our Lord has deigned to call to His holy grace and to the font of baptism. May you never dare, accursed one, to violate this sign of the holy cross, which we now place upon their forehead; through the same Christ our Lord, who shall come to judge the living and the dead, and the world by fire."*

It is evident that deliverance ministry was central to Jesus' mission and remained a key practice among Christians for centuries. Unfortunately, in some high-church traditions today, deliverance ministry has been restricted to specially trained priests. This approach replaces Jesus' promise that *mere believers* would drive out demons, with a hierarchy of specialists. While specific individuals may be exceptionally gifted for deliverance due to the Spirit's anointing, scripture affirms that all believers are called to this ministry (Mark 16:17).

Other denominations fail to practice deliverance at all—even among the pastoral staff. Such groups typically profess Satan is still working in the Earth, but they fail to do much about it when it comes to delivering people of demonic oppression. I argue both sects of Christianity require reformation in the modern era as the West is returning to pre-Christian practices. Churches that do not utilize deliverance will find it increasingly difficult to feed the sheep of Christ in the coming decades as pagan worship, witchcraft, and oppressive spirits in the form of suicidality and anxiety are on the rise.

Having cast out thousands of demons, I've developed some practical methods for deliverance. That said, methods are only effective up to a point—they must ultimately yield to the specific guidance of the Holy Spirit. Deliverance, much like healing, cannot be reduced to a formula. Use these practical steps as a foundational guide, but always obey the Spirit's direction.

The first step to deliverance—apart from recognizing the authority one has in Christ and consecrating oneself—is to partner with the Holy Spirit in discernment. You need to know if you're actually dealing with a demon or not. Some common demonic symptoms I have seen include panic attacks, chronic nightmares, sleep paralysis, unabating depression, suicidality, irrational anger, unabating anxiety, addictions of all kinds, self-harm, intrusive thoughts (lustful, critical, blasphemous, paranoid, self-loathing, etc.), sexual deviancy/perversion, insomnia, and a hatred of scripture, church, worship music, or other things of God.

I once had a man tell me that the moment he saw me preaching in the park, he felt great anger toward me and didn't understand why. He said that clued him into the fact he needed to talk to me (this man was later delivered of a multitude of demons).

A symptom that tends to indicate severe oppression or even possession is when an otherwise healthy person experiences memory loss. They may do things or say things and then immediately forget what they did and said; the events will often occur at night. Anytime it seems like a person's consciousness, will, or personality has been co-opted, they are most likely demonically possessed. A good indicator of oppression would be if, while reading this chapter, you've become anxious or angry; you might feel the same way when the Spirit is moving heavily in a church service.

When it comes to sickness, many of the demonic symptoms I have seen include pain that moves in the body, autoimmune disorders, cancer, undiagnosable illnesses, incurable diseases, symptoms that change over the years, most forms of arthritis, and some forms of blindness. Even if the pain was caused in the natural (such as from a sports injury), I have seen people need deliverance from a spirit keeping that wound from healing. It is usually something related to despondency ("I'll never be healed") or religion ("God doesn't heal anymore"). I believe all sickness is demonic at its root, but not all sickness is caused by a demonic spirit inhabiting someone's body that needs to be driven out.

If words of knowledge don't come easily to you, I recommend diagnosing demonic oppression by asking simple questions: "What are you dealing with? Do you have panic attacks? Do you deal with chronic nightmares? Did you ever think you would not be healed?" Some people wonder why I ask them so many questions, and my simple answer is that a medical doctor does the same thing. We are in the business of getting to the root cause of affliction. Biblically speaking, though, Jesus also asked questions.

"So they brought [the demonized boy]. When the spirit saw Jesus, it immediately threw the boy into a

convulsion. He fell to the ground and rolled around, foaming at the mouth. Jesus asked the boy's father, 'How long has he been like this?' 'From childhood,' he answered. 'It has often thrown him into fire or water to kill him. But if you can do anything, take pity on us and help us.'"

- Mark 9:20-22

Notice this intriguing question Jesus asked: "How long has he been like this?" This is the question I ask more than any other in deliverance ministry. Typically, I phrase it as, "When did the symptoms start?" The follow-up question is usually, "Did anything traumatic happen around that time in your life, such as the loss of a loved one, a prolonged period of depression, or another significant hardship?"

I ask these questions to identify the entry point the demon may have used. More often than not, the person will respond with something like: "I went through a divorce," "My mother died," "We adopted our son," "I almost died in an accident," "I was a heavy drug user," "I gave birth to my second oldest," "I lost my job," or "Our company was being sued." Demons frequently exploit trauma as a doorway for oppression.

For example, I recently ministered to a woman suffering from an autoimmune disorder that had begun a decade earlier. As I probed further and asked what had happened in her life eleven years ago, she said, "All of my sickness started after the death of my father."

Once the doorway that allowed the unclean spirit in is exposed, the next step is to work on closing it. Often, this involves inner healing and forgiveness—something I will explain further in the next chapter.

The entry path may have been things like sin, witchcraft, idolatry, or generational curses. Things outside the will of God open us to the enemy; we must guard our hearts and minds. If any of these things are discovered, I'll have the person renounce (come out of agreement with) them. Sincere repentance is in order, and verbally speaking against these things will mitigate the hold demons have on the person. Sometimes repentance is more than just a verbal thing; it requires the destruction of physical objects such as idols or occult books.

I've ministered to a plethora of people claiming Christianity who wear evil-eye jewelry or keep nick-nacks of African gods they brought home from vacation. Plenty of other resources list various entry paths for the demonic; my goal is not to write a book on deliverance. As you grow in this ministry through serving the afflicted, you will notice some patterns that will help you become a more efficient minister. The bottom line is to locate the path of entry and remove it.

After achieving this, I will drive the evil spirit out of the person. Very simply, command the spirit to leave the person. You can name the demon anything you want (Jesus often called it an "unclean spirit"), but I typically refer to it by its specific affliction—for example: "spirit of death," "spirit of depression," "spirit causing fear," or "spirit of sickness." This approach works well for most "low-level" demons or for people who are merely afflicted, rather than fully possessed (losing their will or consciousness).

Often, you will need to be persistent when driving a demon out. Sometimes, the thing will leave immediately, sometimes dramatically, but at other times, it may go quietly or not leave at all. Use discernment, work with the Holy Spirit, and stay on the case. If a demon is not leaving someone quickly, it could mean you need to spend more alone time with Jesus in prayer or fasting as a lifestyle; it could mean the person still requires inner healing, repentance, or to forgive someone; it could mean a curse needs to be broken, or it could mean you're dealing with a very nasty spirit.

We know from Matthew 12:45 that there are spirits "more wicked" than other spirits—a hierarchy in the demonic realm. Many of these demons have names such as Leviathan or Jezebel. Such spirits will have lesser demonic spirits underneath them operating within a person. As the deliverance minister begins to rebuke these more powerful demons, typically, more minor powers will come out of the person instead. It is like the chief demon is sacrificing its servants to save itself. These scenarios require patience and persistence. Let's carefully read the story of Legion (another demonic power with a name):

"They came to the other side of the sea, to the country of the Gerasenes. And when Jesus had stepped out of the boat, immediately there met him out of the tombs a man with an unclean spirit. He lived among the tombs. And no one could bind him

anymore, not even with a chain, for he had often been bound with shackles and chains, but he wrenched the chains apart, and he broke the shackles in pieces. No one had the strength to subdue him. Night and day among the tombs and on the mountains, he was always crying out and cutting himself with stones. And when he saw Jesus from afar, he ran and fell down before him. And crying out with a loud voice, he said, "What have you to do with me, Jesus, Son of the Most High God? I adjure you by God, do not torment me." For he was saying to him, "Come out of the man, you unclean spirit!" And Jesus asked him, "What is your name?" He replied, "My name is Legion, for we are many." And he begged him earnestly not to send them out of the country. Now a great herd of pigs was feeding there on the hillside, and they begged him, saying, "Send us to the pigs; let us enter them." So he gave them permission. And the unclean spirits came out and entered the pigs; and the herd, numbering about two thousand, rushed down the steep bank into the sea and drowned in the sea."

- Mark 5:1-13

If you read this story too quickly, you'll be prone to miss verse 8, "For [Jesus] was saying to him, 'come out of the man, you unclean spirit!'" Notice, Christ was rebuking this demon, but it was not leaving the demoniac. Like the man Jesus laid hands on twice to receive his sight (Mark 8), Jesus did not give up on this poor soul bound by Satan. Instead, our Lord responded to the demon's cries by asking for its name.

A demon speaking out of a person is not common, but it does happen. When it happens, you must employ the gift of discernment by the Holy Spirit because demons will frequently lie to you. I don't recommend conversing with them as a new believer, but if your powers of discernment have been trained by constant practice (Mark 5:14), talking to the spirit can lead to its expulsion. By giving Jesus its name, Legion exposed itself completely and became subject to the Name above all names (Philippians 2:9-11).

One time, our ministry team at church was doing deliverance on a young woman who was manifesting heavily—slithering around on the carpet and shaking violently. She was afflicted by multiple spirits, so after the slithering one had left (some sort of serpent spirit), we still had to deal with the chief one afflicting her. Through questioning the woman, I gathered some vital information: She had dealt with a hidden lust addiction, been sexually assaulted in the past, and was having chronic nightmares about her death. The fourth piece of information came to me as I began to command the hiding spirit to manifest itself—I felt the physical symptoms of arousal start inside of me.

Now, that's not a happy thing to have to write, but I want you to know that during deliverance ministry, demons can make your flesh respond in various ways. One time, after a man had given his life to Jesus, I began to drive demons out of him. Immediately, his head snapped up; he looked me directly in the eye and stated darkly, "You have no power here." The moment the spirit uttered those words, fear gripped my flesh. Simultaneously, the Holy Spirit inside me rose in a burst of angry tongues and drove the wicked spirit out. Other times, I have been in the process of deliverance when the feeling of light-headedness overcame me. It felt like I was going to pass out. All of these af-flictions—arousal, fear, fainting (and probably more) have merely affected my flesh during deliverance and nothing else. They also quickly subsided once the spirit was driven out of the person.

Kneeling next to this woman, as that feeling started to manifest, the Lord dropped a single word in my mind, "Jezebel." I immediately commanded, "In the name of Jesus, Jezebel, come out of her!" The woman wretched, her back arched, and the sound of vomiting ensued as she collapsed to her side—Jesus freed her.

In the Bible, there is an actual woman named Jezebel (1 Kings), who is a Baal and Asherah worshiper. She marries the King of Israel, Ahab, and has the prophets of God persecuted and slaughtered. In the New Testament, Jesus compares a false prophetess in the church of Thyatira to Jezebel (Revelation 2), who seduces the believers of God into sexual immorality. These desires to control, manipulate, seduce, and oppress the prophets of the Lord are found in the demon called Jezebel. They manifest in the person it inhabits. This spirit is not the only one that will try to give you feelings of arousal to get you to stop the deliverance. I have also seen it in incubus/succubus spirits that were afflicting a former sex-worker Jesus delivered.

I have also had spirits lie to me about their name. One time a demon told me its name was Dagon during a deliverance. As I began to recall how Dagon was humbled by the Lord when the Ark of the Covenant was brought to its temple, the demon laughed at me and said it lied about its name. So again, don't trust everything you hear from a demon, but always trust what you hear from the Holy Spirit. He is your guide, and He is the one actually driving the demons out of people as you command them to go into the abyss.

Long deliverance sessions will exhaust people, and they may need to sleep for some time to regain their energy. One of the things I love about deliverance, though, is that there is almost always an immediate improvement in the person's life. When depression lifts, they can feel it. When a spirit causing nightmares goes, the person sleeps well that night. When a demonically caused illness is broken, they usually immediately recover.

After the demon has left a person, and I'm confident Jesus has swept them clean, I baptize them in the Holy Spirit. I'll frequently lead them through a simple prayer, "Heavenly Father, thank you for forgiving me of all my sins and freeing me. I ask that you'll send me the good gift of the Holy Spirit; fill me, and cloth me in power to advance your kingdom." Then, I'll lay a hand on their forehead and say, "Receive the Holy Spirit." Glorious things tend to take place.

The final step is to warn them to stop sinning if that was the cause of their affliction (John 5:14), to tell them to start practicing the basic disciplines of Christianity (such as being involved in a local church, reading scripture, praying daily, etc.), and to engage in spiritual warfare when those spirits try to come back. I go into post-deliverance instructions for maintaining freedom in a booklet I wrote titled *Jesus Has Delivered You (now what?)*. This is a very brief overview I give to people and ask them to read within 24 hours of their deliverance.

Chapter 18
Inner Healing

We were ministering in a public park in Nashville, TN when my wife and I came upon a woman asking to be physically healed. Sensing deeper wounds in her soul, I began to tell her what I felt the Lord wanted to deal with in her. She confirmed these things, so I took her hands and prayed, "Holy Spirit, would you come and do what only you can do? I know your word says, 'a bruised reed I will not break, a smoldering wick I won't put out.' You are near to the brokenhearted. Will you come now and bind the wounds in her heart?"

At the end of the prayer, I blew on her, and she fell to the ground under the weight of the Spirit. When she got back up, my wife came to her, and they hugged for a solid five minutes, both weeping. The woman was then able to forgive people who had abused and neglected her.

About a week later, this lady posted on social media, "On 8.2.24 Jesus radically SET ME FREE from so.

Many. years. Of depression, anxiety, panic attacks, trauma, eating disorders, betrayals, heartache, and hopelessness. All the pain in my heart and in my mind GONE. The obsessive thoughts and ruminations GONE. The dark cloud that followed me around GONE. The weight of the past LIFTED. The hurt in my heart HEALED."

She went on to write, "I haven't quite found the words to explain it or share a long-form story, but what I can tell you is that whatever you've done, whatever you've been through, whatever you've been diagnosed with, whatever you struggle with—God has a miracle waiting for you. He is the redeemer, the restorer, the healer. He makes all things new. You weren't meant to carry all this weight, friend. Give it to Him. Let him heal you. It's time to be set free."

In ministry, you will run across two types of people: those who have been abused or neglected who say, "I *can't* forgive them," and then those who have been abused or neglected who say, "I don't *want* to forgive them." God can do immeasurably more with the former than the latter. The type of person who wants to forgive but can't needs only one thing done in his/her life to jump that hurdle: a supernatural God to remove pain from their heart supernaturally. It would be easy for them to forgive if there was no pain.

If every time the face of an abuser crossed their mind, or a memory "just so happened" to crop up, and it didn't stick them in the side of their brain like a hot poker, they could forgive. The problem is the pain is there, so even though they may want to forgive someone, they can't in their own strength.

Forgiveness is a Divine trait. I do not believe it is human to forgive—instead, we crave vengeance and to carry victimhood. God said vengeance was His, though, so that option is not on the table for the believer (Romans 12:19). Simultaneously, the Bible says we are "more than conquerors" in Christ, so victimhood is not on the table (Romans 8:37). The only door God has left open is forgiveness. Indeed, it is not only open to us, but Jesus compels us to step through it. Only by our disobedience or ignorance do we cling to the pain.

A minister friend of mine once had me hop on a video call with a missionary in a foreign country. This missionary was dealing with a host of incurable diseases, and her family had begun seeing demonic entities in their home. At the start of our call, she plainly stated, "People tell me I must do something to be healed, but I disagree with them and don't want to have to do anything to be healed." I told her I agreed, that Jesus paid for her healing on the cross, and all she had to do was receive it.

What the missionary failed to tell me, which became more evident as the call went on, is past ministers had told her she needed to forgive her abusers. It wasn't for healing either; it was to be free from demonic oppression. I quickly figured that out as I prayed for her. The Lord then highlighted an issue with her father. The man had abused her growing up and then similarly abused her daughter.

I told the missionary what God thought about her father's actions, but I also told her Jesus declared boldly, "If you do not forgive others their trespasses, neither will your Father forgive your trespasses (Matthew 6:15)." I went on to ask her if the problem was she didn't *want* to forgive her father, or if the problem simply was she didn't feel like she *could* forgive him.

She thought about it momentarily and finally declared, "I do not want to forgive him." At that point, I asked her if she had ever heard of the parable of the Unforgiving Servant. A demon then manifested; the missionary's face morphed, and it screamed at me, "I shouldn't have to do anything to be healed! I won't forgive!" Shortly thereafter, the call ended.

The parable of the Unforgiving Servant (Matthew 18) has been used to heal more people than any other teaching I've given. In it, Jesus tells a story about a servant man who owes an unbelievable sum of money to his master. The servant asks for patience, declaring that he will pay the debt in time. I believe Jesus uses an insurmountable amount of money (10,000 talents), so listeners would laugh at this point in the story. There is no way the man could ever pay such a debt back.

Instead of asking for patience, the servant should have requested pardon. The master, taking pity on his servant, forgives the whole debt and lets the man go free. A little while later, the servant finds a fellow servant who owes him about a hundred days' wages worth of money. It is a lot of cash, but it could feasibly be paid back. Dropping to his knees, he asks for patience from his co-worker. The now unforgiving servant denies him patience, doesn't offer forgiveness, and has his fellow servant thrown in jail. Upon hearing this anecdote, the master calls the unforgiving servant back in and declares, "You wicked servant! I forgave you all that debt because you pleaded with me. And should not you have had mercy on your fellow servant, as I had mercy on you?" Jesus goes on to state, "And in anger his master delivered him to the torturers, until he should pay all his debt."

Many translations fail to translate the word "torturer" in this passage correctly. The Greek word used is "basanistés," which is often rendered in Bible translations as "jailers," but it actually means "to torture" or "to torment."

Jesus then makes one of the scariest statements in all scripture, saying, "So also my heavenly Father will do to every one of you, if you do not forgive your brother from your heart." People gloss over this passage way too quickly, I have learned. If we take Jesus' words at face value, when it comes to unforgiveness, not only will our sins not be forgiven, but we will be turned over to torturers until we can pay the debt of our sin. I see this as an eternal punishment that begins here on Earth the moment we begin to harbor bitterness toward others.

Interestingly enough, I have only ever seen this applied to believers. Non-believers don't seem to be under the same Kingdom Standards as Christians. Notice the Unforgiving Servant was forgiven of a debt he could never repay. I believe his character represents every Christian believer. The parable itself comes right after Peter asks Jesus how many times he should forgive his brother—and Jesus' response suggests *every single* time.

I have learned most people want to follow Jesus' example of forgiveness, but that pesky pain keeps them from forgiving "from [their] heart." Many can say, "I forgive so and so," but the moment a memory hits them, their heart reveals they've been unable to truly let go. It is a difficult scenario to be stuck in, but Jesus holds the key to their deliverance. Just as the Lord can repair a broken bone in a moment, He can repair a broken heart in a moment. If one desires to forgive, that is enough spark for the Holy Spirit to blow on and turn it into a raging fire.

"The Lord is near to the brokenhearted and saves the crushed in spirit."
   - **Psalm 34:18**

In the documentary *Holy Ghost Reborn*, there is a sequence about a war veteran going through the process of inner healing. He sits on a couch as three prophetic men lay hands on him and wait for the Holy Spirit to show the veteran the most significant source of pain in his life.

Suddenly, the man begins to weep as he is transported to a childhood memory of trauma. Amid the chaos, Jesus shows up in his memory and transforms it from a traumatic experience to one of love. When I first saw that scene, my jaw dropped. It never occurred to me that God would take a person's memories of abuse and rewrite them. I lacked that kind of imagination, but upon seeing it for myself, I began to implement it as the Spirit led me.

The first person my wife and I tried it with was a friend who was trapped by addiction. As he lay on my couch with his eyes closed, my wife asked him, "What do you see?"

"I see Jesus," He responded calmly.

"What is he doing?" Aly asked.

"He's smiling at me."

"Is He saying anything?"

After a long pause, the man replied, "He said if I don't lay down my personal pride, then I will die."

We all knew the Lord was warning my friend that if he did not get help by going to a rehabilitation center, he would perish. Unfortunately, my friend refused to get help and overdosed on heroin one day—causing a heart attack, stroke, and pneumonia in his lungs from vomiting while on his back. Aly and I begged the Lord to have mercy on our friend, and although he lived, he came out of the ordeal unable to walk and with much of his faculties lost.

The second person we tried Holy Spirit Therapy on was a female friend of ours. I put my hand on her head, and I asked the Holy Spirit to bring up any point of pain in her past. Suddenly, our friend saw herself at a young age in the midst of a traumatic experience when she was taken advantage of. She could recall details vividly. I asked her to look around the room to see if anyone besides the attacker was there with her. Eventually, she spotted Jesus! Jesus began to do something that made my friend laugh, and her traumatic memory was wiped and replaced by a new one filled with joy. We then asked the Spirit to continue showing us traumatic points of pain—each time, Jesus would reprogram them.

One time, I was praying for a man with cancer on my couch. I put my hand on his head and asked the Spirit to show us anything He wanted to deal with. The man began to weep. He could hardly speak as he told me, "I'm in my bedroom; I've set up a noose and am about to take my life. My aunt is banging on the door, but I've locked it." This was a memory the man had from his teenage years. "I looked out my window," he said, "And I saw a bright light that distracted me. I didn't take my life that night because of that light."

Immediately, the Holy Spirit gave me a word of knowledge, "It was an angel! God sent an angel to save you that night!" The man wept and received inner healing.

Another time, I was praying for a man in my life group. He was going through a divorce and was dealing with depression, anxiety, anger, and more. There's a time to tell demons to leave a person, and there is a time to ask the Lord to heal their heart. I encourage you to listen to the Spirit's guidance because sometimes we want to go in aggressively when *He* wants to go in gently and do deeper work. This was one of those times. I put my hand on the man's forehead and asked the Lord to show him the place of pain. Suddenly, he found himself crying as a kid in his childhood closet. The Lord showed me the same vision, and I told him, "I see your parents arguing in the kitchen."

"That's where they always argued. I'd cry in my closet so they couldn't hear me," he responded.

The Lord revealed many other things that night, and this man was set free from trauma that had been with him for decades. As such, he was also delivered of a generational spirit of anger, as well as depression and more.

Over a year ago a woman prophesied to me, "God will send bitter ministers to you that are burned out." A person who meets this criteria almost always shows up at our meetings. One such woman came to a revival night in Centennial Park in 2024. She was a missionary whom God pulled off the mission field and told her to be settled in America. Her heart had grown cold and become filled with anger toward the Lord. When people are angry at God, it is usually because they've lost sight of their enemy. I argue it is impossible to be angry at God if we're objective.

On the one hand, people mistreat us, we misread words from God, and we sin. On the other side—the thief comes to steal, kill, and destroy. But God, He is holy and good. He is for us. So when people are bitter toward the Lord, I don't believe they must forgive God. Instead, they should repent and ask for forgiveness. They should recognize they have a real enemy who hates them, Satan, and see God as their salvation. So long as a person holds onto their pitchfork against the Lord, He will oppose them. But the Bible says He "gives grace to the humble (James 4:6)."

Unlike the former missionary, this one was willing to submit to the Lord no matter how difficult. I led her through inner healing, forgiveness, and then prayed for her physical healing. That night, I went home dismayed. Having prayed for several people's healing, I didn't see any of them restored, including this missionary. A week later, though, a message from her came to me:

"The pain has been less since you prayed, but that is not the best thing that happened. The peace that came over me was evidence of the Holy Spirit, and then the image of me as a daughter in the king's palace was simple yet very important to me. I've been a Christian for 43 years, and not feeling loved or accepted by God has been a recurring theme. God will show up and convince me, but then it pops back up. So, right now, I absolutely feel completely loved and accepted by God. When I don't feel it, I still believe it, but it is nice to feel it too, and know it in my heart, and right now I do. I also do not feel

any resentment or unforgiveness toward God, my-self or my husband."

This woman went on to accept her new assignment in America and immediately began evangelizing people at the supermarket. She returned to praying in the secret place regularly, and from her testimony of inner healing, she convinced her sister to come to a Freedom Night, where she also received healing from Jesus. Through the Lord binding the wounds in this minister's heart, He also restored her to a functioning part of the Kingdom of God. Between you and me, I believe she will return to foreign soil again one day to bring good news.

Inner healing is not the same as deliverance, but it typically *leads* to deliverance. If you find a demon won't leave someone, they could be trapped in bitterness and unforgiveness. Because of their pride in this area, the Lord has turned them over to the "torturers," which I believe are unclean spirits. Some of the worst sicknesses I have seen, such as dystonia, akinesia, and POTS, have been dealt with through inner healing paired with deliverance in the name of Jesus.

It may be the person isn't angry toward the Lord and has forgiven all of their enemies, but they refuse to forgive themselves.

The vast majority of auto-immune disorders I have seen are tied to some form of self hatred. This mindset is usually put on people from a young age via trauma or neglect. Satan foments it with constant accusations against their self-worth and state of salvation. These people rarely believe they are worthy of being healed, so you must start with scripture (truth), move to inner healing, verbal forgiveness of themselves, and finally, deliverance.

Alternatively, the Lord can do all of these things in a moment during a worship service or simply when a minister grabs their hand.

Those who grew up under religion may believe carrying guilt and shame is healthy, but I assure you it is not. The enemy wants to keep us under condemnation because it makes us impotent. The Bible says "no condemnation" exists for those in Christ Jesus (Romans 8:1). Thus, this, too, becomes a matter of repentance. We must come out of agreement with our enemy, out of accord with religion, and out of agreement with our own accusations against us.

The primary scripture I rely on to help people forgive themselves is 1 John 1:9, "If we confess our sins, he is faithful and just to forgive us our sins and to cleanse us from all unrighteousness."

This passage assures us we are forgiven for the sin we have confessed. If the person agrees, I will explain, "God is the Judge, and you are not. If God has forgiven you, then you must agree with His word over your own. You must forgive yourself; you are not the Judge." Dozens of people have been freed from this simple explanation of truth. It is often like watching a light switch on in their minds.

C.S. Lewis wrote, "Christ died for men precisely because men are not worth dying for; to make them worth it." My goal in healing ministry is often to help someone understand this fact. They are worthy to be healed, they are worthy to be freed, not because of anything they have done, but because of what Jesus has done for them. It would have been easy for a person to say, "I'm not worthy of Jesus dying for me," until

Jesus laid His life down. After that moment, all believers must admit they are worthy of the death of Christ because *He* thought they were. Failure to understand this puts us at odds with the one we are trying to please with our false humility.

Ultimately, for effective inner healing, the person's focus must turn away from themselves, from their spiritual enemy, from their abuses, and onto Jesus. A particularly self absorbed individual, prone to self-pity and starved for attention, can be the most challenging person to see healed precisely because they possess these traits. Insecurity, in many cases, is even harder to let go of than pride because some people believe they *deserve* to remain insecure due to the rejection and pain they've endured.

I have ministered to several individuals—typically late middle-aged women—who struggle to be still and listen to what the Lord is trying to tell them. In these moments, we will have an entire team of ministers contending for their freedom, yet instead of focusing on receiving healing from the Lord, they relish that people are *actually* interested in talking to them. This type of brokenness is hard to overcome, and those who exhibit it remind me of a character from *The Great Divorce*.

In this magnificent book written by C.S. Lewis, the ghost of a woman who is damned to Hell, but offered a second chance at salvation, comes to the outskirts of Heaven, where she is to listen and cooperate with saints and angels to learn how she can enter paradise. Unfortunately, the character merely goes on and on about how poorly she was treated during her life on Earth without stopping to take a breath. Every sentence is tinged with self-pity and umbrage. The author goes on to write:

"The shrill monotonous whine [of the woman] died away as the speaker, still accompanied by the bright patience at her side, moved out of hearing. "What troubles ye, son?" asked my Teacher. "I am troubled, Sir," said I, "because that unhappy [woman] doesn't seem to me to be the sort of soul that ought to be even in danger of damnation. She isn't wicked: she's only a silly, garrulous old woman who has got into a habit of grumbling, and one feels that a little kindness, and rest, and change would put her all right."

"That is what she once was. That is maybe what she still is. If so, she certainly will be cured. But the whole question is whether she is now a grumbler."

"I should have thought there was no doubt about that!"

"Aye, but ye misunderstand me. The question is whether she is a grumbler, or only a grumble. If there is a real woman-even the least trace of one-still there inside the grumbling, it can be brought to life again. If there's one wee spark under all those ashes, we'll blow it till the whole pile is red and clear. But if there's nothing but ashes we'll not go on blowing them in our own eyes forever. They must be swept up."

"But how can there be a grumble without a grumbler?"

"The whole difficulty of understanding Hell is that the thing to be understood is so nearly Nothing. But ye'll have had experiences . . . it begins with a grumbling mood, and yourself still distinct from it: perhaps criticizing it. And yourself, in a dark hour, may will that mood, embrace it. Ye can repent and come out of it again. But there may come a day when you can do that no longer. Then there will be no you left to criticise the mood, nor even to enjoy it, but just the grumble itself going on forever like a machine."

I have met several people closer to a grumble than a grumbler—people who cease to be humans with pain in their heart and become pain itself. Such people have become so accustomed to their state of affairs that they can't imagine life differently. A group of us once ministered to a woman who had been shut up in a house for seven years with demons. She raged against prescription pill manufacturers—blaming them for her illnesses. She joined social media groups to commiserate with others dealing with the same sick-nesses. After spending several hours with her, a half dozen demons left, as well as her symptoms. She was free!

We told her she needed to walk out of the house the next morning and go to church for the first time in seven years. Scared of what a life of freedom looked like, she did not do as instructed and eventually was reshackled by many of the demonic illnesses and fear.

Have you read about people who spend decades in prison having a difficult time transitioning into the real world? Faced with freedom, prison bars seem safe to them. The Hebrews were freed from slavery, but groaned their lives were better when they were slaves (Exodus 14:12). The same is true of many people afflicted by our enemy.

My team has ministered to people who could not tell us when anxiety became a bedfellow for them—they had been imprisoned by it since childhood. Such people begin to identify with anxiety—it becomes a pet or a characteristic of their personality. Detaching that demon from them becomes an exercise in long suffering. A minister better be ready to patiently walk people like these through a long process of dismantling demonic mindsets.

The moment a person begins to internalize their pain or plight, it will open them up to oppression like they've never experienced before. In essence, such people are agreeing with Satan about their life and rejecting the Lord. There's a vast difference between saying, "My anxiety" and "I'm afflicted by anxiety." There is power in what we speak, and out of our mouth will come curses or blessings. When I minister to people who have been trapped for years, I often have them practice speaking blessings over their lives.

I argue scripture tells us to disassociate from our afflictions. For example, "God has not given you a spirit of fear" indicates that fear is first, a spirit, and second, something given to us. It is presented by our enemy and is separate from our being. We do not have to claim it; instead, we are charged to resist it (Isaiah 41:10).

The same is true of our pain; these are the fiery darts of our enemy. Pain in your heart can feel like a dagger. Don't accept it as part of your being; rather, understand it came with an assignment to destroy you. But Jesus still lives to mend broken hearts and to remove such daggers. So, if you find it difficult to forgive others or yourself, turn to the Lord, admit you can't do it in your strength, and ask Him to help you forgive until you genuinely do. One day, you'll wonder why you haven't thought about a person or an event in a long time and search for that familiar pain—incapable of finding it. It will be nailed to a cross.

Chapter 19
Prophecy

As mentioned in my previous book, I spent twenty years of my Christian walk ignoring the Holy Spirit. During that time, I was an avid debater and apologist for faith in Jesus—forming groups at every stage of my life where people could reason with one another. One such group was called *Theology and Brotherhood*.

Most active participants were cessationists, including a good friend of mine whom I've always respected for his gift of wisdom. As the Spirit began to wake me up, I started to reason with this group that Jesus still healed people today through the laying on of hands. The further I walked down that road with God, the more pushback I received from my skeptical friends, and candidly, the less I cared about their opinions.

Years after that group died, the friend I admired for his wisdom asked me to lunch. On the way to our meeting, I asked the Lord for a word for (we'll call him) Jack. Little did I know, Jack was seeking wisdom from me this time around as he felt a calling into ministry. I gave him the word I heard, and he began to laugh. I didn't understand how it applied, but my friend immediately did, and it encouraged him. Halfway through our meal, I struck up a conversation with our server—a kind man wearing black from head to toe. As I began to "look" into the man, I saw creativity and then had a vision of him designing sneakers; he was not saying or wearing anything that would indicate these truths. In front of my cessationist friend, I took a shot and asked the server, "Are you artistic? Do you do design, such as designing sneakers?"

The man was shocked. He looked at me intently for a moment and then pulled out his cell phone. He found his social media page, where he posted photos of his sneaker designs, and told me no one really knew about his hobby. I said, "Well, isn't that interesting that I'd know about it?"

The server opened up about his former life as homeless, addicted to drugs, and a criminal. He allowed me to pray for him, and as I did, I received a vision of a sneaker design I believed God was going to birth through the man for His glory. Additionally, I saw his younger brother.

"Do you have a younger brother?" I asked.

He did!

"I see he is going through many of the hardships you went through when you were younger. You don't believe you have much influence in his life anymore, but I want you to know a sliver is still there. God is calling you to intercede for your brother," I told him.

He acknowledged everything I spoke by the Spirit was accurate, and my cessationist friend witnessed a demonstration of the power of God to prophesy he could not deny.

Prophecy has become my favorite spiritual gift. Often, while out in public, I'll just stare at someone, "looking" into them by the Spirit. Very quickly, a word or a vision comes to my mind, and it isn't always even applicable to ministry. Sometimes, God will show me hobbies or relatives. Other times, I will see visions of abuse. Frequently, a simple word comes to my mind, such as "mother," followed by "neglect" or "sick." One time, I saw a vision of a small kid on a skateboard doing something dangerous, and the interpretation came to me, "Growing up, was your mom apathetic about what you did? She didn't care if you engaged in dangerous activity?"

The woman responded, "Yes, actually, I could be gone from the house for a week, and she wouldn't even check in on me."

I then got a vision of a crown worn by a queen and followed up, "Do you ever feel like Cinderella, that your mom expects to be waited on like a queen?"

This, too, was accurate, and so the Lord continued to speak to her wounds in this way.

A female college student came to one of our Freedom Nights and watched as the power of God struck her friends. This group witnessed Jesus drive demons out of people for the first time, which stirred up spirits in them as well. As the young woman came forward, exhibiting hallmark signs of anxiety, I took one of her hands. Immediately I received an impression from the

Lord concerning a past boyfriend. "You are young and seem happy, but I wanted to know if you've recently come out of a relationship with a man, perhaps while you were in high school, that wasn't healthy?" I asked. She broke down, and tears streamed from her eyes.

As we ministered to her, she fell to the ground, convulsing. My wife tended to her and drove an unclean spirit out as one of her friends watched in horror—unable to take in the confronting sight of her companion manifesting a demon.

What I didn't tell you about this group was that they all belonged to Lipscomb University, a Christian institute of higher education founded by the Church of Christ (a cessationist denomination). There were roughly twelve individuals—one of which made Jesus her Lord that night and was water baptized and delivered. Maybe five individuals were struck by the power of God, several more laughed at us as we ministered to the group, and at least one particularly religious woman had the worst thing to say. She told her friend, who had just become a new believer, that it was "impossible" for God to free her of fear like that.

"...having the appearance of godliness, but denying its power. Avoid such people."
 -   **2 Timothy 3:5**

On the other hand, there was a young man that night I'll call Jake. The Holy Spirit would not leave Jake alone as he practically hyperventilated under the power of God. We were ministering to him when Ethan received a word of knowledge, "Would you say that you're particularly religious? That the power of the Spirit is something you reject?"

"I do not like the gift of prophecy. I believe people use it to show off and make themselves look good," he responded.

"Jake, your generation needs you walking in power. Out of this whole group of college students, I guarantee you that at least three of them have contemplated suicide. They need you filled with the Spirit so God can do something about it through you," I reasoned with him.

Ethan then led Jake through a prayer of repentance from a spirit of religion. The fire of the Lord came upon Jake in great glory, and weeks later, we heard a report that he was blazing for Jesus. We also heard what happened to this group of twelve. Five or six were in active revival, another four or so were angry about what happened, and the rest were somewhere in the middle—mostly curious.

The prophetic gifting has a way of stirring things up. There's a scene in the bible where Jesus used words of knowledge to grab the attention of a Samaritan woman drawing water out of a well:

"Jesus said to her, 'Go, call your husband, and come here.' The woman answered him, 'I have no husband.' Jesus said to her, 'You are right in saying, 'I have no husband'; for you have had five husbands, and the one you now have is not your husband. What you have said is true.' The woman said to him, 'Sir, I perceive that you are a prophet.'"
   - John 4:16-19

The gift of a word of knowledge is when you know something that you couldn't possibly perceive by natural means. Since Jesus had not met the woman before and was not part of her community, the knowledge He possessed about her having had five husbands proved to her that He was a prophet. I presume Jesus had many more words of knowledge for this woman than are recorded based on what she tells her community:

"So the woman left her water jar and went away into town and said to the people, 'Come, see a man who told me all that I ever did. Can this be the Christ?' They went out of the town and were coming to him."
   - **John 4:28-30**

In this instance, the prophetic gifting revealed Jesus to a town of people.

One evening, my friend Jaqualin visited my home to train our team in prophetic ministry. After the lesson came demonstration, and Jaqualin began to pray for people one at a time as the Lord led him. Many miracles happened that evening, but one stands out to me. My father came, slightly skeptical but open-minded. As Jaqualin took my dad's hand, he began to see the internal organs of my dad like a diagram in his mind's eye. Finally, Jaqualin pinpointed the area of healing needed—the bladder. The thing is, no one knew my

father was having issues with his bladder except my
mother (they even hid it from me). On the way home
that night, my mom recalled Dad admitting that the
prophetic gift must be genuine because of that fact.
Yes, Dad's bladder was healed to the glory of Jesus!

Some friends and I were headed back from a revival
meeting in Georgia when we stopped at an Italian restaurant for lunch. Our server was excellent and ac-
commodating for such a large party, but there was
something God wanted to do in her life. It wasn't an
accident we chose to eat there at that time. I asked the
Lord what her issue was, and immediately, "drug use"
popped into my mind—specifically addiction to pills.

She didn't look like a drug user, but that's one thing
Jaqualin warned us about the prophetic. He said,
"You're better off gouging your eyes out than using
them. They are of no help to you." I have seen, time
and time again, this nugget of wisdom prove itself
true. We tend to judge people by appearances, but
God looks at the heart (1 Samuel 16:7). You may be
praying for a tatted-up gothic-dressed person and
think they need deliverance when they don't. You
might look at someone's tired eyes and believe they

aren't sleeping well, and they actually are. We must learn to use our spiritual senses over our natural ones.

At the end of our meal, I broached the topic with our server. She admitted she not only dealt with addiction to pills but a host of other controlled substances, too. Her life was a constant fight to stay sober. We began to trace back to the root cause of her addiction (the pain that pushed her to turn to pills to start with) and prayed for her inner healing.

Finally, we began to drive the demon of addiction out of her in the middle of the restaurant. It manifested momentarily; the woman almost collapsed, and then she was free! She thanked us through tears as Ethan noticed the woman was wearing an "evil eye" bracelet and warned her about New Age practices. She happily removed the jewelry, and we tossed it in the garbage at the nearest gas station as we resumed our trek back home.

One evening, while out to dinner with my wife and a couple of pastors, I looked at a server in the Spirit. Immediately, I heard the word "shoulder." Stepping out of the boat, I asked him if his shoulder was injured. He was stunned that I could know such a thing and proceeded to demonstrate how, every time he tried turning his neck to the right, it triggered severe pain that extended down his neck and across his right shoulder.

I told him, "I believe if you let me pray for it, God will heal it." Sure enough, after laying my hand on his shoulder twice and commanding it to be healed, the pain completely left. The man was absolutely blown away. He knew nothing about Jesus, so I had the privilege of being the first to share the gospel with him that night.

At its base level, prophecy is "revealing the heart of God." Savannah Ramsey adds that it is also "preparing the way for the Lord." When we look at who Jesus said was the greatest prophet, John the Baptist, we see both definitions at work in his life (Matthew 11:11). John was born to prepare the way for the Messiah, and his message was to "repent" for the Kingdom of God was near. Under this loose definition, we are prophesying anytime we preach similar things. In fact, anytime we read scripture out loud, we engage in prophecy as scripture reveals the heart of God and prepares a way for unbelievers to receive Him.

The word "prophesy" in Greek means to "speak forth" or to "declare beforehand." When we look at it in Hebrew, we come to the term "Navi," which is a noun meaning "prophet" and has connotations of "bubbling up" or "boiling over" to deliver a divinely inspired message.

Interestingly, some Old Testament prophets are called "seers," such as Samuel (1 Samuel 9:19). There is great variety within the prophetic gifting—some dream, some smell, feel, taste, and hear in the Spirit, while others "see." This seeing may be physical, it may be simply in their mind's eye, or it may be an open vision. Often, seers will receive a vision or a dream well before an event occurs. In contrast, many Navi-type prophets will begin to prophesy on the spot as the need arises.

I primarily operate in the gift of prophecy as the Navi might—the Spirit will come upon me, and He will begin to speak over someone in the moment. I first noticed this occurred as I would be praying for people. It wasn't that God would give me a word for them, and then I'd pray. Instead, I'd be praying for an individual, and out of nowhere, words would come out of my mouth, bypassing my brain, and they would be things I couldn't possibly know by natural means. I call this *speaking prophecy*. As a believer is already speaking, the Spirit will hijack the message.

I've also seen people prophesy "ecstatically," which I define as an almost complete overtaking by the Spirit of God. The person may begin to behave strangely, become hot and tingly, and out of their mouth will flow an oracle from the Lord with great passion. I have done this at least once during a prayer session before church, which I recalled in this book's chapter on Revival.

Every sense you possess in the natural your spirit-man likewise possesses in the spirit-realm. Feeling in the Spirit can be such a gift, but it is also a double-edged sword when not paired with discernment. Sometimes, during altar ministry, I will feel someone's ailment in my body. For example, once, I went down a line of people praying for their healing when I came upon a middle-aged couple. Immediately, I began to feel faint, as if I were passing out.

Gathering my strength, I asked the husband and wife, "Do either of you deal with fainting spells?" The wife pointed at the husband, who admitted he would occasionally start to pass out. Suddenly, my back became excruciating. It made me double over in pain. I asked the couple again, "Do either of you deal with back pain?" Again, the husband admitted it was him.

This gift of feeling someone's physical pain in my own body is one I want to walk in more. I believe it is an amalgamation of discernment and prophecy.

Pastor Joel was once walking through a ticket line when his ears began to ring. That was not an ailment he dealt with, so he discerned it was an issue someone nearby was having. He approached the ticket booth and asked the man behind the counter if he had dealt with tinnitus. Sure enough, the man did. Joel prayed for the ticketer's healing, and Jesus healed him!

One time, I was ministering in Asheville when a woman who claimed to be cursed by witches came to me. As she drew near, I began to pass out. I understood immediately it was a demonic attack meant to keep me away from her, so I rebuked the curse, and it lifted. I saw this same thing happen to my friend Ethan when we were praying for a woman who was abandoned by her parents at a young age because she refused to join their religious cult. Ethan thought she dealt with fainting spells, but it was actually witchcraft upon the woman's life (for she had done many New Age practices).

After Freedom Night late one evening, a friend brought one of his buddies to my home. Aly told us we had to minister to the person on the front porch, but while I was out there getting sleeted on and freezing, I determined to let the man in our home (this was an error I later apologized for). As we began to minister to him, he became more and more belligerent—trying to get ministers to say the N-word and cursing, for example. Ethan received a word from God, "pearls before swine," and checked out completely (Matthew 7:6).

On the other hand, I continued to minister and prophesy over him. But I was shaking out of my shoes the entire time. In my heart and mind, I was not nervous one bit, so I did not understand why I was exhibiting such symptoms. The man said he needed Jesus, and to repent, but told us he wasn't ready—so we walked him to his ride. Later, I found out that my wife was gripped by fear the whole time we were ministering to the man. I put two and two together to understand that my nervous feeling was me discerning what Aly felt, in the Spirit.

This happened again one day when I was in a restaurant trying to minister to my server. I received what I thought was a word from God for her, but as I went to deliver the word, I began to feel nervous. Instead of giving it, I asked, "Do you deal with anxiety issues?" It turned out she did, so I was able to pray for her deliverance.

One time, I was called to a home to deliver a man from a demon that was choking him in his sleep and driving him to suicide. As I traveled to do this task, I began to tremble—I believe I was picking up on the fear the demon was going through that knew its time had come. All of these examples are instances of *feeling* in the Spirit.

I have not personally heard the audible voice of the Lord, although some have. Instead, *hearing* in the

Spirit primarily comes as a thought or impression in my mind. I was ministering to a woman over the phone when I thought, "You're just like your mother." I intrinsically knew this was a voice the woman wrestled with, so I asked her if she ever dealt with that accusation. She revealed to me that it was a constant fear of hers. She saw herself growing more like her mom each year—overcome with anger and mental illness. To combat this, I began to share how her identity in Christ supplanted anything she received from her mom and drove out a lying spirit.

I once prayed over the phone for a man who had been experiencing terrifying nightmares three nights in a row. Each dream was vivid and featured a shadowy figure stealing something vital from him. Every night, he woke up screaming.

As he told me these things, the Lord said, "Ask about the son he no longer has." In obedience, I told the man, "I have several questions, and the first one is really strange, but *did* you have a son?" After a long pause, he told me he had a son for about 5 years but found out the son wasn't biologically his, which created a divorce, and that son was taken from him through court proceedings. There is no way I could have guessed about a son he once had, but no longer did, without *hearing* it first in the Spirit.

For several weeks in 2024, I dreamed of the Lord healing my eyesight. Being severely myopic from a lifetime of reading books, playing video games, and staring at my phone, I have often asked Jesus to restore my sight. After the second or third dream of God touching my eyes and the blurriness leaving, I woke up with a thought: maybe the Lord is healing my spiritual eyesight? As I mentioned before, part of the prophetic gifting includes seers. Such people see the spirit-realm like most of us see the natural world. Savannah Ramsey is a naturally gifted seer who recalls being able to see in the Spirit realm since she was a child. In college, she remembers going to a dance club and being repulsed because she could see demons crawling all over people. Seeing in the spirit fomented fear in her life until the day she met Jesus. In fact, I've had seers tell me they wish they didn't have that gift.

The Lord has begun to open the seer gifting in my life, and although I have few examples, I'll give them to you in case they help you discern what might be happening in *your* life. One night, as I woke to use the bathroom, the Lord said, "Are you ready to see a demon? Look up." The prospect unnerved me so much that I actually told the Lord, "No," and put my head under my covers. A week of conviction went by, and I determined I would not refuse Him if the Lord spoke to me like that again. It wouldn't be long before I woke up another night, and the Lord repeated the question, "Are you ready to see a demon?" I told Him, "Yes, Lord," and immediately fell back asleep.

Shortly thereafter, I dreamt of the face of a man I did not know. Suddenly, I could see inside the man's mind, and there was a demon. It looked like an amoeba with a central body surrounded by tentacles touching different parts of the man's brain like some parasitic sea creature. I woke up, and the man's head faded, but before me was that demon which stayed for a flash and then was gone. I began to worship Jesus and thanked Him for showing me what He did.

During this time of my life, I often saw shadows and lights out of the corner of my eye. These objects had no proper form and were only briefly visible, catching my attention momentarily and engaging my mind thereafter. Then, one day, I visited a friend's rental home with several others. As we sat down for dinner, smoke burned in the center of the table, about 20 inches in the air. It lasted for several seconds and then faded away. I have seen smoke at least one other time.

The best and most helpful example of operating in this gift was when I was ministering to a man on a video call. Not too long after he joined, I physically saw a demon on the video screen inside the man's throat. A while into the conversation, I asked if the man had dealt with any issues in his throat or ever felt like he was being choked. He responded that it had been painful to speak since we had started the call, and he could barely get any words out. At that moment, the demon manifested entirely; the man's eyes rolled into the back of his head, and he began to foam at the mouth. Jesus delivered him, and for the first time, I saw something in the Spirit which led to a man's freedom! I pray that the Lord will find me faithful with this gift and increase it in my life.

Smelling in the Spirit is quite interesting, but I don't believe I have ever experienced it. My friend Ethan says the presence of God smells like freshly baked bread, and my wife says our promised property smells like cherry jolly ranchers. Some people say that when the evangelist Kathryn Kuhlman died, the whole hospital wing was filled with the smell of roses. One time, a couple came to my house for prayer. When the Lord freed the wife from an unclean spirit, she reported smelling a bouquet of flowers, but no one else in the room could sense it.

It is wise to note that simply because we have not experienced something phenomenal doesn't necessarily mean the anecdote is false. Remember, Job 33:14 says, "For God speaks in one way, and in two, though man does not perceive it." I believe the Lord is always speaking and that the spirit-realm is more alive than the natural one. The problem is, we don't always perceive it—our spiritual senses must be opened.

"'Father, glorify your name.' Then a voice came from heaven: 'I have glorified it, and I will glorify it again.' The crowd that stood there and heard it said that it had thundered. Others said, 'An angel has spoken to him.' Jesus answered, 'This voice has come for your sake, not mine.'"

- John 12:28-30

In this event, multiple people heard something, but only some perceived a voice, while others perceived thunder. A similar thing happens when Saul meets Jesus on the road to Damascus. Acts 22 says some of Saul's companions saw the same light he did but did not understand the voice that was speaking. It could be true that when I've seen little flashes of light, I am perceiving angels as the Lord has enabled me to. I know others have seen angels in far more complexity (my wife once saw them as men).

Encounters and visitations (by Jesus or angels) seem to be adjacent to the prophetic gifting, and many seers will have them consistently throughout the bible—such as the prophet Ezekiel or the Apostle John. The evangelist Evan Roberts, whom I've previously mentioned, testified to a time in his life when the anguish over Christianity's failure goaded him into extended prayer for revival. Then, one night, the Lord woke Evan up at 1 a.m. and took him to heaven where they talked face to face until 5 a.m., when Evan was returned to Earth.

This happened for three to four months. Born out of these encounters was the Welsh Revival, which saw over 100,000 people saved, jails emptied, and bars shut down for lack of demand. Encounters like these will radically transform individuals. Take Thomas Aquinas, for example.

Aquinas was a highly influential medieval theologian and philosopher who wrote dozens of volumes. On December 6th, 1273, during Mass, he had a Divine encounter that rendered him speechless. After, he famously stated, "All that I have written seems like straw to me," and then he never finished his monumental work Summa Theologica. Something about experiencing God renders merely talking about Him insufficient. I hope to be raptured by the Spirit one day to experience more extraordinary revelations of the Lord before I die. My most consistent prayer is to see the face of Jesus.

If you're like me, you want to know how to receive and grow practically in the prophetic. You may crave the voice of the Lord, or you may feel the lost would be more easily reached if you could get words of knowledge for them. The good news is you are already completing step number one—eagerly desiring the gift of prophecy.

"...earnestly desire the spiritual gifts, especially that you may prophesy."
   -   1 Corinthians 14:1

God desires to give us good gifts (Luke 11:11-13). Likewise, I believe He gives us good desires.

"...for it is God who works in you, both to will and to work for his good pleasure."
   -   Philippians 2:13

So when Jesus said, "Blessed are those who hunger and thirst for righteousness, for they shall be satisfied (Matthew 5:6)," I believe even the hunger for righteousness was gifted by God, and the result was yet another gift—righteousness itself.

Similarly, when we begin to desire to prophesy as Paul told us to (1 Corinthians 14:5), it is most likely the Lord who has given us that desire. If He gives us the desire, He will also satisfy that desire within us. The only place we can go to find that satisfaction is in Him. For the Gift is the Holy Spirit (Acts 1:4), and He is also a gift Giver (1 Corinthians 12:11). One of His gifts is prophecy.

To boil this mystery down, let me put it this way: If you find yourself desiring a particular gift of the Spirit, I believe you can rest assured that your Father in Heaven has given you that *desire* because He also wants to provide you with that specific *gift*. Then, it is only a matter of receiving that gift. The way to receive it is to pursue the Holy Spirit and recognize that He is more important than the gifts He brings. In other words, seek first the Kingdom of God (Matthew 6:33), and in due time, the gift you desire, that God desires for you, will come.

Notice it is a gift, so it cannot be earned, but you can certainly ask for it and wait patiently like a child waiting for Christmas to come.

Once you begin to prophesy, recognize the gift will never leave you, but it will only increase as you exercise it and remain obedient to the Spirit, or it will atrophy as you neglect it. Thus, obedience to the Lord becomes your doorway to moving in more power. If you've ever found yourself in a position to prophesy over a line of people, you'll feel yourself drift into a prophetic river of sorts. Words from the Lord will start to come very quickly as the need in the hearts of those listening grows. If you're faithful in delivering a word to the first one, God can trust you to deliver messages to the next ten.

The same is true in public ministry. If God gives you a word to deliver to someone, you must deliver it. I have found myself overcome with the fear of man, driving away from people the Lord told me to minister to. I've barely gotten out of the parking lot before the Spirit's rebuke comes, "Are you going to be disobedient?"

There's a biblical principle of stewardship always at play. Remember the parable of the talents:

"For it will be like a man going on a journey, who called his servants and entrusted to them his property. To one he gave five talents, to another two, to another one, to each according to his ability. Then he went away. He who had received the five talents went at once and traded with them, and he made five talents more. So also he who had the two talents made two talents more. But he who had received the one talent went and dug in the ground and hid his master's money. Now, after a long time, the master

of those servants came and settled accounts with
them.

And he who had received the five talents came forward, bringing five talents more, saying, 'Master,
you delivered to me five talents; here, I have made
five talents more.' His master said to him, 'Well
done, good and faithful servant. You have been
faithful over a little; I will set you over much. Enter
into the joy of your master.' And he also who had
the two talents came forward, saying, 'Master, you
delivered to me two talents; here, I have made two
talents more.' His master said to him, 'Well done,
good and faithful servant. You have been faithful
over a little; I will set you over much. Enter into the
joy of your master.' He also who had received the
one talent came forward, saying, 'Master, I knew
you to be a hard man, reaping where you did not
sow, and gathering where you scattered no seed, so
I was afraid, and I went and hid your talent in the
ground. Here, you have what is yours.'

But his master answered him, 'You wicked and
slothful servant! You knew that I reap where I have
not sown and gather where I scattered no seed?

Then you ought to have invested my money with the bankers, and at my coming, I should have received what was my own with interest. So take the talent from him and give it to him who has the ten talents. For to everyone who has will more be given, and he will have an abundance. But from the one who has not, even what he has will be taken away. And cast the worthless servant into the outer darkness. In that place, there will be weeping and gnashing of teeth.'"

- **Matthew 25:14-30**

If God has given you a gift, the last thing you want to do is bury it in the dirt. On the contrary, you want to steward it well so it advances the Kingdom of God. If the Lord can't trust you to deliver the prophetic words He has given you, why do you expect to receive more? If you are a servant who can be trusted with some power, realize this is a sure principle of the Kingdom: you will be given more power (Luke 16:10).

A man once complained to me that he wanted to hear the voice of the Lord like several of our friends but couldn't. I asked him what types of things he was putting in his eyes and ears and if he had forsaken substance abuse. We must recognize the Spirit is Holy and Living Water (John 7:38-39). The world is filled with pollution (2 Peter 2:20). Let us make every effort to keep the water in our spirits pure and undefiled by the world! We do this by vigilantly guarding our hearts, eyes, and ears.

A man once asked a pastor I know, "Why do I always see pornographic images while I'm trying to worship God in church?" The pastor's response was, "Well, do you watch pornography?" To the man's credit, he admitted he watched pornography that very morning before coming to church.

Ask yourself, how can you receive a prophetic vision when your inner sight is corrupted by something like pornography? And it isn't only sinful things that inhibit our ability to prophesy. Many prophets refuse to watch television, drink alcohol, or listen to secular music. None of these actions are sinful, but they are unhelpful in hearing the voice of the Lord.

There have been times when I went to pray for someone's freedom and a jingle from a video game I had been playing bounced around in my head. It was not an evil jingle, but that earworm was distracting me from listening to the voice of the Lord at that moment. The same can be true of our dream lives. Often, we dream about the things we overindulge in during the day, such as television or video games. This is our mind's way of processing and cataloging—maybe even solving problems. But such things take up limited time in the night we have for dreams from the Lord. One trick Ethan taught me here is to pray in tongues before I go to bed. If we want to see more visions and hear more words, we must make space for those things by culling the world.

Additionally, start taking risks with the Holy Spirit. A woman came to one of our Freedom Nights in the park, stayed the whole time, but never came down for prayer. On the way out, I introduced myself and asked if she wanted to pray for anything. She bashfully responded that there wasn't anything, so I asked if I could take her hand and bless her. A few seconds into holding her hand, the phrase, "She runs herself down," entered my mind. Then, I saw the woman as a prepubescent girl. I asked if she had a habit of tearing herself down and told her it started even as a child. She admitted these things and broke down crying.

Prophecy

The Lord met her in that space and brought healing to her heart—delivering her in the process. Notice, I did not have a word for the woman until I stepped out in faith—expecting the Spirit to speak and for me to hear.

Many people don't see in the Spirit because they never take the time to look. What are you doing when you're out in public? Are you on your phone? Or are you looking for those God wants to highlight to you? Don't expect the voice of the Lord to interrupt you. He does do that, but I hear from Him most when I'm listening. I see the most when I'm actively looking. This gifting has reached a point in my life where, if I look long enough, I can see *something* in many people. When you're "looking," go with what comes to your mind first—especially if you have no reason in the natural to think of that thing. Chew on what you hear or see for a while, ask the Spirit for clarification, and then test the word with the person it is for.

I was picking up a car from the mechanic once when I heard the word "back" for the man behind the counter, followed by "heart."

Now, people with back issues are a dime a dozen, but I hadn't heard in the Spirit about someone with a heart issue before that I could remember. It was unique enough for me to step out and ask, "Do you have an issue with your heart, medically speaking?"

He admitted he did, so I told him God revealed that to me and it means He wanted me to pray for his healing. He said it was odd I'd ask because the past two days he woke up with bad headaches - reminding him that he was out of blood pressure medication.

I once looked by the Spirit into a man who was being delivered by other ministers on our team. The word "gambling" popped into my mind. The fellow didn't look like a gambler—which convinced me I was hearing accurately from God. It turned out he used to be a prolific gambler, as was his father.

When you present what you're hearing, do so humbly. Ask them if it rings true, and assure them they are free to reject it. If that first word is accurate, should you continue to "look," more usually comes. Often, the Lord will present a *golden thread* to us. It is the very thing that needs to be said or dealt with to unlock that person's heart. You can see anything about someone theoretically, but a word in season is what you want (Proverbs 15:23).

A very genuine and godly man once prophesied over my wife and I, "The Lord is about to move you. He says, 'Didn't I tell you to enlarge your tent?' It will be to a town nearby, and there will be a lot of land for your children to play on. There's even a small creek running through the property, and there will be blueberries."

If you read my last book, you might recall when the Lord told me to sell our townhome and build a house. God provided a large tract of land and a home I could not have imagined in my wildest dreams. Yes, the land has a small creek running through it, and yes, the Lord did give me the word about enlarging our tent. And interestingly enough, our property has massive blackberry bushes on it. The prophet was absolutely seeing in the Spirit about a very specific promise God had given me, but the word was out of season. It was a word from a prior season of my life. Timing seems to be the bane of almost every prophetic person's gifting.

We are prone to "fill in the gaps" of what we see and hear. We do this, typically, because we want to be helpful to a person. But it can sometimes backfire and leave people unsure about the authenticity of the prophetic word. Before releasing a word, it is safest to consult the Lord on the right time to speak the message. Additionally, we should ask the Spirit if what we are "seeing" is a future, present, or past event. The vision may not be literal; thus, it requires additional interpretation. Often, that interpretation will be apparent to the hearer rather than the one delivering the prophetic word. Therefore, the best course of action is to tell the person what you see, hear, and feel, but reframe from interjecting what you think about those things.

A prophetic message essentially has four distinct parts. The first part is the *word* itself. The second is the *interpretation*. The third is the *application*, and the fourth part is the *timing*. You will not always get all four parts when you hear a word, so holding your tongue on the ones you do not have is essential. For a long time, I struggled to get the interpretation. I saw visions and desperately desired to know their meaning, but that knowledge seldom came to me. Still, I remained faithful to convey the vision I saw and had many conversations that went like this:

"I see a duck sitting next to a pond. Does that mean anything to you?" I'd ask.

"Not that I can think of," the person would respond.

"Ok, ignore that then," I'd say with a grimace in my heart.

One day, I was prophesying over a different man when I saw ducks on the water, but this time, I also received an interpretation that made perfect sense to the hearer because he and his father would duck hunt together. But just because you have the word and the interpretation, that doesn't mean you know the application. Far too often, I have expanded on words of knowledge into words of wisdom based on how my mind would apply them. These are different things, though: a word of *knowledge* is knowing something supernaturally, but a word of *wisdom* gives direction to a person's life. The application of a prophetic word would, in my book, often be a word of wisdom.

I once prayed over a married couple when I saw a vision of a new home (in the yard was a "Just Sold" sign), and a newborn baby was in the wife's arms. I conveyed what I saw to the couple, along with the interpretation that I believed God would have them move and a baby would come. But I did not tell them when this would happen, nor advise them to make it happen themselves. Thus, I gave the word and the interpretation but not the application nor the timing because I had neither.

Obviously, the great fear believers have about the gift of prophecy is "getting it wrong." In the New Testament, we are given safety nets to help strain out words produced from the flesh or demonic rather than the Spirit. 1 Thessalonians 5:20-21 tells us, "Do not despise prophecies, but test everything; hold fast what is good." There's a temptation for people who have been burned by the prophetic to reject it altogether. Paul is telling us we should not throw out the baby with the bathwater, but instead test the prophecy so we can retain the good ones. Discernment is required by every believer to constantly test what they hear from the Lord—including dreams, visions, and words.

"Beloved, do not believe every spirit, but test the spirits to see whether they are from God, for many false prophets have gone out into the world."
- 1 John 4:1

If someone prophesies to me, I first check whether the Holy Spirit in me confirms what is being said. Sometimes, I will feel a "leaping" sensation inside, for example, and I know it is the Spirit telling me that what I have heard is true. The second thing I do is weigh what I hear against scripture when I've had time to digest it. Can I find any biblical precedent for what has been spoken? Do I see the word resulting in sin or contradicting the written word of God? If I find it does not align with the bible, I throw it out. The third thing I do is ask the Lord to confirm the word by another prophetic means.

"Let two or three prophets speak, and let the others weigh what is said."
- 1 Corinthians 14:29

One time, a highly trusted prophetic voice in my life spoke to one of my friends about marriage, but I was not present when it was delivered. He was told the

woman he planned on marrying was not "the one"
God had for him. This word was given just weeks before his wedding. My friend did not tell me what was
troubling him the night it was presented but decided
to discuss it after taking it to the Lord. I stayed late at
the event, and on my way to my car, the same prophet
gave me the word, presumably because I had influence
in my friend's life and was officiating his wedding.

The moment I heard the word, I was consumed by
shock. There was no peace, no "leaping" sensation,
but I was troubled by it. Politely, I told the prophet I
would pray into what she had delivered. Eventually,
my friend and I sat down and discussed the predica-
ment. Being a God-fearing man, he would choose to
follow Jesus over his passions, but not without confirmation this was indeed the voice of the Lord.

The problems were transparent: My friend felt he had
already received confirmation from the Lord that he
should marry his fiancé, the word did not confirm
with his spirit, and although we searched scripture, we
could find nothing that substantiated "the one" in
marriage was a biblical belief to hold. Further, my wife
and I had ministered pre-marital mentorship to my

friend and his fiancé—and found they were compatible and fit for marriage from a wisdom perspective.

Yet, until this point in our life, if you had asked me which of my prophetic friends was to be trusted the most to hear the word of the Lord, I would have told you it was the one who gave this word to my friend. And he agreed with me on that. So, harkening back to scripture, I told my friend he needed to ask other trusted prophetic people to "weigh" what had been said. He did that but ramped up the challenge by approaching two women in our church and saying, "I have received a word from God through a prophet I trust. I need you to ask the Lord what word I received and tell me whether I should reject the word or not." This challenge was very similar to one given by an Old Testament king of Babylon:

"In the second year of the reign of Nebuchadnezzar, Nebuchadnezzar had dreams; his spirit was troubled, and his sleep left him. Then the king commanded that the magicians, the enchanters, the sorcerers, and the Chaldeans be summoned to tell the king his dreams. So they came in and stood before the king. And the king said to them, "I had a dream,

and my spirit is troubled to know the dream." Then
the Chaldeans said to the king in Aramaic, 'O king,
live forever! Tell your servants the dream, and we
will show the interpretation.' The king answered
and said to the Chaldeans, 'The word from me is
firm: if you do not make known to me the dream
and its interpretation, you shall be torn limb from
limb, and your houses shall be laid in ruins. But if
you show the dream and its interpretation, you shall
receive from me gifts and rewards and great honor.
Therefore, show me the dream and its interpretation.'"

- Daniel 2:1–6

The magicians told the king that only the "gods"
could give him the dream itself, which set the stage for
the prophet Daniel to come in and not only give the
interpretation of Nebuchadnezzar's dream but also tell
the king what he dreamt.

You might be tempted to think my friend was putting
a great demand on the two prophetic people in our
church, but honestly he was putting a great demand
on God Himself. My friend is a man of faith, so he
knew this would be a small thing for the Lord to work

through His servants, according to scripture. In the end, both prophetesses, separately, were able to tell my friend what the word was. "They have called into question your marriage," one of them said. And both women likewise gave this word of wisdom, "Disregard the word you received."

I got to marry my friend off to a woman who would go on to be a wonderful help-meet to him. I hold no ill will towards the original prophet and still believe she hears accurately from the Lord and submits to Him far more than most people.

Let's say you receive a word that sounds great but hasn't come to pass yet. It isn't something unscriptural, and it sits fine with your spirit. My best advice for you is to let it sit on a metaphorical "shelf" until the word comes to pass or bears more relevance. Do not guide your life via rhema (spoken) words from God delivered by others. Always guide your life by the Lord's graphe (written) word as illuminated by the Holy Spirit. Far too many people have a penchant for hearing a prophetic word and shaping their life around it. This is an error in my book. It is better to let such a thing sit until the Lord unfolds it.

The prophetic gift is so broad, yet nuanced, eventually I will write an entire book on it as well as the gift of *discernment*.

Chapter 20
Tomorrow's Church

I had a dream on October 13th, 2024, around 2:30 a.m. The first half of the dream pertained to my ministry, but the second half was a word for the Church at large. In the dream, a storm had blown through my parents' neighborhood. As I drove down their street, I noticed a tornado had hit. Some houses were reduced to rubble, others were gutted, and some remained un-touched. I assumed my parents' home would be pris-tine, but when I arrived, although the outside looked fine, the inside was destroyed—every door and window had been blown out. I called my parents to let them know; they were out of town at the time.

I went inside to survey the damage. Teenagers were looting the house. Adults were there too—mostly pas-tors I had once known. They weren't looting but simply observing the destruction. I became livid and zealous to protect my parents' property. I went outside to my car, and a large teenager got into the passenger seat to steal it. I told him he needed to leave, and if he and his friends didn't go, I'd shoot him. I was bluffing, but I pretended to reach for a gun in the console. I had forgotten that I actually kept a little black .380 in there for self-protection. As I reached for it, the kid shoved past me, saw the gun, and picked it up. He was going to shoot me. We wrestled for the weapon, and I managed to get it away from him. He kept reaching for it, so I pointed it at him and shot him in the gut. He stumbled away, stunned—neither of us thought I would actually shoot him.

I returned to the house, grabbed a pair of pliers, and told all the teens to leave. If they didn't, I'd use the pliers to squeeze their skin until they left. I even used the gun on some of them to get them out. There were about twenty of them in the house. People started leaving, but a pastor I recognized stayed. I didn't bother him or the other ministers. Once most of the people were gone, I looked around. My parents' house was a wreck. I went outside to get into my car, but it was missing—it had been stolen. I flagged my wife down, who was driving through the neighborhood, and asked her to pick me up. Before we could leave, I noticed many people in my parents' backyard. When I went to investigate, creeping around the left side of the house, I found that in the dream, my parent's backyard had become a thriving auto mechanic shop— massive! My dad's big blue truck was there (someone was straightening out the door on it), and my dad was directing a crew of 40 to 50 men fixing vehicles. Despite the storm damage elsewhere, this place was bustling. I saw many cars in the garage, then hopped into my wife's car back out front. We drove off, and then I woke up.

I've spent a good deal of time praying into this dream, and the interpretation is one filled with God's judgment, the enemy's advancement on a sleepy Church, and a remnant of hope found in Jesus' plan for His bride moving forward.

My parents' neighborhood represents the Church at large, with individual homes symbolizing individual church communities.

Some churches are standing unscathed; others are damaged but could be repaired; still, some are beyond repair. The Lord sent this tornado to judge His Church. Like Revelation 3:17, many Christians say, "'I am rich; I have acquired wealth and do not need a thing.' But [they] do not realize that [they] are wretched, pitiful, poor, blind and naked." In Revelation 2:5, Jesus warns, "Consider how far you have fallen! Repent and do the things you did at first. If you do not repent, I will come to you and remove your lampstand from its place." In my dream, many of the churches had their lampstand removed.

Coming to my parent's home, I thought it would have survived the storm, but I found all the doors and windows were blown off and that it had been invaded by thieves. All the while, the owners were on vacation (not vigilant), and the pastors within were meandering about—not doing anything to stop the ransack. I believe the looters represent demonic forces that have infiltrated the Church while its shepherds stood idling by. Tasked with confronting wolves, the American pastorship has failed—allowing every kind of evil to participate in our churches and even run many of them.

The overwhelming anger I felt at the sight of this was the Lord's anger at the desecration of His Church. In the dream, my car represented an evangelistic ministry (a "home" on the move). Something that stood out to me was the vehicle model, which was my old car that I no longer have. This indicates that evangelists are under equipped to perform their tasks in the modern American Church. When I hopped into my driver's seat, there was a looter in the back who fought me for control of my ministry. I had feigned toughness by threatening to shoot him with a gun I didn't think I had. But to my surprise, the firearm was actually where I pretended it would be. This gun, along with the pliers I later used, represent our weapons of warfare. The Holy Spirit, in particular, must be partnered with again to drive the demonic out of our ministries. He has always been there, but the Church has forgotten Him in the console—the center of our vehicles.

Heading back into the church, I began to drive out the demonic forces which had invaded. This tells me that a remnant of Spirit-filled believers will begin this difficult work as the old guard, which has failed to partner with the Spirit, looks on. On the way out, I found my car had been stolen—indicating how Satan has hijacked evangelistic ministries. Isn't it strange that so many churches in the modern era do not have evangelists on staff? But even where evangelistic ministries exist, they aren't always fruitful.

I was meeting with a leader of a well-known high school outreach for tea one time. I wanted to get my ministry, Freedom Collective, into a local high school, so it made sense to network with other ministers who had already achieved that feat. When the barista brought our drinks, I stopped momentarily because I felt like the Holy Spirit had a word for him. Later, as my conversation with the fellow evangelist ended, I asked him, "Do you want to make a fool of yourself for the gospel with me and come talk to our barista?" To my dismay, the man demurred. It was a shame, too, because the word I had was accurate, which led to me praying for another person's freedom in the coffee shop; this other evangelist could have seen the glory of God and missed out.

Similarly, as I spoke with him to gauge synergy between our ministries, I asked, "How many students have you seen come to Christ since starting?" His answer was candid, "None." I asked how his organization did outreach, and it was primarily through events and bible studies. Prying further, I wondered out loud if they ever presented the gospel message and did altar calls at these events. Sadly, the answer was "No." Friend, nine ministers from this national outreach organization were assigned to this high school. Many evangelistic ministries are loaded with cash but not fruit. The Church has been robbed by the enemy and judged by the Lord. The evangelistic ministries have been stolen while dark evangelists have been incredibly effective. What is the Lord's plan to rectify this situation?

In the dream, I saw my father as I rounded the corner of my parent's house. He was directing the repair of a large number of vehicles that would be sent out from the disheveled "church." My father in the dream represents our Heavenly Father, who is currently mobilizing a fleet of evangelistic ministries that have, or will, survive this storm. They must be nimble, fast, and "sent" by the Father.

Out of the rubble, I believe our God will respond by raising the Stephens and the Philips—those who walk in the power of the Spirit and are willing to live and die for Christ. The Church will be rebuilt, but I pray it won't look the same as it has in my lifetime.

One of my wife's friends came to a Freedom Night where she got rocked and saw the glory of God on display as people were healed and freed from demonic oppression. She hastened back to her home church, asking one of the leaders, "Is this true? Does God still heal people like this and drive out demons?" The leader responded in the affirmative. In desperate disbelief, my wife's friend asked, "Then why don't we do this at church?"

"Because it would make people uncomfortable," the leader replied.

"That's not good enough!" my wife's friend stated in frustration.

A member of my family had helped plant a church and offered every aspect of his life to see it thrive—helping design and establish it while leading a life group and donating large sums of money. The Spirit interrupted him, though, and he began to pursue the gifts of God—especially prophecy. Soon, he was receiving prophetic words for individuals and his local church. And although his pastors believed in the gifts, they were uncomfortable openly practicing and fostering them. My relative met with them and asked to be allowed to teach on the gift of prophecy and to form a prophetic ministry team. They rejected this proposal, citing he had never gone to seminary.

Once, I visited two churches in another part of the country simply because I was already in town for ministerial purposes. During worship at the first service, the Spirit came strong upon me, and I began to receive a word for the church. Many specific things were said, but the primary encouragement was that the church pleased the Lord because of its deep hunger for Him. I vividly remember, upon initially walking into this building, feeling the presence of the Spirit and His joy.

I then visited the second church, which felt like it was trying to crank the ignition switch, but the car wouldn't start. The presence of the Lord was not very strong, and the enthusiasm to worship King Jesus was only upon a few members. I asked God what He felt for this church and heard, "I have been knocking." Immediately, I was reminded of the Laodicean church in Revelation, "Behold, I stand at the door and knock. If anyone hears my voice and opens the door, I will come in to him and eat with him, and he with me." I asked the Lord if the head pastor would receive such a word and heard, "No." He had me deliver it, anyway.

Can you hear Stephen crying out? "You stiff-necked people, uncircumcised in heart and ears, you always resist the Holy Spirit. As your fathers did, so do you (Acts 7:51)." He spoke these words boldly—right before being stoned by the spirit of religion.

I believe these are the types of churches that God will judge to varying degrees. They refuse the Holy Spirit and reject the primary weapon of warfare given to them to defeat a voracious spiritual enemy. That enemy isn't knocking on the door of our churches; he is already inside. Satan isn't someone we should be debating over, but curb stomping. The Holy Spirit isn't Someone we should be debating over but yielding to. As it stands, too many of our churches are rejecting the Holy Spirit of God and failing to confront demons. Nevertheless, God will have His say. Perhaps we are like the Hebrews, having come out of Egypt, but stuck wandering in the desert. A generation may die there, but God will bring that generation's children into the promised land.

Jesus will have a pure Bride, unstained from the world, not betrothed to demon gods but only to Him. Jesus will have a Church set on fire by the glory of God Himself, the Holy Spirit. Jesus will have a people who obey the Father and seek His will. The love language of God is obedience. "If you love me, you will keep my commandments," Jesus encourages us (John 14:15).

"It is hardly complimentary to God that we should choose Him as an alternative to Hell: yet even this He accepts. The creature's illusion of self-sufficiency must, for the creature's sake, be shattered; and by trouble or fear of trouble on earth, by crude fear of eternal flames, God shatters it, unmindful of His glory's diminution. Those who would prefer a Hell to a Kingdom can be allowed to make their choice. Those who choose Heaven will find that they have been chosen for it; those who choose Hell will find that they have been chosen for Hell. You will certainly carry out God's purpose, however you act, but it makes a difference to you whether you serve like Judas or like John."
   - The Problem of Pain, CS Lewis

I want to serve like John for the rest of my days. If I am to be a tool in the hands of the Lord, make me like David rather than Nebuchadnezzar. One submitted his life to the Lord in faith; God *used* the other for expediency. Babylon glorified God by executing judgment on Israel, but I don't want to be used in such a way because, at the end of the day—I would still be Babylon. The ruins of so many churches, littered with the failure of leaders who bred apostates through "church hurt," will be used to glorify Jesus. He will wash His bride, and out of her ashes, she'll be cleansed. Agile evangelistic ministries will blossom as they yield to the One who came to seek and save the lost.

God, don't let this next generation resist your precious Holy Spirit! We need the fire of God more than ever. We need a movement of people who, once they've caught that fire, will run with it.

Kathryn Kuhlman once said, "God is not looking for golden vessels, He's not looking for silver vessels, He is looking for yielded vessels."

Friend, my challenge to you is to yield. Throw away the false doctrines of our ancestors concerning the

Spirit of the Lord. Divorce religion and marry Jesus. He is the only Bridegroom worthy of your affection— and He calls you to obey His commandments: heal the sick, drive out demons, cleanse the leper, raise the dead, and preach that the Kingdom of God is at hand. Consecrate yourself, the Lord is calling us out of the world. The Spirit is being poured out lavishly upon people who have forgotten Him; we must respond.

Appendix
Healing Miracle Stories

I have seen about a couple thousand miracles at this point in my life. The only drawback has been remembering all of them. Some days, before I teach on healing, I will sit and wonder if I've seen anything at all—it can be that hard to recall specific stories. It wasn't like that in the beginning, when miracles were rare. But miracles shouldn't be rare since the Spirit of the Lord is in the Church.

As in my last book, I've endeavored to recall stories that stand alone for no other reason than to document the things I've seen and heard to the glory of Christ Jesus. For the sake of not making this book much longer, I've only included six stories.

More Than He Bargained For

My wife and I were eating at a local hipster spot when a nearby man struck up a conversation with us about our two young daughters. He was a relatively new father keeping tabs on his daughter, who was playing with my own children. As he left our table I asked the Lord if He had a word for the man, and I heard "arm." Dinner wrapped up, so I decided to approach the new father and his wife. We struck up a conversation filled with small talk, and eventually the man revealed he was a military veteran. By this time he knew I was an evangelist, so he divulged something to me he hadn't told many people; he suffered with PTSD to the point he would see demons in his room at night.

The gift of discernment allows a person to understand whether something is of the Lord or not; it looks into a situation. But it can also draw things out. If you're the type of person perfect strangers confide in, and they don't even know why, there may be a gifting of discernment upon your life.

"Let me ask you this. Since you were in the military, did you come out with any injuries—perhaps in one of your arms?" I asked.

"I do have an injury in my shoulder, but it isn't from the military," he responded.

"Well, I pray for people and God heals them. I'd love to pray for Him to heal your arm," I explained.

The man was willing, and he told me that he was a new Christian believer, but he belonged to a denomination that did not pursue the gifts of the Spirit. I asked him to show me the range of motion he had with his arm, and it was very limited with severe pain. I put my hand on his shoulder and commanded it to be healed in the name of Jesus.

"Did you feel the muscles move?" he asked me, wide-eyed.

I told him to test his shoulder, and he raised his arm without any pain. I like to say it was as if he saw a ghost. I then explained, "The reason I wanted to pray for your arm was to show you the Lord cares about you enough to heal it. And if Jesus would heal your arm, I'm telling you, He would also free you from your PTSD." I asked him if he wanted me to pray for his freedom then, or if he needed to think on it and we could meet up later. He said he wanted to meet up later, so we exchanged numbers, I invited him to meet, but he never responded.

Ten Seconds is All it Takes

After Sunday service at my church one morning, I walked to the altar to receive anyone that desired prayer. A middle-aged woman made a bee-line for a fellow minister and I, explaining how she fell recently and tore various muscles and ligaments in her leg like a bad sprain. I had her sit on the altar to take pressure off her leg. The other minister and I then laid hands on her (I put mine on her knee) and I prayed simply, "Muscles, bones, ligaments, and nerves, be healed right now in the name of Jesus." As soon as the words came out of my mouth, her foot kicked like it does when a doctor hits a person's knee at a reflex point.

"Did you see my foot move? I didn't do that!" she exclaimed. She stood up and began to walk around, finding no pain in her body. I told her, "Jesus healed you, praise Jesus!" while marveling at how quickly the Lord healed her.

The First Convert

In 2024, while sitting in prayer, the Lord instructed me to hold 6-8 outdoor meetings in Centennial Park, Nashville. Our very first gathering that fall started off slow—only eight people showed up. As worship began,

I fixed my eyes on the Lord and interceded for those in the park. Then, as I stepped onto the stage to preach the gospel, I turned around to a surprising sight—a crowd of roughly 70 people had gathered.

My 10-minute sermon challenged them with some of life's biggest questions, such as, *"Why am I here?"* But at the end, I told them they needed to answer the most important question of all: *"Who is Jesus?"*

I then gave an altar call, and one man came forward, kneeling at the altar—soon followed by nine more. This first convert had spent the past 30 years as an alcoholic, mistreating his wife who had brought him to the event. That night, he surrendered everything, gave his life to Jesus, and experienced deep inner healing. We also prayed for his physical healing, and the Lord immediately restored both of his rotator cuffs. The power of God struck him, and he fell out on the lawn. When he got back up, his back was miraculously healed as well. In a moment of divine grace, his wife forgave him for three decades of hardship, and she, too, was set free—healed from arthritis.

Less than two weeks later, this man passed away unexpectedly. His wife called to thank me, telling me she knew with certainty that her husband was in heaven—and that she had been given the gift of forgiving him before he passed.

She described their last week together as one filled with Bible studies and three-hour-long worship sessions. His newfound zeal for the Lord had dramatically transformed their marriage in a way she never thought possible.

I don't believe his salvation and sudden passing were mere coincidences. I believe they hold a deeper significance for the city of Nashville. There is an urgency now for the lost to be found. Time is always limited—we never know how much we have left on this Earth. Since then, I have adopted a simple yet powerful motto: *Preach as if those hearing don't have another day to live.*

Scan the QR code to watch a clip from my preaching in Centennial Park that first time.

Alzheimer's

One Sunday morning I was told by a pastor that if the Lord gave me a word for the congregation, I could share it after worship. I asked God what He wanted to demonstrate through me, and I received a vision of a brain scan. Hopping on stage, I grabbed the microphone and announced God wanted to heal someone's brain. The service went on as I stepped down to pray for whoever the word applied to.

A middle-aged woman sauntered down the isle, face in hands, weeping. Through distress she told me how her mother suffered terribly with Alzheimer's, and that it ran in her family. She was already starting to notice the diseases' effects - specifically forgetfulness. A demon manifested heavily and the Holy Spirit drove it out of her.

I followed up several weeks later and asked if she had noticed any changes. This was her response, "Hi James! I can tell you that I've noticed significant difference since I went up for prayer. I've been keeping track in my journal. [Before], I had to stop 2 or 3 times when telling a story or speaking to someone, and ask - "what was I saying again?""

Incurable Diseases

I love investigating whether modern science declares a disease to be incurable or not. Turning the wisdom of man on its head is a specialty of my God.

One night, Ethan and I were asked to pray for a friend's dad over the phone. He had suffered with spinal stenosis most of his life - resulting in so much pain he couldn't travel anymore. Likewise, his knee was blown out which made it almost impossible to walk. The Lord brought up betrayal from an ex-wife and ex-business partner, along with many other areas the

Spirit wanted to heal in the man's heart. After about 45 minutes of prophetically led inner-healing and forgiveness, we began to pray for his freedom and healing. By the end of the call all of his pain had left and he could walk without issue. Many days later I asked his daughter how he was doing and she exclaimed her dad couldn't get over the fact he was healed. It was almost unbelievable for him!

I then looked up whether spinal stenosis was curable, and the internet confirmed it was not. Yet by the blood of Jesus this man was healed!

Unusual Miracle

In a future book I'll talk about my time in Kenya, but I want to share a story from my layover in New York concerning a restaurant server Ethan and I had.

I asked our server if he believed in the supernatural, and he started to tell us about his dream life and how he felt he sometimes goes to a different realm, exclaiming of course he believed in the supernatural.

I told him Ethan and I had visions for him and we wanted to know if what we saw was true or not.

I said, "You have an issue with your spine, specifically a disc in your spine. You are also unhappy with your current living conditions."

He looked like he had seen a ghost and replied that these things were spot on. He said he would get high, which would make him cough, and the coughing alone would hurt his spine. He admitted he injured it one time when he was drunk playing volleyball.

Ethan then told him his right knee was injured and had an accurate word about the server's absent father. Again, our server was shocked and told us that under his pants was actually a knee brace on that knee, and the word about his dad was correct.

I told him "it gets better" because he could be healed from those issues in his body if he gave us 30 seconds. I felt the Holy Spirit wanted me to try something new I've seen others do. I handed the server a knife and asked him if it was a regular knife, that there was no way a knife could heal his body. He agreed.

I took the knife back and blew on it, telling him, "I believe when I hand this knife to you that your body will be healed. You may even feel warmth in those areas that are broken."

He was dumbfounded by this but played the game. Taking the knife, he felt his entire body begin to tingle. The longer he held it, the more the manifestation localized in the broken parts.

I took the knife back and told him to check his pain. He squatted down fully and exclaimed he could not do that before. There was still some pain so I took his hand and commanded the knee to be fully restored, and it was!

He had no grid for any of this, but was extremely open minded and grateful. We shared the gospel with him and as we did, he began to tear up. He told us his whole body felt something going on and we told him that it was the Holy Spirit.

Apparently, we were the third group of Christians to witness to him he could remember, and he felt like God was chasing him down.

Ethan saw many more things which we talked to the server about, but in the end he wasn't ready to commit his life to Christ. He counted the cost, but couldn't get there. We're praying the Spirit blows on those seeds.

More Healing Stories

I post healing stories regularly via social media (currently Facebook, Instagram, Youtube, and occasionally TikTok). You can follow me on these platforms if you want to be encouraged by more testimonies from the Kingdom of God.

Facebook: @jthayer2
Instagram: @james.m.thayer
Youtube: @JamesMThayer
TikTok: @james.m.thayer

More Books

Currently, my books can be found online at jamesmthayer.com as well as on Amazon.

If you enjoyed *Somebody Gave Me Fire*, try reading my previous autobiographical work titled *Stepping Out of the Boat (a year of miracles)*.

If you're craving more Holy Spirit content, listen to my podcast: *The World's Last Night* by James M. Thayer.

Please write a review about this book. Thank you!